The Fearful Void

Geoffrey Moorhouse's books, which have been translated into several languages, cover a variety of topics, from history to travel. They include *The Other England* (1964); *Against All Reason* (1969), a study of monastic life in the twentieth century; *Calcutta* (1971, published in Penguin in a revised edition); *The Missionaries* (1973); *The Diplomats* (1977); *The Best Loved Game* (1979), a prize-winning collection of essays on cricket; *The Boat and the Town* (1979), about a deep-sea fishing community in North America; and *India Britannica* (1983), a history of the British in India. His most recent work is *To the Frontier*, which won the Thomas Cook Award for the best travel book of 1984.

Geoffrey Moorhouse is a Fellow of the Royal Society of Literature and a Fellow of the Royal Geographical Society. He lives in a hill village in North Yorkshire.

GEOFFREY MOORHOUSE

The Fearful Void

PENGUIN BOOKS

Penguin Books Ltd, Harmondsworth, Middlesex, England
Viking Penguin Inc., 40 West 23rd Street, New York, New York 10010, U.S.A.
Penguin Books Australia Ltd, Ringwood, Victoria, Australia
Penguin Books Canada Limited, 2801 John Street, Markham, Ontario, Canada L3R 1B4
Penguin Books (N.Z.) Ltd, 182–190 Wairau Road, Auckland 10, New Zealand

First published by Hodder & Stoughton 1974
Published in Penguin Books 1986

Made and printed in Great Britain by
Richard Clay (The Chaucer Press) Ltd,
Bungay, Suffolk

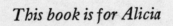

This book is for Alicia

Illustrations

MAPS

DRAWINGS

PHOTOGRAPHS

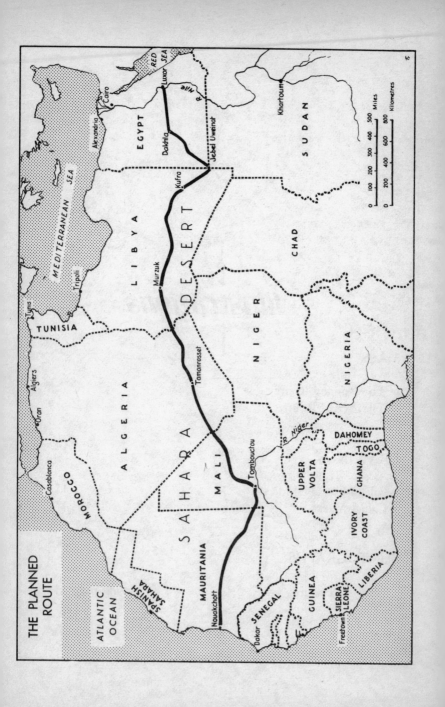

THE PLANNED
ROUTE

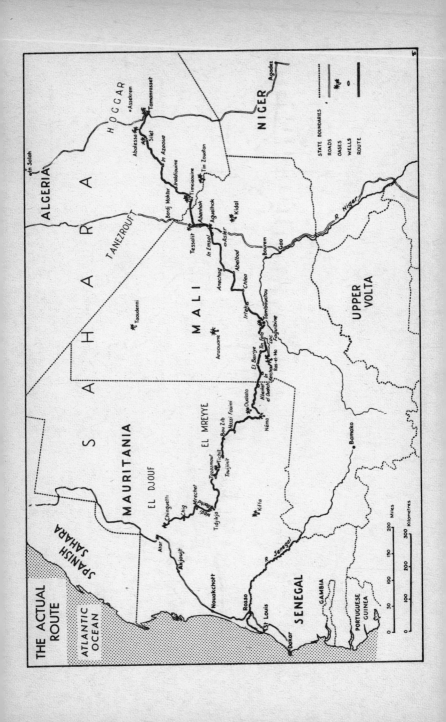

THE ACTUAL ROUTE

1

IT WAS A CHILD, screaming in nightmare, which awoke me. As I rose from the depths of my sleep, sluggishly, like a diver surfacing from the seabed, the corridors of the hotel echoed with those pealing, terrified cries. They poured over the balcony beyond my room and filled the courtyard beneath; they streamed out into a town which was cooling itself, ankle-deep in sand under a new moon, and they were lost, plaintively, among the low dunes scattered to the south and to the east. I reached consciousness to the dimmer sound of a father's voice gentling the infant terrors away, and the night became stealthy with silence again. But the spell of tranquillity had been broken. In a day or two I must leave this room, with its bare security and comfort, and move off into those dunes beyond the mosque, into the awful emptiness that stretched for three thousand miles and more to the east. A man called Mohamed was even now travelling down from his encampment in the desert, to be my companion at the beginning of what seemed to me a very fearful journey.

I, who normally sleep so securely that I have rarely been able to recall my dreams on wakening, had experienced the childish nightmare too, in the past few months. There had been a midsummer night in London when I had dreamt myself deep into the Sahara, among endless sand dunes and a formless, panic-stricken sense of being lost and in peril. I could not tell whether I had failed to find a vital water hole, or whether I was just hopelessly unable to decide which way I must go to safety; the images were inexact, only the torment was penetratingly clear. As I emerged from the horror of it, my body streaming with sweat, my mouth bitterly dry, the woman I loved helped me to safety again.

But now, in this room on the edge of the desert, there was no A to calm my fears. Nor were the fearful images inexact any more. For two or three weeks I had prowled around this rim of the Sahara, preparing myself for my journey. I could visualise its beginning with some clarity, and I now had the name of a companion to give a tiny substance to any event my imagination conjured up. As the child's screams dwindled into sobs and died with a whimper, I lay blankly and widely awake for a while. A couple of dogs barked down by the marketplace, where all the commerce of Islam heaved and badgered and bartered during the day. Then silence and nothing, nothing, nothingness stretching away to infinity around my room. On one side there was an infinity of ocean, on the other three an infinity of desert, all threatening this small remnant of civilisation which man had contrived against nature. What a folly it seemed to abandon that so wilfully.

Gradually, the images crept out of the corners of the room and shaped themselves over my bed. I saw myself asleep somewhere out in the nothingness, then wakening suddenly at some sound. Appalled, I saw that Mohamed was carefully leading our camels away. I was unable to move or call out from my sleeping bag, so transfixed was I by the care he took not to disturb me: he walked them

12

down to the far side of the sand dune before mounting so that I shouldn't hear their protesting noise. By the time I'd struggled out of my bag, he'd vanished, with the camels, our water and our food. I had nothing but a sleeping bag and the dying embers of our campfire.

The sequence ended abruptly there. I shifted uneasily, aware that the blood was pumping through my chest more obviously than is normal at two o'clock in the morning. Then another image crossed my mind. Again I was awakened from sleep in the desert, but this time Mohamed was inert in his blanket nearby. Cautiously I raised my head and saw figures creeping towards us, evidently bent on murder. As one of them approached my companion, I scrambled out of my sleeping bag, kicked Mohamed awake and leapt towards the attacker, my sheath knife already drawn and in my hand. Untidily, the sequence dissolved with me rushing up a dune, pursued by a figure. I stumbled and saw his weapon—a sword, a club or a knife—descending. Then the vision was gone. Much gratified as I was that my fanciful response had been so heroically in the best white man's tradition, I was nevertheless left pondering for several minutes just how I would get out of my sleeping bag in such an emergency, and whether, indeed, I ought to sleep with my knife quite ready for action of that sort.

Impatient by now of these midnight movies, I switched on the light and, reaching for Solzhenitsyn, began to read myself into torpor again. But my body, I noticed, had become a little clammy, though the night was cool. I was afraid.

It was because I was afraid that I had decided to attempt a crossing of the great Sahara desert, from west to east, by myself and by camel. No one had ever made such a journey before, though many men have traversed the desert from north to south. For ages before Europeans ventured into the interior, there were well-defined caravan routes from Black Africa below the Sahara to white Africa fringing the Mediterranean. Slaves were regularly herded from the markets of Tombouctou and Tchad up to Fez, Tripoli and elsewhere on the northern littoral. The Europeans who took to the desert in the nineteenth century—Laing, Caillié, Barth, Clapperton, Nachtigal and others—did so from a mixture of motives. Sometimes it was a straightforward attempt to explore the commercial possibilities of a route into Black Africa. Until René Caillié's successful venture in 1828, a number of explorers had been trying to reach Tombouctou,* chiefly to find out what truth there was in rumours that here was a fabulous city on the southern edge of the Sahara. The motives of such men were always strongly seasoned with a taste for adventure on its own account. But always there was also the possibility of some tangible achievement at the end of their quest; and always this logically meant a crossing from top to bottom of the Sahara. There was never any logic to a journey made from the Atlantic to the Nile, or vice versa. The intervening space had gradually been known from the time of Herodotus to consist of nothing but sand, rock and diminishing savannah. The limits could easily be explored from the sea. The only lateral caravan routes in the Sahara were over relatively short distances, like the one from Agades to Bilma, for the conveyance of salt. There was only an adventurous challenge in trying to cross the biggest desert on earth between its most distant boundaries. Men ignored it until 1963, when a party of twelve Belgians with half a dozen vehicles motored from the Atlantic coast of Morocco right across to the Red Sea.

If I managed to make the first great traverse by camel, I would enjoy my success. I recognised that the moment I first thought of attempting the journey. In the spring of 1971, I was flying home from Sierra Leone at the end of some fieldwork for a book on nineteenth-century missionaries, with vague plans for a later history of Saharan explor-

* Still, in the Western world, more commonly known as Timbuktu or Timbuctoo, but, in Africa today, spelt as above.

ation swilling round my head. It was a thick, muggy day as we took off from Freetown, and we were soon riding high above continuous banks of grey cloud. After an hour or so, this changed dramatically. The earth beneath was now hidden under a vivid orange fog. Whether it was a sandstorm or merely the colour of the desert reflected onto cloud, I had no means of knowing. But certainly it was the Sahara. And this orange pall covered the earth as far as the eye could see from thirty thousand feet. It was the first time that the terrible immensity of that wilderness had been registered on my emotions rather than my intelligence. Three and a half million square miles of desert at once became a staggering reality, instead of a statistic paraded before the bored glance of a mathematical ignoramus.

My emotions produced two responses, in quick succession. First there was an almost sensuous thrill of anticipation; impulsively, I wanted to grapple with the void down there, I wanted to plunge into it, I wanted to stretch myself out to its limits. Instantly, my heart and my body recoiled from the prospect. I have climbed and walked among mountains since my school days, but still I have only to look at the photograph of a climber on some awfully exposed slab of rock, and the palms of my hands become damp with sweat. They became damp now, even as another part of me was seriously beginning to wonder whether I could possibly commit myself to the desert. I was aware that it had not been crossed the long way by one man using the desert's most primitive and traditional form of transport. The fantasy of such an achievement danced into already mixed feelings. Of one thing at least I was certain. I should relish that crown.

The possibility of a giddy and unique success, however, was not enough by itself to set me on my way. One of my weaknesses is a deep need to justify my actions; I have always found it very difficult to do something simply for the fun—or the hell—of it. I did not need to look far for a justification of this journey. It was there in my instant

15

recoil from the prospect of commitment, in the fearful sweat that sprang out of my palms. I would use this journey to examine the bases of my fear, to observe in the closest possible proximity how a human being copes with his most fundamental funk.

I was a man who had lived with fear for nearly forty years. To say this is not to suggest that I had lived in a permanent sweat of terror. I can think of only two or three occasions since childhood when this would have been true. Once, certainly, when I was climbing on the Matterhorn without a companion. I slipped on some icy rock and was lucky not to finish up in the glacier, a couple of thousand feet below—and terrified enough to turn back to the Schwarzsee as soon as I had calmed down. There was another occasion in Calcutta during a particularly turbulent period in local politics. I walked round a corner, straight into a demonstrating mob which at once transferred its attention to me. Maybe a hundred men surrounded me in an intimidating circle, while I sat down and pretended to read about the Bengal Renaissance from a bulky volume with which I hoped to conceal the fact that my knees were shaking spasmodically, and squatted thus for perhaps a quarter of an hour until a truckful of soldiers arrived and dispersed the crowd. Dramatic moments like these, however, have been mercifully rare. To live one's life in fear is something much less spectacular and much more commonplace in everyone's experience, I believe, than most of us are prepared to admit or even able to identify.

It is to act, for a great deal of the time, from negative rather than positive motives. One takes a certain course of action not because one wholly wishes to do so, but because one fears that unless one adopts this course, the consequences may be painful. The habit can become so entrenched in a man's character that he ceases to observe the motivation, producing instead any number of rationalisations that will explain and justify his conduct. The result can sometimes be catastrophic, as I had discovered in my own experience.

For a decade and more, my married life with J had been quite extraordinarily free from expressions of anger on both sides. I don't believe we had known open conflict until the day I confessed adultery to her. There were, of course, tensions from time to time long before this, but neither of us had allowed them to become explosive. They were screened by various devices which could be recognised by such clichés of phrase and habit as "carrying on bravely" and "smiling the thing off." Had either of us been challenged to produce reasons why we didn't explode in each other's face with "You stupid bitch," swapped for "You selfish bastard," we would, I think, have answered that each of us cared for the other too much to hurt him or her with our anger, and that we had both been taught (in very narrow Protestant traditions) that it was sinful and selfish and quite un-Christian to put our personal interests so violently forward that it disturbed the other's tranquillity and sense of well-being. In fact, I believe that our angers were contained basically by fear and not by generosity. We were afraid to speak out violently because it was possible that we might be hurt by the response of the other. We might even—and this was the most frightening thought of all—lose the other and become lonely and insecure again, as before marriage.

This merely exemplifies the calibre of the fear which every man carries with him, unless he is uncommonly wise or strong or lucky. It appears in a great many other forms, almost every day of his life. We hesitate to speak to strangers for fear of a rebuff, a small humiliation. We are loath to act generously because we fear that more may be taken from us than we really wish to give. We will not stand up and be counted in some small but important matter because it may cost us a security or, more frequently perhaps, an advancement. Gradually we become stultified, incapable of giving to each other, waiting instead for the next hostile move from another fearful man, which must be countered with all the craft at our disposal, for the sake of self-preservation.

Yet I also believe in the essential greatness and goodness of the human spirit. Instinctively, for it is beyond measurement, I believe it to exist in the same proportions in every race of mankind. I have seen far more generosity and kindness all over the world than I have seen meanness and viciousness, though I have seen much of that, too; I have offered it myself. The balance between the two is determined by fear; this is every man's spiritual battleground. And while there can be no solution to the spiritual struggle so facile as that expressed by "learning to conquer fear," it is possible to come to terms with it, to grow stronger and straighter through the encounter with it. We must not hope to banish it entirely. It would be hazardous to do so, for fear can in some situations be the only warning of a purely physical danger which may cripple or destroy us physically. What we have to learn and relearn and not forget is how not to be destroyed, crippled or merely reduced in spirit by fear. We have to find our own ways of shedding natural timidities which cause us to decline some possible course of action without even examining it before commitment. For if we do this, if we turn away from the action as a reflex of fear, I think the fear of it follows us for the rest of our days, systematically weakening our spirit in all things. We are reduced in our ability to go forward and meet, recognise warmly and embrace, Life itself and all who share it with us.

Fear can thus be seen as the most corrosive element attacking the goodness of the human spirit, which, untouched by fear, finds itself always in a natural movement towards its fellows. This, if we will notice it, is the way of the child until he has been pained for the first time by an encounter with some other creature. The most insidious form of fear, which is the fear of being afraid, is the most potent force of all against this movement, for it does not simply arrest that movement: it does not allow it to begin. Yet if, in the face of fear, we can summon the strength and the faith to go forward, I think that far more often than not we find that one of two things happens. Either the encounter with the thing feared demonstrates that it is by no means as laden with terrible properties as we had supposed from a distance, a discovery which tends to dissolve the fear itself. Or else, terrible as the encounter may prove to be, it is one which can be endured and which can fortify us in the endurance. There are obviously limits to any human being's endurance, but they can be judged only by being tested, and they are almost certainly much greater than most of us take for granted in ourselves.

I had gradually come to these conclusions over many years, out of my own experience and my observation of others. I had found myself more and more focusing my attention on the part that fear plays in all our lives. In my own case, I recognised that my deepest fears were those of annihilation, of being surrounded by what is hostile, of being unwanted, of loss and of being lost—in several different senses. I doubted very much whether I was at all exceptional in fearing these things. And while I had come to know, over a long period, a great deal of my fearful self, there were still extremities that I hadn't touched, which I hadn't been able to examine, where my belief in the necessity of forward movement had not been tested.

To do these things, it would be necessary to place myself in a completely unknown context, in which imagination might find the most fearful possibilities rampant. Once I recognised the opportunity for such experiment, I did not doubt for a moment the necessity of engaging in it. Having been saddled since childhood with a pathological degree of curiosity, it was natural that I should wish to draw close to these extremities. There was a temperamental logic in the fact that, having recently involved myself in the life of the most crowded place on earth, Calcutta, I should now be contemplating a passage across one of the emptiest.

The Sahara fulfilled the required conditions perfectly. Not only did the hazards of the desert represent ultimate forms of my fears, but I was almost totally a stranger to it. I had crossed a corner of the Rajasthan desert in India by car, and I had motored through the sandblasted hills of Judaea in Israel. I had been on the threshold of the Sahara itself once, in Marrakech, but there it was no more than an exotic and completely safe tourist attraction. On none of these excursions had I spent so much as one night away from the comforts of an hotel. I had never in my life touched a camel, let alone ridden one. I was not even capable of communicating with the inhabitants of the North African desert, for I spoke not a word of Arabic. I could scarcely be less prepared for a long and slow journey from the Atlantic to the Nile upon the back of what was said to be the most intractable of beasts. My only obvious asset for such a venture was a fair degree of physical fitness, laboriously maintained over many years by an addiction to exercises concocted by Canadians for the reduction of weight among obese aviators.

Friends were later to say my idea seemed so preposterous that they assumed I would drop it as soon as I had fully digested its practical implications. But long before I had finished writing about nineteenth-century missionaries, I was quite certain where my nagging wish to know would next take me. And though it might well be that I should be drawn across the desert by the prospect of an explorer's crown, I also knew that, more powerfully still, I would in truth be propelled by my own fears.

2

By the end of March 1972, I was free to begin my preparations for the journey. From the tentative plans which had been forming in my mind throughout the previous year, it had become obvious that I must take the fullest possible advantage of the desert winter. The Sahara was no place for a lone traveller by camel in summer, when the air temperature can rise to 134 degrees F, and where the sand temperature has been known to reach 168 degrees. In such conditions it would be suicidal to attempt an extended journey with very limited water resources. I must therefore be in á position to move away from the Atlantic coast by the beginning of November at the latest, which meant that I must leave England early in October, to allow time for acclimatisation. I had six months in which to ready myself, and there was much to be done.

The first priority was clearly to start learning Arabic. I have never been a linguist. Though I had travelled widely as a journalist, I had never managed to pick up more than a smattering of phrases in any tongue other than French, and even my French was laborious for want of lengthy practice. The prospect of tackling one of the notoriously difficult languages at the age of forty, and trying to speak it well, both deterred and excited me. It was perhaps expecting a little too much of a curiously unreceptive part of myself, yet the possibility that I might gain access to a completely alien culture and tradition by this means was enormously pleasing.

I enrolled as a pupil in a small school hemmed in by kebab cafés off the Tottenham Court Road. It was run by a Mr. Beheit, late of Cairo and points adjacent, of dapper appearance and explosive temperament, who assured me that after three months of his special treatment I would speak Arabic fluently. Whereupon he drew from his desk a postcard which an old pupil had sent him from somewhere in the Middle East, expressing great gratitude and reporting the astonishment of local Arabs that he could converse with them like a native. It was written in English. Mr. Beheit himself spent most of his time coaching businessmen in French, which was destined to equip them for advancement through the Common Market. Through the thin, partitioned walls of his school, one could hear him bellowing in exasperation at some confused entrepreneur: "*Non, M. Jones. 'Je ne suis* PAS *français.' Pas,* PAS, *PAS!*" I was gratified that my own tutor's approach was infinitely softer and less public. Also from Cairo, his name was Ahmed, and he worked in the school as a relief from playing bit parts in English television.

For a couple of hours every morning we would face each other across a small table, while we discussed in meticulous detail the colour scheme of the tiny cubicle, the events in the street below and, once a week, the hair-raising progress of a window cleaner across the curtain-walled building in the next block. In between, bearing in mind the particular interest I had in acquiring Arabic, I would inquire the way to some imaginary oasis, anxiously demand fodder and water for my camels, wonder politely whether the sheikh was prepared to grant me audience now. It was all hard going. I frequently despaired of ever becoming anything like a fluent speaker, though Ahmed assured me that my pronunciation was above average for a Westerner. This, I suspected, was a small Egyptian flattery, for there are a couple of Arabic sounds which not even a gift for mimicry allowed me to grasp for ages. There were, moreover, vast distinctions of meaning conveyed by subtle sound shifts rarely employed in English. And for me the problem was increased by the need to assimilate a vocabulary that would vary from place to place across five essentially Arabic-speaking countries that practised vernaculars of their own: the word for "people" might be *nais*, *sha'ab* or *sooken;* that for "now" could be *taoo*, *hella* or *dilwa'ti*. I was in a similar position to that of a foreigner to Britain who finds himself confronted with men of Glasgow, Dublin, Llanelli, Liverpool, Birmingham and Bethnal Green, each of whom speaks English in the most pungent local dialect.

Each day I was mentally exhausted by the strain of a morning in school, followed by an afternoon struggling at home with a tape recorder. Yet there was relief in the most elementary forms of understanding and progress. When I merely got the drift of a torrent which Ahmed had just released, I was childishly elated. When I managed to roll a complete sentence off my tongue without apparently thinking what I was saying, and it came out right, I beamed like an idiot. I could keep going enthusiastically for a couple of hours after some simple discovery of Arabic etymology; the fact, for example, that the Arabs regarded the umbrella (*shamseeya*) as a protection from the sun (*el shams*) and not from the rain. And the enjoyment of reading and writing the flowing Arabic script was something that did not leave me once I had mastered it. By the end of June, no one could have described me as anything like a fluent speaker of Arabic. I was approximately in the position of a fifteen-year-old who, equipped with a modicum of schoolroom French, nervously awaits his first trip to Paris. But this was something I could improve upon in my own time. I bade farewell to Mr. Beheit, still struggling to drive the French negative into the still confused mind of Mr. Jones.

I had arranged by this time to find out something about camels from the London Zoo. Armed with a temporary employee's permit, I began to visit Regent's Park in the mornings, before the public was allowed in. I had hoped that perhaps it might be possible for me to learn the elements of camel riding there. So it would have been, for the keepers were willing enough, if only the Zoo had possessed a harness and saddle suitable for the single-humped Arabian camels in its care. But the only saddlery in London was designed for the use of small children on the backs of two-humped Bactrians, shaggy creatures from Asia, which are unknown in the Sahara. There seemed little point in learning to sit cosily on one of those. What I could learn, however, was to become used to having camels about me. It was a small but important step. I am not particularly attracted by animals as such and have always found myself much irritated by the sentimentality of urban animal lovers. There's a high degree of nervousness involved in this feeling: let a dog crouch low and bare snarling teeth at me, and I can feel myself tightening up inside under the threat of attack; the last thing I'm ready to do in such circumstances is to try to pacify the animal with soothing words and friendly, confident gestures. A large and lumbering beast such as a camel has always therefore been a potential source of danger.

They had three Arabians at the Zoo, and one of them was a heavily built bull named Fred. As we walked towards his pen for the first time, his keeper told me about the perversity of bulls. You had to be careful of them at all times, he said, but particularly during the rutting season. They were liable to attack without provocation, with necks outstretched, and they always went for a man's belly with their teeth. There were cases, he said, of natives having been disembowelled this way. I remembered Wilfred

Thesiger writing * about an old man and a child who had been savaged to death by a bull as they sat by a campfire in Arabia.

Fred was sitting down when we arrived at his pen. As we entered, he shambled to his feet and padded over towards us. A single pace away, and his neck arched high in the air. Then something half ridiculous, half revolting happened. There gradually emerged from the side of his mouth a pink bubble, a membrane which slowly expanded into a great drooling balloon that went slithering obscenely down the animal's neck, before it deflated and disappeared inside the maw again. From somewhere within there came the sound of slobbering, sucking turmoil. Down into our faces swept the sweet stench of decomposed vegetation, mixed with heaven knows what stomach juices. Thus the bull camel betrays his excitement when confronted with a cow on heat. I stood my ground, manfully, while Fred's keeper grinned at us both.

"He fancies you," he said.

The feeling never became mutual, but my familiarity with this ponderous beast became such that one day, wondering just how strong the camel's neck was, the keeper and I swung from it together, like a pair of children, legs in the air, while the bull stood patiently, showing no sign at all that he noticed the sudden weight around his windpipe. By then I had so far overcome my initial timidity that when the younger of the Zoo's two Arabian cows ran at me, partly in play, partly to test what she had from the first sensed as weakness, I turned to face her and smartly clouted her under the eye. She backed off and never chased me again. I was learning.

After these early-morning excursions at the Zoo, I went home to grapple with Arabic, or else I spent afternoons in the library of the Royal Geographical Society, reading the reports of various expeditions into the Sahara. The evenings were increasingly spent in stargazing. It was

* In his book *Arabian Sands*.

vital that I should become a proficient navigator, which meant a great deal more than an ability to use a map and compass. This I had been able to do since my days in the school cadet corps, twenty-five years previously. On more than one occasion since then, I had been grateful for that early training, when caught in cloud or mist on Dartmoor, in the Lake District and the Scottish Highlands. The problem of finding a way across the Sahara, however, would obviously be much more like that of crossing the Atlantic safely than of reaching Bassenthwaite in one piece from rough ground northeast of Skiddaw. Before you can set a compass course, you must know as precisely as possible where your starting point is. Which means, in default of charts as blessedly detailed as those of the British Ordnance Survey, being able to use a sextant and work out a position by celestial navigation.

I had occasionally handled a marine sextant during my time in the Navy, but that was just after leaving school, and I had long since forgotten even the basic principles of its use. In any case, I now found that a marine sextant was of little use in the desert. One needed a bubble sextant, as devised for aircraft navigators, with an artificial horizon which would be as necessary when travelling among ranges of sand dune as when flying at 25,000 feet. I finally tracked down a secondhand instrument, recently calibrated, in a ship chandler's emporium. I got myself a handbook of instruction in what appeared to be a witheringly mathematical art, a *Nautical Almanac,* and a set of sight reduction tables; these, at least, superseding the logarithmic tables which navigators had to rely upon until quite recently, should help to take the weight off my notorious incapacity with figures.

In one respect, however, I was determined to ignore the most up-to-date methods of calculation. I would not be taking a transistor radio with me into the desert, for it would have represented something alien to the spirit of the journey I wanted to make. At the same time, an inability to receive time signals increased the likely difficulties of accurate position-finding. For in taking a sight of the sun, the moon or any other heavenly body by sextant, it is of absolute importance to note the exact moment of the shot; someone has estimated that every second in error of time leads to a quarter of a mile's error in longitude if the observer is at the Equator, more as his latitude increases from zero. I decided to risk something of error by taking with me an electronic watch, whose daily variation would be very small and, more important, constant. Given that I could adjust it against time signals every few weeks—which seemed a reasonable supposition—the safety margin should not be disastrously affected.

The methodology of navigation seemed, when I got down to it, to be much less complicated than I had expected. But when I actually came to use the sextant in practice, the results were hopelessly inaccurate. Night after night, A and I trudged across Hampstead Heath, trying to distinguish Aldebaran or Capella in the great orange glow that dimmed all but the brightest stars in the heavens above London. For a start, the Great Bear, the Pole Star and Sirius were almost all I could identify with certainty. But identification was not the greatest difficulty I found myself in. Having reached certainty in picking out half a dozen stars, I could theoretically begin to obtain fixes from them, but the fixes I was getting were distinctly at variance with what I knew my position to be. We would rush home and work out the results of the sextant observations, which appeared to have been taken from somewhere in the middle of the South Yorkshire coalfield, when I knew perfectly well that we'd been standing on Parliament Hill Fields.

I assumed that my feeble mathematics were failing me in the most elementary sums of addition and subtraction, so I persisted through many cold and semiobscure nights to plot myself west of Bristol, east of Tolpuddle and at a number of points right in the middle of the English Channel —anywhere, in fact, except in North London. In some desperation I canvassed friends with some knowledge of navigation, asking them to check my methods. They could see no fault in them. Yet still the massive errors continued. Finally I conceded that the sextant, newly calibrated though it was, might just possibly be at fault. An acquaintance in the RAF arranged for it to be tested at Farnborough. A few days later I was informed that there was a perpetual error of 2 degrees 17 minutes built into the wretched thing; which meant that I could not possibly have found my position to within less than 137 miles of where I stood. Farnborough returned it to me "rectified beyond the theoretical limits of accuracy." Next day I took a couple of sun sights, morning and afternoon, in the back garden and worked out a two-shot transferred fix. This time, I was only five miles out.

I would need to do better than this in the desert, but at least I could be confident of my instrument, with only the errors of inexperience to overcome from now on. No seaman would worry overmuch if he knew he was fixing his position in mid-Atlantic to within five miles. In mid-Sahara, however, the problem would be different. There would be water holes to find, literally no more than holes in the ground, that might easily be missed unless one arrived within a mile or so by navigation. This much was clear from the rather sketchy charts on which I had plotted the routes I intended to take. It would obviously be impossible to try riding across the desert in a straight line, as though one were sailing a yacht across the ocean. One's course was essentially determined by the need to move from well to well and from oasis to oasis.

In choosing the Mauritanian capital of Nouakchott as my beginning I was selecting a place virtually on the seashore of the Atlantic, where I might expect to obtain camels. From there I would ride in a southeasterly curve across Mauritania and into Mali, to reach Tombouctou. There I could probably rest a little and replenish my stores before heading northeast, towards the Algerian oasis of Tamanrasset, almost exactly in the centre of the Sahara. This would be my halfway point, before moving east across the Libyan desert, by way of Murzuk and Kufra. At Kufra I would be within six hundred miles of the Nile, but a direct march to the river through Dakhla Oasis was ruled out by an intervening sand sea, devoid of water and consisting of one range of high dune after another. Instead, it would be necessary to turn south at Kufra, to the mountain of Jebel Uweinat, standing at the junction of Libya, Egypt and the Sudan, and then to go northeast to Dakhla, before cutting due east to reach the river at Luxor.

As the English explorer Wilfred Thesiger pointed out to me when I sought his opinion, this was not the most intelligent route to be taken by a man intent on making the first camel crossing of the Sahara from Atlantic to Nile. It swerved needlessly all over the place, far beyond the requirements of finding food and water, and probably put the best part of a thousand miles on the most direct route. My choice as far as Tombouctou would have been fine, but after that it would have made more sense to continue almost due east across Niger, Tchad and the Sudan, striking the Nile somewhere above Wadi Halfa.

That I had no intention of trying to cross that way was not mere perversity on my part. My primary aim in going to the desert was not to establish a record, much as I might enjoy doing so, but to explore an extremity of human experience. The Nile was a physical objective to be aimed for and reached if at all possible, for it would have been as pointless to set off vaguely into the interior of the Sahara as it would be to embark upon a cross-Channel ferry with no notion of the direction one would take at the other side, or the distance one was prepared to travel. Moreover, I still wished to write my history of exploration.

With this in mind, there were three places I much wanted to see. One was Tombouctou, which had been the objective of so many nineteenth-century explorers. Another was Tamanrasset, where that strange, compelling mystic Charles de Foucauld had hidden himself for a decade before being killed by marauding tribesmen. The third was Murzuk, an old slave market on one of the main caravan routes north to Tripoli. My way across the desert was predetermined by these three points quite as much as by any well or oasis.

If I reached the Nile by the chosen route, I would have ridden about thirty-six hundred miles. Assuming that I could cover about twenty miles a day, which all expert opinion seemed to agree upon as a reasonable rate of progress by camel, this would have meant about six months of riding. But, as Thesiger said, it was quite impracticable to suppose that one would maintain twenty miles every day, from start to finish. There would be inevitable delays from time to time, when one would make no progress at all. No one set of camels would be able to cover anything like the full distance; they would have to be replaced at different stages, and buying fresh ones would take time. There was always the possibility of falling ill and having to stay put until the sickness passed. Thesiger's view was that unless I managed to reach Murzuk by the beginning of March, I had no chance at all of getting across the Libyan desert before the onset of summer; and to be caught in that emptiest quarter of all the Sahara in summer was probably to perish. He didn't believe I could reach Murzuk in time. It seemed that I would probably have to be content with spending the summer there, before continuing my journey in October. With luck, I might reach the Nile by Christmas 1973.

Thesiger's advice had been valuable, but it was full of doubts and what seemed to me spectacular pessimism. When I asked him what he thought about the chances of travelling entirely alone, he was incredulous.

"You don't seem to realise," he said, "that camels represent wealth to the Tuareg, and if they see a lone Englishman crossing their territory with a string of beasts, they'll bump you off without compunction."

This was not quite the impression I had formed of the Tuareg from other sources, which seemed to suggest that what had once been the fiercest and most warlike people of the Sahara had moderated since their struggles against French colonialism into a rather simple, poverty-stricken and passive race of herdsmen. Thesiger most certainly knew more about primitive desert life than any other Englishman, but most of his remarkable explorations had been in Arabia, his knowledge of the Sahara was comparatively slight, and I found myself wondering whether perhaps he was not unconsciously transferring his experience of one area to the other. I suspect that he thought my enterprise little more than a stunt.

There was only one man whose advice about the desert could carry more weight than Thesiger's, and he was Theodore Monod, whose whole life has revolved around the Sahara. Monod is one of the polymathic figures of our time: an ichthyologist by training, a geologist by extension, an Orientalist by taste, a gifted linguist by nature who is, among many other things, France's chief connoisseur of English doggerel verse. He is also a formidable explorer and desert traveller. For nearly half a century he crossed and recrossed the Western Sahara by camel, and some of his journeys are still legendary among people who know the great emptinesses of Mauritania, Mali and Algeria. A great deal of what is known about the structure of the Western Sahara, about its prehistory, derives from his field work on these journeys, and it has not yet been superseded. If you study the North African collection at the Musée de l'Homme in Paris, you find that many of the specimens, almost all the landscape photographs—in sepia, blotched with age and a little flyblown now—were supplied by Monod.

The contrast between him and Thesiger could scarcely be more complete. Where the Englishman is tall and heavy, the Frenchman is short and wiry. Where Thesiger lopes along in great deliberate strides, Monod scuttles like the White Rabbit. Thesiger is rather blank, with penetrating eyes that look as though they haven't seen much to laugh about; Monod is very warm and he grins in a fetching way at small things. At seventy he has the physique of forty-five, the mental attack and verve of thirty. He drives his battered Mercedes saloon with all the dash of a playboy at the wheel of his first sports model. He has enthusiasm, and he shares it.

For two or three months we had corresponded about my plans, Monod offering a variety of suggestions seeded with quotations from Edward Lear. In August, A and I went over to France to collect the best available charts of the Sahara from the Institut Géographique National in Paris. We went on to Colomieres, the Monod country home near Sens. In his library, a converted barn which probably contains everything that has ever been printed about deserts, the Sahara in particular, he bubbled with the enthusiasm he had already transmitted in his letters. He provided much practical guidance, culled from his long experience. You must never, he said, place a guerba on the ground overnight, or you may find that most of the water inside the goatskin has disappeared into the sand by morning, by the process of osmosis. You must always allow your beasts to browse wherever they can find grazing, however impatiently you may be delayed, for in the next few hundred miles there may be nothing at all for them to eat.

Even more important to me than such droppings of wisdom was Monod's buoyant assumption that I was not on a fool's errand, that my journey most certainly could be accomplished with reasonable luck, provided one set about it intelligently. He doubted whether it would be possible to travel without any companions at all, as Thesiger had, but his reasons seemed to me more realistic. Monod didn't believe that one man could cope physically with all the hard work involved in an extended camel journey. He himself, he said, would never have dared to try it. But not once did he imply that I would be an idiot to make the attempt myself.

"Perhaps," he shrugged, "it is that I am not bold enough." He entered into the spirit of my adventure as though he were planning to come with me. Why didn't I, he said, as we pored over the charts in his library, why didn't I try to cross from Oualata to Arouane, en route to Tombouctou? "Why not try that, if you want adventure? It's never been done, you know. We really have no idea of the country between those two places." The country between, even on the informative IGN charts, was about three hundred miles of totally unmarked desert.

By the time we returned from France, there was little more than a month left before I must be away. Gradually I completed my preparations. I collected a variety of inoculations and I put together a small kit of medicines. I listened to what the School of Tropical Medicine in London had to say about salt intakes and minimal water requirements. Not less than eight pints a day was their advice, based upon experiments conducted in the Arizona desert. But expert opinion on this subject was as much in conflict as it was upon the matter of how far a camel could be expected to go without water. Wilfred Thesiger reckoned to have travelled for twelve days in Arabia on no more than a couple of pints a day, but a colleague in the RGS told me that once, when he had found himself reduced to two pints for a couple of days in Libya, in an emergency, he had been very ill indeed. Monod said that six pints should be sufficient except in summer, when one might well need twice that amount.

As for camels, Thesiger put the absolute limit at twenty waterless days when travelling. An American who rode from Morocco to Tombouctou just after the war claimed that his beasts would not survive for more than five days without water. The experienced Swiss traveller René Gardi has suggested seven days. Desert journeying was evidently even more of a hit-and-miss affair than I had supposed.

I assembled my pieces of equipment and stowed them in two kit bags. Almost everything was severely practical, but if I was to spend a year or more in the Sahara, I would need something beyond my natural resources to prevent my mind from vegetating. A gave me a pocket chess set and some problems, which made a decent start. But when I considered the number of books I had promised myself that I would read one day, given sufficient spare time, I was defeated by the amount of choice at my disposal. In the end, I settled for Dawood's translation of the Koran, into which I had only dipped so far, Solzhenitsyn's new novel, *August Nineteen Fourteen*, and Archibald Wavell's classic and affectionate anthology of verse, *Other Men's Flowers*; it was an old standby, even though by the nature of its compilation it omitted a number of my favourite poets, like e. e. cummings and R. S. Thomas. I also carried my Arabic dictionary. It occurred to me, as I was packing these books, that they did not represent a very venturesome selection. I would be much in need of old standbys, emotional and intellectual, if I was to manage the months ahead, and I recognised this clearly enough on the brink of departure. Whatever lay in store for me, I should not be capable of burying myself totally in the desert.

My vision had foreshortened sharply over the past few months. At the start of my preparations, I had seen the journey as a sweeping movement from Atlantic to Nile. But it slowly became impossible to contemplate the whole vast project and all its implications; this was an enormity far beyond my imagination once I had settled down to working the thing out in its manifold parts. By midsummer, I found my resolution limited to reaching Tombouctou, with a very vague subconscious acknowledgement that I must then proceed into a blankness beyond, but with no desire at all to think through that blankness into some concrete perspectives. Eventually, I was not even thinking as far ahead as Tombouctou. I was wholly preoccupied with the immediate tasks of acquiring the right inoculations, setting my domestic affairs in order, and obtaining permission merely to set foot on Mali with a camel. Even after a prolonged negotiation at the Paris Embassy of the republic, that issue was still in doubt. It would be necessary to visit Bamako, Mali's capital, deep in the African bush, before I could set any kind of course across the Sahara for Tombouctou. If I failed on that mission—and I was given the impression that my chances of success were no more than even—then my expedition to the Nile might founder before it properly began.

I had also reached a point of tension that was not immediately connected with, yet was inseparable from, all my fears. In the preceding months I had known moments of great calm, and they had followed a consistent pattern. They came after I had accomplished some small constructive thing: merely writing to Monod for advice was enough to create tranquillity. Or else they succeeded and healed the moments of nightmare that had recurred from the beginning: after the horror of being lost, being attacked, being finished had subsided, I found myself still secure, still whole, still resolved, therefore calm. Or was I merely living in a fool's paradise before plunging into an idiot's self-destruction? The nightmares and the calms, however, had now given way to a tautness of the spirit that lifted me beyond the reach of either and was slowly creeping through the tissues of my body. I realised one day that I had not for weeks listened to any of the music that I loved, for fear that it would release the sluice gates of emotion, relying instead upon a diet of the most unmemorable jingles in the pop charts. A said that my face was now habitually clenched, as with concentration, but I knew that this was only partly so. I was braced against the onset of fear just as much as I was applied to the tasks still to be done.

I relaxed only when I was with my children, enjoying them dreamily and watching them more carefully than I could remember for a long time. Andrew and I walked across Dartmoor one weekend, ostensibly so that Dad could practise compass work on a Saharan training exercise and Andrew could feel he had a hand in all this, but really so that I could watch him grow for forty-eight hours and leave another small mark on him. Conceivably it might be the last one. I had no palpable sense of doom, but I recognised that at the bottom of all the fear lurked the real possibility of catastrophe. I spent the last weeks frugally, and there was much tenderness in them. A and I lingered over everything we did together, trying to make it last, in case we never happened again. J and I discovered that we could hug each other again, as we hadn't been able to for years. We had become close once more, across our accepted separation.

Early in October I left London for Paris, to lobby the Mali Embassy again before flying on to Africa, and to see Monod for final instruction. In his apartment high above the quai d'Orléans, with the Seine swirling round Notre Dame just below, we lunched off Madame's fish stew, plum pie and vehemently nonalcoholic fruit drinks, while this boundless man demonstrated the superiority of the French liquid compass over the English one, discussed the sometimes impenetrable topicality of Giles cartoons, and wondered where on earth he had mislaid his diary of a crossing to Tombouctou forty years earlier.

His almost last words were very characteristic. "Take plenty of string," he said. "It's always very useful." Then he was away down the quai at the dash, eager for another encounter with his students.

I had one more appointment, and I kept it a few hours before catching the plane to Dakar. I went to the Russian Orthodox Church for the Sunday morning mass, as I had got into the habit of doing whenever I could, over a number of years. Originally drawn there by the quality of its choir, I was more and more impelled by a presence in the place, of which the singing was only part. I had long since rejected most of Christianity's codified faith, where it seemed to be intellectually doubtful and spiritually crippling in the teaching I had received. Yet I could never deny its attraction, both intrinsically and as a possible passage to enlightenment. I could admire and accept the ethic, I could venerate the man who first pronounced it, I could certainly acknowledge the mystery of something beyond the tangible; but further than this I could not go.

Yet here, in the spell cast by those rumbling basses and those skirling Slav sopranos, by the drift of incense and by the operatic movements of the priests and acolytes, I had increasingly come to feel that I was close to some aspect of truth that had hitherto eluded me. There was a deeply restrained sadness in that place which marked the émigré faces of the congregation as they watched the movements around the tabernacle with obedient, wondering eyes. At the same time there was something that transcended the sadness, expressed crescendo and diminuendo in the voices of the choir. I never left without feeling calmer and stronger, surer of goodness and rightness in mankind, than when I entered.

On this morning the tourists, as always, crowded self-consciously near the back of the church, intimidated by its strangeness and its quintessential power. Old ladies in black, with woollen mufflers scarved round their heads, threaded their way through to the space at the front, kissing the icons and lighting candles before them, then settling down in attitudes of prayer. The archpriest arrived at the west door, an ancient man in a soup-stained cassock, with wide and staring eyes above his ragged old beard. The cantor, he of the slicked-back hair, the brushy moustache, the richest diapason of all, had come to meet him. So had two acolytes, and they now began to clothe the archpriest in gorgeous cope and maniple, stole and mitre, while he leaned, semi-invalid, upon his staff.

While this was going on, while the cantor swung the smoking censer from its chain and the choir climbed and dipped gently through the introit, I found my mind drifting away through multiple definitions of God. This was the oldest conundrum of all, which had plagued me since that day in late adolescence when I had for the first time asked myself a serious question about the pious atmosphere that had always suffused my family.

In an instant, my reverie was startled by a totally new conception, the sudden linking of two terminals that produced a burst of illumination. It was not only new to me: it could not possibly have occurred to me until I had started to prepare for my journey. For I had discovered, in the past few months, that in celestial navigation, in astronomy, there is a thing in the universe called the Point of Aries. This is the place in the heavens where the path of the sun (the Ecliptic) intersects the celestial equator (the Equinoctial) on March 21 each year. It is, in a way, the invention of astronomers and navigators. Nothing exists there, in a physical sense; there is no single heavenly body called Aries. But all the heavenly bodies in our zodiac are related to it. They swivel about the Point of Aries in definable trajectories at predictable moments, and they do this unceasingly throughout time. It is because Aries exists that the navigator is able to make his calculations, and so fix his position on earth. This is the focal point of activity for all those millions of light specks which we call stars. It regulates their relationships. It also gives man, trying to find his way across the wildernesses of the earth, a security that he can find it, if only he learns the secret of using Aries correctly.

Perhaps—I wondered, as I watched the priest being clothed, as the incense climbed indolently to the apse, as the chant lifted the spirit high above the rue Daru—perhaps God should be thought of as a spiritual Point of Aries. Insubstantial, without a material presence, but nonetheless our focal point and our security. Without awareness of this God, without a sense of common relationship with God and with each other through God, without being able to refer to God, we are quite lost; people spinning helplessly and hopelessly through a fearful void of the spirit.

This was not a concept to set theologies atoppling. I had no grand illusion about it; for all I knew, it was already regarded as a commonplace in some insubordinate Dominican priory or other. But I was glad that I had come by it now, at this time and in this place. As I walked out along the rue Daru, where the autumn leaves were starting to untidy the pavements, all the old fortifying influence of the Orthodox mass was with me again. There was something else this time, though. I felt released, as from some burden that had chafed at me long. I would never be more prepared for a journey across the wilderness.

3

I STAYED IN DAKAR only long enough to be plundered by the most rapacious taxi drivers in creation and to discuss my immediate plans with the British Embassy. The Foreign Office had advised its North African missions of my venture, and this had already produced from our men in Cairo a memorandum, which awaited me in the Senegalese capital, about mines the Egyptians had recently laid in their southern desert. There was also a letter from Monod, which he must have written within hours of our parting three days before. He had found the missing diary and copied the itinerary of his 1934 crossing of Mauritania to Tombouctou. It had taken him fifty-seven days but, he warned, "that kind of calculation is, in fact, very silly; there is really no accurate possible count; so many things may happen, so many incidents. . . . A camel trip has nothing to do with a railway timetable. And should not!" It was a warming send-off from a tireless and generous man, but for the moment the impediment of bureaucracy lay between me and my attempt to follow where he had led; and Egypt was so remotely in the future that the warning about the land mines could register as nothing more than a vague shape upon a dim and hazy horizon.

I flew on to the southeast, across the oozing delta of the Gambia river and over the arid bush of sub-Saharan Mali, to present myself, with a letter of recommendation which I had finally wrung from the Paris Embassy, to the Director-general of the Security Services in Bamako. This M. Bagayoko, I had been told by friends in Paris, was a man more powerful even than the President of the Republic himself. All the corridors of power radiated from his office, every position of influence was in his gift, and no foreigner could remain in the country for more than seven days without personal supplication at his headquarters. As my passage across Mali by camel was liable to take anything up to a couple of months, it was imperative that I get this matter settled before I set off from the Atlantic coast. The Foreign Office had warned me very severely against being found inside the republic without the correct documentation from Bamako, and I had no wish to add unnecessarily to the natural hazards ahead. I had no doubt that imprisonment in Mali might last a long time and be excessively unpleasant.

I never, in fact, set eyes on M. Bagayoko, although I arrived with a letter of introduction to him from the cultural attaché in the Paris Embassy. A succession of interviews was conducted by his deputy, a dumpy man with a wide and encouraging grin which somewhat offset what I took to be his professional habit of prevarication. For almost a week I marched and countermarched across the dusty little capital, bearing indecipherable pieces of paper from one office to another on what appeared to be fairly aimless errands of national security. I spent many hours in a dilapidated anteroom at security HQ, reading the weekly handouts of the Russian news agency Novosti and the cumbersome and interminable thoughts of Kim Il Sung, President of North Korea—"*respecté et bien-aimé* Leader [sic] *de son peuple*." I spent many more hours in my room at the Grand Hotel, relic of French colonialism with crude murals of Alsace and Provence still daubed upon the dining-room walls, reading Solzhenitsyn and playing myself at chess.

In between, I walked steadily up and down streets decorated with the banners of revolution, bearing such emancipated sentiments as "*Justice égale pour tous. Pas de justice de classe.*" At the very least, I could profitably begin my programme of acclimatising to temperatures a good 40 degrees higher than those I had just left in England, working my body hard, pouring in as much liquid as I could contain and proportionately increasing my intake of salt, in accordance with the prescription issued by the School of Tropical Medicine. I was in no mood to investigate the local culture, beyond what was visible in public, for this was Black Africa and almost as alien to the desert as my own land. I wanted to be out of it and on my way, and I fretted irritably at the diversion that had been imposed upon me by the insinuating philosophies of Kim Il Sung and the Moscow Politbureau.

In the end, with only a few hours remaining before my seven-day visa expired, I emerged with a passport much stamped upon, much cancelled, but with a final and unblemished permission, *aller et retour*, to catch my plane out again. I hoped it would be sufficient to convince any security forces I might meet in the Sahara that I had M. Bagayoko's approval. I had no energy left to ask yet again for some more tangible proof of his blessing. And I was too relieved at having my passport back; one felt awfully vulnerable, even for a few days, without it.

A weekend in Dakar, and I took plane for the last time. We flew straight out to sea, then turned north over the spangled waters of the Atlantic and continued thus for an hour or so before swerving in to the coast and our landing. I caught myself pondering the curiosity of this route, a choice presumably made after some thought about safety.

41

Was the desert so hostile, then, that even in his most power-ful and sophisticated travelling machine, man preferred to have the ocean beneath him rather than that barren waste of land?

As we climbed down from the sky above Nouakchott, I think I expected to see the earth ruddy or silvery, devoid of everything but rock and sand. I anticipated no romantic spread of date palms, for I was aware that Nouakchott was a very new and inorganic township, an artificial capital created midway between the borders of Spanish Morocco and Senegal when Mauritania gained her independence from the French. A dozen years before, there had been nothing at this point in the wilderness except a police post and a huddle of fishermen's huts a mile or two from the beach. But now, as I could see, there were sprawling blocks of low concrete buildings, almost encircled by a perimeter of tents. The land was a browny-grey, under a sun that became less luminous and distinct as we came to ground, and there was a great deal of scrubby and dessicated vegeta-tion about. As I stepped out of the aircraft, a chilly wind laden with sand swept down the runway, causing the robes of the bystanders to billow and swell like spinnaker sails. There was a film of grit over everything in the rudimen-tary customs hall.

At ground level, that windy evening, Nouakchott ap-peared unlike any town I had ever visited before; yet, at the same time, it was a queer amalgamation of several famil-iar places. There was something in it of the English sea-side resort that has seen better days, maybe a Herne Bay out of season, needing a lick of paint here and there to give it that old enticing polish, and many more people to restore an air of vitality. There was something of the decayed small town of Texas portrayed in the Bogdanovich film *The Last Picture Show*, with puffballs of dust rolling along derelict boardwalks. The shops of Nouakchott were also ranged in lines shaded by verandahs, but instead of board-walks, one trod upon fraying linoleum tiles. The bar of El

Oasis Hotel was packed with heavy white men, sinking much beer in noisy affability, glad to be turning their backs together upon the alien world outside. They were almost all French, and their business was to ransack the desert for oil, but I had seen their like before in the Yukon, where other gregarious vagabonds were also drawn into a wilderness by the prospect of mineral wealth. There was a single main street laid with tarmac, ceremonially wide, with a strip of no-man's-land bearing neon lights down the middle. But even here the sand had drifted so thickly that vehicles moved with no more than soft crunching sounds, as they would in Europe just after a heavy fall of snow. Grey and fine was the sand, fine enough to trickle through an hourglass; but containing in each handful a million fragments of pulverised seashell.

In the heavily filtered light of that landfall, it would have been a very dull place had it not been for the bright sky-blue of the Mauritanian national dress, the great flapping robe which they call the boubou. Practically every man wore it, I was to discover, unless he was in uniform, in superior government service, or in the more mobile employments of the Western oil companies. It mattered not whether he was a true Moor, descendant of the race which had once colonised Spain and left its intricate mark upon the Alhambra at Granada and elsewhere, or a Negro with his origins in Black Africa, once subservient to the Moors and now living in an occasionally uneasy independence with them. The vivid, swirling boubou made Mauritanians of them all; though, this being a self-proclaimed Islamic republic, the women were almost invariably cloaked in a discreeter black.

As I stood outside my hotel that night, disappointed that the stars seemed quite as obscure as they could be on Hampstead Heath, a couple came along the road, their feet skidding gently backwards in the yielding sand. The woman was singing in a high, thin, childish voice the verses of some tantalising Arab chant whose words I could not

43

pick up. Between the verses, the man broke into a nasal snatch of chorus, a roundabout plangent tune with only sound to it: *la-la la-la li-larra-li-la, la-la la-la li-larra-li-la*. . . . Until that moment I sensed that I had come to some bastard place, conceived haphazardly in a union made mostly at the insistence of Europe. But on hearing that duet, I felt the old thrill of the strange, the mesmerising and the faintly intimidating, come creeping up my spine. I knew I was on the track of what I was after.

By extreme good luck, there was an Englishwoman highly placed in the Government service here, a widow whose husband had been a Mauritanian diplomat. Jean Abdellahi had long since offered her assistance, and she now introduced me to the head of her secretariat, Ahmed ould* Die. He was a boyish, slim man with an engaging habit of laughter, whom I was never to see clad as the majority of his fellow countrymen were. He preferred trim suitings in his office, which he exchanged for hipster gear at parties, where he liked to go jitterbugging with a dazzlingly attractive Danish wife.

For all his youth, he was a very powerful man in Mauritania, hereditary chief of an up-country tribe as well as head of the republic's tiny tourist, communications and radio departments. He was more than willing to help me get started. Within a day or two of my arrival, he had planned to obtain one of his tribesmen to accompany me on the first stage of my journey into the desert, if I thought that one man would be sufficient for my purposes. I was determined that this should be so, for, although Theodore Monod had advised me that the best unit for extended desert travel consisted of three men and five beasts, I very badly wanted it to test me at the limits of my own capacities. I still hoped that after I had served my apprenticeship with a companion at the beginning, it would be possible to push on entirely alone.

* "Ould" means "son of."

Ahmed warned me that almost certainly I would have to begin my journey elsewhere, for in Nouakchott, he said, there were very few camels to be had, and they of extremely poor quality. Mauritania was now entering its fourth year of drought, the desert was littered with carcasses, and beasts strong enough for a long passage into the interior were more likely to be found further north, at Akjoujt, where there was still good grazing. Moreover, I should not expect to get away before the middle of November, for Islam had just entered Ramadan, the month in which the Koran was revealed to Mohammed, and Ahmed's kinsman would not wish to leave his encampment until the great fast was over. In the meantime, it might be an advantage if I spent a few days out of town, in camp with some nomads, where I could learn how to ride camels and begin to pick up a little Hassaniya, the local dialect of Arabic, of which I so far knew nothing.

It was an excellent proposition, and for the next few days I strode about town in high spirits. There was a low range of dunes to the south, and towards noon each day I walked out to them to take a midday sight of the sun with the sextant. It was a very short journey, past the concrete tenements that flanked the main avenue, down a street of ruder, single-storey dwellings, out through the encirclement of tents and the scattered garbage of community. But the high wind which attended my arrival in Nouakchott had died, the sun shone fiercely out of a cloudless sky, and I was already experiencing the effects of exposure by the time I was on my way back. Standing on the dunes, I could feel the sand burning through the soles of my sandals, and the sextant became unpleasantly hot to handle. After no more than an hour and a half in the open, my lips had dried out and the spittle had become bitter on my tongue, thick and gummy at the corners of my mouth. I could see how men might die in the heat of the desert.

I investigated the marketplace, a small square behind the tenements, formed by tiny shops. There was just as much commerce in the open, among heaps of dates, sacks of grain, packages of many things tightly sewn up in skins, bottles full of what looked like eggnog but which was rancid fat for cooking, and dismembered pieces of meat pestilential with flies. Women sat before mats covered with gaudy articles, beads and trinkets and all manner of decorations. Men squatted together in rows, all sewing busily with needle and thread, all of them Negro. "It's the blacks," said a European oilman, "who do all the work while the Arabs guard the till."

In one of the shops I bought some clothes for the journey: a boubou and a serwal, which was a pair of baggy silk trousers reaching down to the calves, and a howli, which was simply four metres of black cloth to be wound round the head as protection from the sun. I had no great taste for fancy dress, but these things had been evolved out of the environment into which I was consigning myself for a long time, and it made sense to adapt as much as possible to local conditions. Apart from any other consideration, I had as little wish to be conspicuous in European clothing among desert nomads as I would have had to wear Arab clothes in my own country, or even in Nouakchott.

I went south down Mauritania's only tarmacked highway, in a Land-Rover packed with provisions and great drums of water, which my host for the next few days was taking home to his camp. This Mafud was a trader, with interests in both Nouakchott and Rosso, a small border town by the Senegal River. He divided most of his time between the two, but at weekends and occasionally in midweek he would repair to the tent where his family awaited him. It was one of a dozen or so spread out over a couple of square miles, some distance inland from the highway.

The landscape here undulated in great rolling waves of sand, but there were many trees in it, some of them in leaf. There were clumps of grasses, all of them brown and dry, and almost all of them an absolute plague upon human beings. Most widespread was the cram-cram, which cast into the wind fluffy seedlings equipped with tiny sharp hooks that attached themselves to clothing and flesh alike, pricking and scratching intolerably. Another variety dropped hard spiky shells upon the ground and these, slipping easily between the soles of the sandal and the feet, would penetrate excruciatingly up to half an inch in depth. Even the trees were armed with long lancet thorns which tore at the careless passerby. There seemed to be nothing at all in this wilderness which might encourage a man to put down roots. Here these people would remain, until their small flocks of sheep and goats and camels had eaten what little edible vegetation there was. Then they would move on, to find fresh grazing for their animals, and settle down again for a while, in the endless, timeless, enervating rhythm of the nomad existence.

As we drove up to Mafud's tent, a gang of children came scampering out, antic with excitement at our arrival. A handful of men emerged more steadily, murmuring "*Marhaba*—Welcome." Only Mafud's wife lingered dutifully behind, spreading cane mats and putting down cushions to ease the homecoming of her lord and master, and the stranger he had brought with him. Then she busied herself with a great basketwork tray laden with millet, which she winnowed vigorously, while the children withdrew to a corner and eyed me curiously with many giggles. The men had thrown themselves down in a circle, full of gossip as they casually started the long conversational process of making tea. As I was to discover interminably over the next few months, this was paramount in the life of the desert, an operation that could easily be made to extend over an hour or more, with repeated infusions progressively sweetened in one small pot, poured deftly from some height into tiny glasses and swigged like a shot of liquor.

"*Bismellahi!*" * the drinker would cry, as he tipped

---

* An abbreviated form of the phrase "*Bismelleh er Rahman er 'aDheem* —In the name of Allah, the compassionate and merciful." In full, it comes as preamble to many prayers, as well as to each chapter in the Koran. The abbreviation, however, can be used as an exclamation in practically any context imaginable.

back his glass, just like a boozer shouting "Cheers!" Then the pot would be refilled with water, a larger chunk of sugar would be added, and the talk would continue for another space while the mixture bubbled quietly upon the glowing embers of charcoal.

Mafud urged me to change my clothes, to be like them, and this I did awkwardly while the children shrieked with laughter, the men shouted encouragement, and even Mafud's wife grinned discreetly behind her hand. I doubt whether they had enjoyed such entertainment for some time, but better was to follow after dark. Having shown me how to wind the howli round my head into a compact turban, so that it would not disintegrate into swathes of cloth upon my shoulders, my host proceeded to conduct me on a small tour of the encampment. If I felt thirsty, I should draw water from the goatskin guerba hanging from the thorn tree over there. If I needed a flashlight in the night, I would find it in the corner of the tent, just there. Then he led me a little distance away, just over a rise in the ground, and proceeded to instruct me in the art of what he fastidiously called *le cabinet*. You dropped your serwal thus, under cover of the encircling boubou, you squatted thus and, having attended to your affairs, you concealed all traces by scuffing the mess over with sand.

An hour or two later, unable to delay the operation any longer, I stole out of the tent, flashlight in hand. As I rose from the ground, I realised I had made a cardinal error by removing my serwal entirely, under the cover of the bou-bou. The serwal was an enormously baggy garment, with very tiny holes for the legs, lost somewhere in the many folds of silk at the bottom. I shuffled to one side to get onto clean sand, while I began the struggle to find the leg holes, totally enveloped in the tentlike structure of the boubou. Suddenly, I heard a rustling sound nearby. I froze, for might this not be a snake? Then I switched on my flash-light, and I could scarcely have been more appalled had there been a reptile by my side. There in the sand, already dismembering my dung, were half a dozen of the biggest black beetles I'd ever seen in my life, each quite an inch and a half long. Their eyes were set on stalks, and these glowed pinkly in the beam of light. Worse, they were starting to roll the pieces of steaming dung towards me. I leapt to one side with a shout and for a moment or two hopped round on one foot, desperately trying to find the second leg hole in my serwal, trying just as hard not to step on the hem of my boubou and bring myself crashing to the ground, trying most of all to get out of the path of those ghastly dung-rolling pink eyes. Then I realised that the entire family had rushed up to behold the Nasrani * dancing like a dervish, one-legged, in some eccentric ritual ablution of his own, upon their sand dune. There and then I decided that these were probably the most inconvenient clothes ever devised by man. I was never seriously to revise this opinion.

There was much merriment around the tent next morning at the prospect of my initiation as a camel rider, the children beside themselves with glee as they awaited more ludicrous happenings to the Nasrani. An old man named Gul Mahomed arrived with a great grey bull already saddled for my use, but first there was tea-making and an hour of desultory talk before he indicated that he was ready to begin instruction. It would have been unthinkable otherwise. A folded blanket was placed as a pad inside the saddle and I was motioned forward to mount. The beast was couched on the ground and the trick was to place your right foot on his back, just forward of the saddle and just behind the beginning of his neck, to spring up and make a half turn to the left in the process, landing neatly in position with both legs astride the pommel. I leapt and, while I was in midair, the camel decided to rise, but I managed to gain my seat and stay put with a bump. Great applause from the onlookers, and I a much happier man than the night before.

* Literally "Christian," but used to denote Westerners indiscriminately.

With Gul Mahomed leading the beast by its head-rope, we lolloped off across the sandy scrub, in a rocking motion that could easily, I guessed, become soporific once your body became accustomed to the hard wooden edges of the saddle. Gradually I began to learn things. You carried a long riding stick, and with this you tapped the camel on the right side of his neck if you wanted him to veer left. If you wanted to break into a trot, you cut him smartly on the rump, or dug your dangling heels into his neck, like a jockey. To stop him, you hauled hard on the headrope. To make him couch so that you could dismount, you tapped him on the back of the head and hissed at him until he went down on his knees.

After a couple of hours, it seemed to me that the discomforts of camel-riding had been greatly exaggerated. True, it was tricky work rising from the ground, when you were flung heavily backwards, then forwards, then backwards again, as the animal came up onto its knees, then to the full extent of its hind legs and finally all-standing on its front feet too; and vice versa when coming to ground. Otherwise, it seemed largely a matter of allowing the body to sway back and forth with the beast's motion, flexibly, without straining to sit tight—though at the trot one bounced and bumped ungracefully in the rahhla, the huge saddle, with its great butterfly wings at each side. The tendency was then to hold on to these.

Thus I acquired my beginner's confidence, and only once in the next few days was it shaken. We had reached the stage where I was allowed to hold my own headrope, with Gul Mahomed walking alongside, in pace with the camel. He had fallen behind for a moment to remove a thorn from his foot when, without warning, the bull went down like a plummet, with me barely managing to keep my seat. No sooner had he hit the ground than he started to roll over to the right, in spite of the burden on his back. As a reflex more than a thoughtful move, I brought my leg from under his falling flank and went sprawling into the sand a few yards away. Spread-eagled there, I heard Gul Mahomed shout, *"Ma'aloo, ma'aloo*—Fine, fine," and I raised my head dizzily, to see the bull standing calm again, satisfied with his only half-completed dust bath. I jerked his head down crossly to make him couch for remounting, well aware that I had narrowly missed a broken leg and a journey finished before it had even begun.

At the tent, when we returned, they told me that in just such a fashion had Ahmed ould Die's father been fatally injured, badly crushed when his camel stumbled and fell at the gallop. It occurred to me that one's chances of surviving any accident far out in the desert were probably very small indeed.

A pattern of days developed in which Gul Mahomed would take me riding for a couple of hours before midmorning, when the sun began to grill the earth and sap the life out of a man. After this there was little activity away from the shelter of the tent. Men would come and go on the briefest of errands, refreshing themselves at great lengths with tea in between. The household's religious tutor, a shy and gentle young man called Sidi Mohammed, would sit with the children and begin the day's instruction in the Koran. Large curved boards, beautifully smooth from generations of use, were brought out of the tin trunk which contained the most precious family possessions. On these loakh, Sidi Mohammed would inscribe in black ink the texts which each child had to learn by heart. To one he would give el Fateha, the verse which comes as an exordium before anything else in the sacred book of Islam; to another he would offer el Shehahda, the witness to the oneness of of God and the primacy of his prophet Mohammed. The children would sit in corners, peeping at the loakh and murmuring to themselves until they thought they had the verses memorised; then they would step forward to be tested by Sidi Mohammed, who dreamily corrected them while he doodled in the sand with his writing stick.

Meanwhile, Mafud's wife and sister were hardly ever

51

idle, except in the most stifling heat. Always there seemed to be grain or rice to be prepared for a meal. Or there would be tattered garments to be stitched. Or simply children to scold. When there was no other task pressing, they would make zrig, a refreshing mixture of camel's milk and water, with sugar added: they poured it all into a bald goatskin, tied the end tightly and churned the contents backwards and forwards until they amalgamated and came out unappetisingly grey, but tasting rather like diluted yoghurt. On the days when Mafud's return to the tent was expected, Xenoba, his wife, would spend hours daubing the palms of her hands and the soles of her feet with a repulsive-looking muddy substance; it was henna, which she kept in place by drawing socks and then plastic bags over the hands and feet, and which eventually stained her a deep arterial red.

Mafud used to return like a warrior prince, though he was hot merely from the commerce of Nouakchott or Rosso. He would leap down from his Land-Rover with a rifle in his hand and stride straight to the back of his tent, where a mattress had been quickly laid for him. There he would sit, bolt upright and cross-legged, with his newly hennaed wife sitting at his right side and the rifle placed carefully on the ground at his left. In front of him everyone else would sit in a half circle, like a court exchanging obedient simplicities with its monarch. Not till Mafud had given a sign would someone move out of place to start making the first ritual round of tea.

He was a man cleft in two by conflicting cultures, and so were his closest friends. He had a cousin, Hussein, who was also deep in the business life of Nouakchott. One weekend this man came out to the camp, arriving clad in boubou and serwal at the wheel of a very shiny Peugeot saloon, which he had driven dramatically across the low duneland from the highway, swerving round the trees and flinging up a wake of dust, while music played from a cassette tape recorder in the dashboard. He, too, was armed with a rifle, complete with telescopic sights. That weekend was spent mostly in marksmanship of hair-raising carelessness. Mafud and Hussein loosed off round after round of ammunition at bottles stuck in the sand only a few feet from the track where people were in the habit of passing. Children skipped and danced inches from the muzzles of the guns, wanting to be first in the collection of spent cartridge cases.

At some pause in the musketry, I asked Hussein whether he would choose his Peugeot and the sophistications of Nouakchott or a lazier but infinitely less comfortable existence here in the camp, if it came to the point. As I spoke, he was combing his hair with careful, urbane movements. Then he grolched noisily, the spittle landing in the sand with the sound of a falling cowpat.

"I prefer the traditional life," he said, with a gleam of teeth. "The tent, the desert, the camels, the hunting." I wondered: but the two gestures—the hair-combing and the spitting—surely marked him for the hybrid he had become.

As for Mafud, he was if anything more deeply divided in his loyalties. He was the local secretary of the ruling Party; it was for this reason quite as much as for the payment of £4 a day that he had undertaken to be my host at the camp. As such, he was committed to the reforms by which the Government was attempting to shift this primitive and resourceless land into the middle of the twentieth century. When one of the nomads, visiting the tent one day, picked up my belt and demanded outright that I should make him a present of it, Mafud rounded on him angrily.

Then, turning to me, he said, "You must never give these people presents, though they will always be asking you for things. They have to learn that we are not a race of beggars."

Yet he himself possessed a slave, a Negro whose life at the camp was somewhat better than that of a faithful family retainer in Victorian England, but a slave nonetheless—forbidden to marry any girl who was not similarly born into the bondage of true Moors, obliged to remain thus unless Mafud should wish to make him a free man.

Awkwardly I had clothed myself before these people; awkwardly I fell as best I could into their ways. I discovered what it was to be pinched with cold night after night, then withered with heat day after day, and no proper protection from either cold or heat. The differences in temperature were astonishing. One morning at seven o'clock there was frost, white upon the windscreen of Mafud's Land-Rover. Yet a little after noon the temperature in the shade of the tent was 101 degrees F; when I held the thermometer in the open air, it registered 110; when I stuck it into the sand outside, the mercury climbed to 131. That night I felt frozen stiff in a down sleeping bag, and the cold kept waking me up.

A few days later a sandstorm blew up and clouds of dust gusted into the tent from its open, southern side, to settle in a thick coating on and inside everything. I wrapped the sextant tightly in a plastic bag before replacing it in its box, but the sand penetrated even that. My teeth became gritty through a firmly closed mouth. Like everyone else, I rolled myself up in my boubou so that no part of my body was exposed. At once I found myself breaking into a sweat all over, though normally one was aware of no moisture except under the armpits and in the crotch; elsewhere it evaporated as soon as it came to the surface of the skin. Once or twice I got up and peered out at this sandblasted wilderness. At the start, the horizons were as indistinct as in England when swathes of rain sweep across a landscape, though the sand seemed to be driven along no higher than the treetops. But by evening, when the wind had died down, the sky had been changed from bright blue to a muddy colour, full of dust particles; the sun was transformed into a gleaming disc, silver as a moon and surrounded by an umbra of blue.

I could see little to romanticise in this life. The food disgusted me, though I have never been a delicate eater. I was surprised how little emotion I felt the first time that Mamadoo, the slave, hauled a lamb from the little thorn corral by the tent, and slit its throat on the spot; I felt nothing more than dreamily sad. But when the meat arrived after the briefest contact with the camp fire, and I was urged to gorge myself on something that was tepidly raw, I had difficulty in getting it down. We ate much meat in that camp, and always it either dripped blood or else it was on the way to putrefaction after days of hanging in a tree, encrusted with flies. Otherwise, we ate mounds of plain, boiled rice or couscous, totally without spices or seasoning, and extremely dull.

Everything was so very grubby; even the delicious zrig had plenty of things floating on top, with a sediment of sand in the bottom of the bowl, so that I took to sieving it crudely through my teeth. And my hosts would not stop hectoring me to eat as much as they did, which was a considerable amount each day, far more than my normal intake of perfectly palatable food.

"It is," they kept saying, "full of vitamins and protein"; on the subject of which someone had evidently done a sound job of education in Mauritania. Perhaps it was, but it left me feeling heavy and windy and badly in need of a good wash, which was virtually impossible. Ablutions were almost confined to a ritual hand-washing over the brass bowl which Mamadoo brought round before and after eating, pouring water from a kettle onto the fingers of the diners, who would murmur *"Bismellahi,"* as they wrung them dry. Within a day or two I had started to smell rather powerfully, with grease and stale milk well in the foreground of the bouquet.

Most trying of all was the lack of privacy. Apart from the delicate matter of *le cabinet*, everything one did was with half a dozen onlookers sitting within a few feet, scrutinising, commenting, implicitly participating. When I opened a kit bag to search for some article or other I was conscious of eyes wishing to examine all the contents, and

I had no desire to reveal to these people everything that was in my baggage—or in myself. They were friendly and they were boisterously warm, but their ways were utterly alien to me and I did not wish to surrender myself to them. They took no delight at all in silence, which was something to be driven away by conversation or by any kind of noise that might be extracted from Mafud's transistor radio or his tape recorder. Stillness did not fall on the tent till midnight, when the radio was finally switched off, bodies rolled themselves in blankets and pressed close to each other for warmth, and the only sounds were those of the dying campfire, the occasional bleat of a lamb from the thorn corral, or the clank of a tin basin kicked over by some goat that had come foraging round the tent for refuse. A new tension was added to the ones I had brought with me, and to release it I would walk off into the dunes whenever I decently could, to be alone, to talk to A, to remember things fond and behind and within me.

Sooner or later, on these walks, I would observe someone coming towards me from a distance. Almost always I turned away, so that I should not meet them. This was partly my unreadiness for an encounter in which I should not be able to communicate properly. But at bottom it was fear of the strangeness in these people, an anthropomorphic thing about native savagery, based upon lunatic folk myths with which I had been impregnated in childhood, as much as historical incident. Would they suddenly turn nasty? What would become of me if they did? I knew that this fear would not die until I could unthinkingly move towards these strangers as a friend. I was not prepared to do this yet. Instead I gazed to the east, towards my destination, and tried to bring my journey into focus. This thing, I told myself, could be accomplished so long as I could keep moving towards its outcome. But without this movement I was done.

More than once, I found myself playing an old absentee game. Last week I was in Dakar, a fortnight ago today

56

I was in Paris, three weeks ago today I was at the Greenwich Observatory with the children, a month ago tomorrow A and I were drinking wine on the beach at Deal. . . . On all my other journeys, there had always been a comforting corollary: three weeks hence, the day after tomorrow, I'll be home with her, with them. . . .

Not this time, though.

I returned to Nouakchott a few days before the end of Ramadan. I had learned as much as I was likely to about camels at the hands of Gul Mahomed. Although he seemed content to walk miles each day, with me riding near him, he refused to let me out of his sight. The bull was very strong, he said, and if I rode off alone it would gallop away with me "*bareed, bareed*—far away"; and his gestures towards the horizon suggested that I might well end up in Tombouctou far ahead of schedule. I was not sure whether he was more concerned for the fate of me or of his animal, but there was no arguing him out of his obstinacy. Until I had a beast of my own, I was obviously not going to learn how to gallop or how to cope unaided with any sudden problem that might arise. I might as well spend the rest of my waiting time in some comfort and some privacy; once I got moving, it might be quite a while before I enjoyed either again.

In the town once more, I busied myself with the sextant each day, gradually refining my sighting errors until I was consistently getting fixes to within three miles of where I knew I was, latitude sights to within a mile. I marched round and round the place until there couldn't have been a corner of Nouakchott that I hadn't revisited half a dozen times. I walked to the Atlantic one afternoon, a four-mile hike across the municipal refuse ground and then into some high dunes which hid the ocean from the town. There were people on the beach, but I found an empty spot well away from them, and they left me alone to enjoy the green swell breaking and creaming in out of a smoky horizon. Dunlin strutted and prodded at the water's edge, and I wondered whether they were migrants from the Essex mud flats. Balls of fluff seemed to be blowing about the beach but, on looking closely, I realised they were crabs, feathery creatures moving with remarkable speed on fine, stilted legs; though, if you took one step towards them, they vanished instantly down holes in the sand. The afternoon was balmy and peaceful, with a band of coolness coming in from the ocean just above wave height, and heat from the sun just above head height. I ached for A to be with me. It was too easy here to recall Deal, where we had sat on a shingle beach with our picnic while fishing boats came rushing out of the Channel with their catches, to be winched laboriously above the tidemark. Perhaps that was why I had come here: to feel lonely with and without her. Next time I looked upon such waters, I thought, I'd be flying over them, on my way home.

The following night a holy man, a marabout somewhere in the north of Mauritania, spotted the first trace of a new moon. Ramadan was over. In the morning I followed crowds to the mosque on the outskirts of the town, near the airport. Thousands of people were drawn up in a huge circle around a dais outside the building, where the imam stood in front of three microphones. Closest to him was a multitude of men, all clad in robes which were new and stiff with starch, not just Mauritanian blue, but white and black and yellow as well. Outside this great circle stood a thin line of women, at a respectful distance from the rites. Slowly the imam chanted el Fateha and el Shehahda. Responsively the multitude, with slippers off and prayer mats on the ground, knelt and bowed backs and heads in unison, till each brow was smeared with dust. Then they straightened up and fingered their rosaries, while the imam continued his prayers.

When it was over, they drifted back into town, full of gentle pleasure, with smiles all round, at the prospect of the feast that marked this day of Fit el Idr. Up the road, in the courtyard of some tenements, a man was preparing the

58

carcass of a sheep. It had been skinned and was hanging by its hind legs from a tree, neat and bald as a plucked chicken, while the fellow studiously disembowelled it onto a sheet of linoleum laid upon the sand. At the gate of my hotel, there was a puddle of dried blood, and a blood splash on the wall where another animal had been slaughtered in full view. These people concealed so little from each other. My people concealed so much.

My time on this fringe of civilisation was running out, and I was impatient to be away. I began to pester Jean Abdellahi, marching down to her office in the Presidency each morning to ask what news there was of Ahmed's kinsman, grumping with irritation when there seemed to be little that was reliable. He would be flying in on Saturday, from an airstrip at the oasis near his camp. Then he would be coming by Land-Rover, which meant that he would not be here till Tuesday. Sorry, the Land-Rover had returned without him, he must be coming by truck; things took time in Mauritania. I went to a party at the American Embassy, where they showed a film purporting to demonstrate the democracy of a Presidential election. I went to another party in a multiracial household, where I watched Ahmed jitterbugging in his hipster gear and caught myself wondering whether he was betraying something better than he knew, or taking some fine step forward into a more golden age. I heard the child scream in nightmare in the next room to mine. I watched the fearful images take shape in the darkness above my bed. I sweated coldly in the night. I read more Solzhenitsyn.

I returned from stargazing one evening to find a note from Jean. Ahmed's kinsman, Mohamed, had arrived in town. We could be away next day, if I wished. Would I report to the Presidency in the morning to meet him? My spirits soared, and I began to move around the room humming tunes as I folded maps, parcelled books, checked medicines and stowed things into my kit bags. I slept soundly and woke eagerly in the morning, breakfasted well and went over to meet Mohamed, to discuss the terms of our contract. I returned alone to the hotel, where a man from Agence France Presse was waiting to interview me. We talked for a little while over a beer, he wished me bon voyage, then he rose and said he must be off.

As the door of my room closed behind him, I was suddenly panic-stricken. My hands began to tremble slightly and I felt a little sick. I was committed now. Before, there had always been at least a theoretical chance to withdraw. Now I was completely in it. "Please-God-help-me" kept running through my head. What was A doing? Within the hour I must be on my way. Yes, I *did* wish I'd never dreamed the idea up; the whole thing suddenly seemed a monstrous folly, with no hope of pulling it off. The man from AFP had said that it was a very British thing to do. He couldn't know that it was much more a very Moorhouse thing; plunging into something that stretched his imagination, then having to face self-extrication.

My head whirled with these trembling thoughts, and others. I hadn't managed to find in Nouakchott a drug I'd been advised to obtain as an extra precaution against malaria. One of my sandals was becoming unstitched. They said boil all water, but how could you insist on it when camping with nomads; how could you even slip a purifying tablet into a common drinking vessel? Mohamed had gone to buy a lock for his baggage; was he afraid of thieves in the night? Please-God-help-me. . . .

My desert clothes lay on the bed, waiting to be worn again. Very deliberately I stripped off and began to put them on. Then I bundled up my shirt, my jeans and my jacket—*my* clothes—and stuffed them in a kit bag. My hands had stopped trembling by the time I'd finished. The nausea had left my stomach. I was tense, but the panic had died down. I shook my head wryly at this fainthearted creature who was supposed to be attempting something that no man had ever done. Then I walked out into a day that glared and throbbed with heat.

4

I LIKED THE LOOK of Mohamed ould Moctar ould Hmeida as soon as I saw him in Ahmed's office. He was a small wiry man, very dark, a Kounta from the Tagannt plateau, country through which we must pass in the next week or two. His hair was flecked with grey, his nose was short and flat and he had a lot of hard creases in his face. He was about my own age, a former *goumier* who had served first with the French Camel Corps, later with the Mauritanian Army, and there was still a great deal of the old soldier in his bearing. He sat motionless on his chair, while Ahmed recited the details of the agreement that was to be made between us. Mohamed would accompany me as far as Oualata, an oasis close to the border with Mali, possibly as far as Tombouctou itself, and he would discharge his duties at my convenience. For this I would pay him the equivalent of £2 a day, plus his food and equipment, and I would find the fare back to his encampment, by whatever were the swiftest means available. It was agreed that I should hand him £60 of his money as we passed through his own region, so that he could leave it with his family.

As Ahmed ran through each item, Mohamed signified

61

assent with a series of affirmative clicks; he scarcely uttered a word from start to finish. Most of the time he looked at the floor, not subserviently, but like a footballer being harangued by the referee. Just occasionally he lifted his eyes to take me in, and when he did, it was a very level look. The sergeant, I thought, weighing up the green new officer who doesn't know one end of a rifle from the other. I was much comforted by his presence. At Mafud's camp I had met no one with whom I would have cared to commit myself to the desert; they had all become just a little too softened by their proximity to the capital. This man was different. He exuded toughness, and I was ready to trust him with my life. He clearly took the affair very seriously. Almost the first thing he said when we were alone indicated this. We were gathering our baggage before finding a vehicle that would take us north when he put his finger to his lips, his eyes widening with emphasis.

"You must not," he said, "tell anyone where we're going, or the purpose of our mission."

We travelled through the dusk towards Akjoujt, crammed with half a dozen other men inside a battered Peugeot station wagon. It had been arranged that we should spend the night there with a cousin of Mafud's, one Hamid, a garrulous fellow who had doubtless broadcast the whole of our business around the town before we had got as far as the camel market next morning. Only a handful of beasts were hobbled there, awaiting buyers, and not one of them looked as strong as the animal I had been riding the week before, though the prices asked seemed exorbitant. According to Jean Abdellahi, I should have been able to buy a camel for £66, but here men were demanding £100, according to Mohamed. I was not sorry when he suggested that we should move on to Atar, where, he was certain, the prices would be much cheaper. Akjoujt was a depressing place, built in the shadow of the great steel works which produced almost the whole of Mauritania's national income. The town seemed to consist of nothing but dust—dust blowing, dust mixed with garbage, dust packed into blocks

62

and constructed into habitations, dust almost paved with flattened tin cans in all the side streets.

Here the tarmacked highway finished, and our station wagon drove northeast across a sandy plain dotted with trees, not unlike the area round Mafud's camp, before it climbed the first of Mauritania's three successive plateaux. The contrast was dramatic. Here was a wilderness not of sand, but of rock shattered by aeons of scorching days followed by freezing nights. I would not have cared to tramp far across it in climbing boots, let alone in sandals while leading a camel. Though a track had been driven and flattened across these boulders by bulldozer, twice we punctured and stopped to repair the damage. It was night again before we reached Atar and went stiffly in search of lodgings.

We found them in the house of the local baker. Atar was a substantial town, celebrated throughout the land for the quality of its date groves, and Sidi Ahmed the baker was known throughout Atar for his generosity to strangers, whom he would lodge in his own bedroom rather than see turned away. He took us in without question when we appeared at his door, together with an old man who had travelled with us from Nouakchott and who seemed to have taken some fancy to this Nasrani who dressed as he himself did: he would sit by my side when we were both conversing with others, gently kneading and stroking my leg with his hand, making no sexual advance, but merely offering me his warmth and his affection.

We had been there only long enough to consume a dish of couscous, about a dozen of us squatting together in the courtyard, when Mohamed edged over to me and asked my permission to go out into the town for a few hours. "Of course," I said, wondering what on earth would keep him from an early night, for the journey had been fatiguing. I was fast asleep by the time he returned and did not discover the purpose of his errand until the following evening. He then suggested we walk together round the town, to visit some old friends of his.

We ambled silently through slender alleys, under a brilliant moon, until we came to a low door in a long mud-brick wall. We walked through a courtyard and entered a room more decorated than any I had been in so far. There were two or three crude tapestries on the walls and a couple of silver vessels on a small shelf. A young woman, light-skinned, rather attractive, dressed in white, with the very faintest suggestion of a coquette, greeted Mohamed as though he were an old family friend, and he exchanged a word with a small girl sitting on a mattress in the corner. We sat down and talked about the day's events, while the woman prepared tea. After the first glass she reached for one of the silver vessels, took a pinch of incense from it and flung this onto the charcoal burner. Then she took down the other vessel, upended it over Mohamed and me in turn, sprinkling our boubous with a sickly scent. Quite suddenly, the atmosphere had become arch with sexual intrigue.

The woman leaned over Mohamed and whispered in his ear. They giggled together, and Mohamed stretched himself sensuously on the mattress. It was a side to him that I hadn't suspected, and I was fascinated. Turning to me he said, "She wants to know if you have need of a woman."

I tried to sound more casual than I had started to feel. "Perhaps," I replied, and waited to see what would happen next.

What happened next stunned me for a moment. Mohamed called out sharply to the little girl. She rose and, facing the wall, slipped off her frock and put on a black shift. Then she lay down on the mattress and drew up her knees, with her legs apart. I felt myself go rigid with shock. Surely not, for God's sake? This was a child of perhaps twelve; I had a daughter like her in England. Should I turn on Mohamed angrily, telling him he was an evil little shit? Should I get up and walk out without another word? Or what? I sat still, mesmerised, while a critical moment lumbered slowly past. Mohamed's flirtation with the woman started up again. We drank more tea. He took out a bank note and tickled her nose with it. She coyly wasn't having any now. Occasionally she glanced at me. The child still lay there, stroking her thighs, listlessly contemplating the ceiling. Had Mohamed simply ordered her to bed, with all the false authority of a visiting uncle? I could not tell, and I still don't know.

Suddenly my companion arose, tired of his fruitless game, and said, "Let's go!"

We walked back to Sidi Ahmed's house, both of us wrapped thickly in a resentful silence. I would have given much to know what was going through his head, but there were no more words I wished to exchange with him that night. I was tainted by what had happened in the presence of that child. Unfairly, perhaps, I held him responsible.

For two days we lingered in Atar. In the marketplace here were many more camels than at Akjoujt, and they looked in much better shape. Two or three times we scrutinised them, while men came up and interrogated Mohamed about the Nasrani, flicking their eyes sideways at me as they did so. Most of the camels were cows, their udders protected by bags of netted cord to prevent the calves sucking milk that the nomads themselves wanted. Nevertheless, each cow was attended by its calf; they would be sold in pairs, useless for our purposes, for they would have neither the speed nor the staying power for a journey across the breadth of Mauritania.

It had occurred to me that we might have a better chance of striking a bargain if I remained in the house of Sidi Ahmed, while Mohamed bartered for beasts as though he were buying for himself rather than for a European: but no, he said, it was important that they should see he had a patron. After each excursion to the marketplace we returned to the house, and there, before long, one of the prospective salesmen would find us and, over Sidi Ahmed's tea, begin a lengthy dissertation on the excellence of his camels. Mohamed took little part in these proceedings, seeing it as no function of his to shield me from the strain of bargaining with his countrymen. He merely mentioned beforehand that at Tidjikja, the oasis nearest his encampment, the very strongest camels could be bought for £60. The prices in Atar were outrageously higher than that. One man offered me two bulls, together with their saddles, saddlebags and bellybands, for a total of £400. When I laughed in his face, he muttered something angrily to Mohamed, his one good eye gleaming blackly at me, his other, milky with trachoma, glaring ominously in the semidarkened room. Mohamed chewed a stick and said not a word.

We bought no camels in Atar, but we assembled much equipment and food. We wandered endlessly in and out of tiny workshops, fingering saddlebags, testing the strength of ropes, rummaging among guerbas, saddles and buckets. Elsewhere we poked sackfuls of rice, prodded dates sewn up into skins, carefully weighed great cones of solid sugar, sniffed suspiciously at boxes of green China tea. Buying these things was a cumbersome, repetitive process, involving much idle conversation and frequent visits to each place in turn before a sale was arranged and some urchin was recruited to carry the goods to an increasing pile of our possessions heaped in Sidi Ahmed's courtyard. That good and openhanded man never once complained of imposition. Instead he busied himself on our behalf, finding a metalworker who would make the complicated lock for the tassoufra, the great leather bag, richly decorated, in which we would carry our foodstuffs behind the saddle.

Once more we moved on by vehicle. Our stores were pitched into a high-sided truck, our two saddles were lashed to the backboard and we climbed up to join a score or so of people spread-eagled in confusion above an already heavy load of boxes, tin trunks, sacks and bedding rolls. With many a cry of "*Bismellahi!*" to the bystanders, we lurched out of the marketplace and rumbled across the town. Then we stopped. A man with a rifle climbed up, hauling a wife and five children after him. Many household possessions followed. So did half a dozen sheep, bleating with anguish. It was not to be a comfortable journey, for either man or beast.

We rocked and rolled around the edge of a long escarpment, ascended a pass and moved into low undulating sand dunes, with scarcely any trees and even the clumps of brown grass becoming fewer and farther between. Thrice we bogged down and had to drag sand mats under the wheels to start moving again, but these were welcome diversions, allowing us to get off and stretch our cramped and stiffening limbs. We descended the sides of a dried-up wadi, down banks so steep that sheep were tumbled on top of children, men were flung into each other's ribs, and those squatting nearest the sides of the truck were banged sorely against the ironshod rails. The mood of the passengers progressed from carnival gaiety to subdued endurance to almost silent weariness and exhaustion. We had been buffeted together for nearly ten hours, though we had covered no more than eighty miles by the time the truck drew up in moonlight at the oasis of Chinguetti. Mohamed and I bedded down for the night in a corridor of the old French fort at the invitation of the man with the rifle, who had turned out to be the incoming Commandant of the military outpost there.

Chinguetti was where Monod had started his long traverse of Mauritania forty years before. I was to do the same. It stood on the edge of El Djouf, the Empty Quarter of the Western Sahara, whose great dunes of sand rolled away for several hundred miles to the north and east, without interruption and almost devoid of vegetation. It fulfilled exactly the conventional image of a desert oasis, as did no place that I had so far visited. Here, set amid thickets of date palms, was a village of mud houses and tents made of hide stretched domelike over latticeworks of palm branches. Facing the village across a great open space, which would have provided an admirable field of fire against an advancing mob, was the old fort. Once the French tricolour had fluttered above its low, crenellated walls, with round towers at each corner, complete with firing slits. If you stood on these battlements in the evening, as the sun began to slide out of the sky, you could still catch a whiff of that old P. C. Wrennery; for from every direction small flocks of sheep and goats, shepherded by sturdy boys on foot or by girls riding aslant donkeys, would come streaming into the sanctuary of the oasis from the sparse pasture out in the lee of the hostile dunes.

Otherwise under the green and gold flag of Mauritania, the fort now had an unbusinesslike air. Its handful of troops seemed to spend most of their time lying in the sand by the front gate, playing interminable games of kherubgeh with little balls of camel dung versus rows of tiny sticks. They were, as often as not, competing with their new garrison commander, a simple man who wondered whether England was to be found next door to Guinea, and who one day proudly showed me his framed certificate of service before inviting me to turn it round. On doing so, I found myself regarding a portrait of Morocco's King Hassan, who has long wished to add Mauritania to his realm. The Commandant seemed quite unperturbed when I congratulated him on being ready for every eventuality.

For three days we camped in the fort, while Mohamed made what seemed to be desultory forays round the village to inquire about beasts. I had some time since shed the innocent notion that the purchase of camels was comparable to buying a motorcar in Europe, merely a matter of identifying a salesman, discussing the matter with him for an hour or two, handing over the cash, then driving the vehicle away. Most of the animals owned by the men of Chinguetti were grazing in pasture halfway back to Atar; it would take days to fetch them and more days to talk about them before ever a price was agreed.

It was now past the middle of November. I had impressed upon Mohamed the urgency of getting under way, but still he seemed to prefer idling his time in the company of distant relatives to any great show of activity. Even more than Mafud and his family, he insisted on my keeping pace with his own insatiable appetite for food, becoming truculent when neither my stomach nor my emotions could absorb another mouthful of half-cooked meat, tasteless rice or millet made sloppy and revolting with the addition of rancid fat. At ten-thirty one morning we applied ourselves to the entire liver and one leg of a lamb butchered by the Commandant in the fort. At noon I was invited to attack a huge pile of couscous in a tent, surrounded by children snotty with mucus and crawling with flies. Twice again before sunset, Mohamed demanded that I should eat with some friends or be thought gravely discourteous. And when, to avoid this stigma, I had taken a mouthful or two and then refused more with embarrassed explanations of sheer inability to proceed, he muttered *"Ilhamdu Lillah—My God!"* and lectured me upon the necessity of following the customs of Mauritania, not of Europe, while his friends silently watched this small humiliation of a Nasrani by one of their own. Testily I repeated my explanation, and saw Mohamed lapse into a sulky condemnation of my manners.

Uneasily, I began to wonder whether my first assessment of him had been premature. The farther we had travelled from Ahmed ould Die's office in Nouakchott, the more assertive had my companion become while I, the complete novice in this environment, was in no position to question his authority, even when my instinct told me it was overdone. We had a long way to go together, and this was far too soon for strain between us.

Next day he announced that we must wait until we reached Tidjikja before purchasing camels, but that a couple of beasts could be procured instantly for hire, to take us on the first stage of our journey. A shepherd lad would travel with us, in order to take the hired camels back to Chinguetti, but after that we would be on our own. This was not the beginning I had intended, but it was one I would have to accept, for I could not now afford to lose a day more than necessary of the relatively cool winter weather. I had become restlessly impatient to be off, my nerves were becoming overstrung with the tension of waiting, and I was in no mood to linger any more while Mohamed stuffed himself with food and lay torpidly in various tents for hours on end. Wryly I acknowledged to myself that if I had been temperamentally capable of driving a car at less than the speed limit, which I'm not, I would have found it much easier to adapt to the ways of the Sahara.

We set off early in the morning of November 23, with the shadows still long and wide on the sand, with scarcely anyone about to notice our going. As we plodded up a long hill of sand out of Chinguetti, I experienced for the first time in weeks the sheer contentment of fruitful physical exertion. At last my journey had begun, the time of nagging speculation was over, and for the moment I had nothing to do but enjoy the rhythms of my body, the easy swing of the arms balancing the heavier thrust of the legs in the most relaxing exercise of all. I checked my compass bearing and began to move buoyantly ahead of our tiny caravan, Mohamed and the shepherd lad walking together, leading the two camels by their headropes. I could hear them gossiping behind me and was glad that I did not have to take part in conversation, for even after weeks of talking French and Arabic, communication still exhausted me and I was grateful enough for silence.

At the top of the hill I could appreciate as never before the awful proposition of crossing endless sand dunes. These great hills and valleys stretched, it seemed, to the uttermost parts of the earth. There was a scattering of thin cloud in the sky, and some trick of early light and shade produced quite astonishing resemblances, from afar, to the valleys that lead off Dartmoor, with shapes imprinted upon ridges and terraces that might have been trees or rocks, but were no such thing. There was nothing here but sand, sculptured by the wind into overwhelming cliffs and sensuous crescent curves. At a distance, they had the beauty of abstract patterns. Close to, they had the beauty of texture: there were edges to these dunes so clean and sharp that you wanted to run your finger along them, and the very finest sand was skimmed whitely off the edges like spindrift by the gentlest of winds.

Yet all this beauty was deceptive. It was difficult to hold a compass course when the dunes swerved artfully against the line of march. Each dune had a hard side, packed tight by ages of prevailing winds, and it was important to keep to this, where even a loaded camel would leave no more than a footprint. Let even an unburdened man move onto the soft side of a dune, and he would sink through the surface, sometimes up to his knees. Often there was no avoiding this, unless one was to put navigation at risk. As the sun climbed higher in the sky and braised the earth, descending the soft side of a dune meant not only a dragging weight upon the feet and a growing effort to lift one's limbs out of the clinging morass; it also meant the agony of slithering strides downhill to get bare legs free of the scalding surface sand.

All day we laboured up and down these dunes, eyes screwed up against the flaring white light. In the middle of the morning one of my sandals broke, and I walked barefoot until we rested at noon and I could repair it. When I raised a leg to inspect the growing soreness of the sole, I found that I already had a large blister on the ball of my foot, containing not fluid but a tight packing of sand, which began to trickle out of the puncture by which it had entered. The early exhilaration had already been replaced by tiredness and a perpetual thirst that made the throat sore and produced a number of recurring, liquid images, whenever the mind wandered from the immediate interest of the landscape and the need to be checking the compass.

One was of Andrew and me reaching the end of our Dartmoor walk, parched enough to stuff ourselves with grapes and ice cream before catching a bus into Plymouth. Another was of A arriving at Windermere, where the children and I awaited her after bathing in the lake before her train came in. A third was a pastiche of all the bars around St. Martin's Lane and the National Portrait Gallery, none of which, I think, I had ever entered. Oddly, these images were a comfort and not a torment in this desperately arid place. But as I surveyed my blistered foot and poured a canteen full of water down my drying gullet, I wondered just what shape I would be in after walking all the way to the oasis of Tidjikja, in theory well over a week away.

The Commandant at Chinguetti had repeated to me the rule of the road with camels, just before we set out. You walked with them for the first hour or so of a day's journey, while it was still cool. You mounted and rode until noon or thereabouts. You rested through the worst heat of the day, then rode again until just before sunset, when you made camp for the night. Mohamed had invited me to mount after a couple of hours on the march, but I had refused. I pointed out to him that there were only two beasts for three men, and that if it was impossible for all of us to ride, then all of us must march. I was disinclined to accept special treatment because I was a European and un-accustomed to desert travel. Fairness apart, I was acutely aware that a psychological battle for authority had developed between Mohamed and me. The more points I could score at the outset, the better the relationship might be in the long run. I had to demonstrate that I could do anything he could do, within all possible limits, and I suspected that I could more than hold my own at walking, even in this draining heat.

So we marched steadily all day. Once or twice we had to stop to adjust the load on one of the beasts when it began to roar with the discomfort of a rope cutting into its belly or the hard edge of a cooking pot digging into its bones. This was a laborious business, for each time we had to un-hitch kit bags and tassoufra, guerbas and oddments, then heave them all up into place again. I was very ready to call a halt when the evening's cool began to drift over the sand. Spotting a stunted tree at the foot of a huge dune, the first sign of vegetation since leaving Chinguetti, we agreed to rest there for the night. There was some dead wood for a fire and a scattering of grasses with a little life still in them, on which the animals could graze. While Mohamed gathered a few broken branches together, and I made a wind-break out of our saddles and other possessions, the shepherd lad hobbled his camels tightly by the forelegs, so that they would not stray too far in the darkness.

His name was Mahomed ould Ely, and his identity card bore the vague and bleak information that he had been born *"vers 1945,"* that he was *"illettré,"* with a smudgy thumbprint for his signature. I was glad of his company that evening, for he was a cheerful, open fellow, a welcome counterbalance to my older companion's taciturnity. He was short and stocky, but he had a most beautiful walk, a swift gliding movement in which the feet didn't quite shuffle, in which the arms and shoulders swung almost mincingly, very like the movement of a male ballet dancer across the stage to take position for the next formal sequence of choreography. In spite of his build, there was something exceedingly delicate in all his bearing. When he had hobbled the camels, he would order them to graze by raising his arm as if to throw something, but merely flicking his wrist and hand gently in their direction, hissing at them quietly to be off and feeding.

As the coolness turned to cold, we squatted around our small fire to drink tea, to eat dates and to pluck at fingerfuls of a stodgy uncooked pudding made of unrefined flour mixed with water and what my companions called butter but which was, in fact, rancid dripping from the sheep. This diet would be varied only by plain rice boiled with a little salt, and by meat whenever we could obtain it. I didn't quite see how it was expected to hold body and soul together over a long period, but for the first time I approached it with something of an appetite, for the walk had made me hungry, less mindful of the grubbiness and the disagreeable smell of the fat. The moment we had finished, we rolled into our blankets, for the cold was starting to bite into our limbs. By seven-thirty, there was absolute silence in our little camp and all around. Half an hour later I watched Mohamed steal over to the fire and smother the glowing remains with handfuls of sand. Sleepily, I wondered whether he was anxious not to give our position away to persons unknown in the night, though we had seen not a sign of life since setting off. Intermittently I slept, waking every few hours to watch a pattern of stars which

73

was not the same as the one on which I had practised my navigation at home. It was not until four in the morning that I first saw my old friend the Great Bear come crawling up the sky above the northern horizon.

Within three hours we were on the march again, after shivering over tea and the remains of the stodgy pudding. By the middle of the day we were moving like tightrope walkers along the narrow ridge of a great crescent, treading carefully close to the hard-packed edge to avoid tumbling a hundred feet down the almost sheer slope of soft sand on one side, or the gentler incline of firm sand on the other. This was the outer rim of El Djouf and an end, for the time being, to sand dunes. Ahead of us now stretched a different kind of desert, a plain of black dusty gravel on which footsteps left a sandy print. There were occasional heaps of sand, no more than the height of a house, and every few miles a thornbush or two. We fairly strode across this ground, for the going was firm, but it was cruelly hard on the feet. My own were in a painful state by evening, and those of the other two, although hardened by permanent exposure since birth, seemed to be in much the same condition. Both men were as eager as I to anoint their soles with a salve that I brought from the medicine bag.

Tidjikja lay almost due south of Chinguetti, but scarcely ever were we to march on that line. We proceeded instead in a series of doglegs, rather in the manner of a yachtsman tacking up a seaway, for the chief necessity towards the end of every afternoon was to move in any direction that promised some grazing for the camels, and, above all, to move across the desert from one point of water to another. I contented myself with keeping compass checks on our course and marking our position each night with a couple of solar fixes. Later in my journey I would have to assume the whole responsibility for navigation. But for the moment I was happy enough to leave direction-finding to my companions, who lived at the two extremities of our relatively short route to Tidjikja and presumably knew this local landscape well enough not to lose their way. It allowed me to concentrate on the terrain, to see if I could begin to identify the telltale signs that meant there would be camel fodder or water in this direction or that.

We reached our first objective, the well of Chig, on the morning of the fourth day. The previous afternoon we had moved from the plain into low dunes, scattered thinly above a bedding of hard rock. For five hours we had slogged wearily up and down mounds of sand which was always soft and which, in the hollows, was never deep enough to prevent our feet bruising upon stone and clinker. A wind had arisen, blowing grit into our faces, to add to the misery. But then we topped a rise and beheld a sandy valley studded with bushes, with a dark blur of many trees at the far and distant end. We camped at once, and within an hour of starting again after dawn we were among the trees, casting back and forth across the breadth of the valley, searching for the well. I had become so accustomed by now to the loneliness of our march that I was startled to observe two familiar shapes in a patch of shade just ahead. A camel was sitting couched under a great thorn tree and, alongside him, another was lying full length in the sand. I tingled with the anticipation of meeting people again.

"There must be somebody at the well already," I called to Mohamed.

"No," he replied, "there won't be anybody."

It was then I noticed that both these camels were motionless. We had drawn level with the sitting animal before he showed the slightest sign of life, and even then he barely turned his head in our direction. The other never moved at all. Its rear vent had been torn open, evidently by some rodent, to expose raw meat; it could not have been dead very long. Its companion, said Mohamed, would soon be dead, too; certainly within a day or so. The idea seemed ridiculous, for here was not only water, and the camels presumably had been travelling with human beings who could have drawn it for them, but there were many trees in succulent leaf, food that our own beasts had been snatching at hungrily for the past half hour, as they went past. How could these camels die in such a situation? He explained that they had become fatally exhausted. They had travelled too far on too little food for much too long, gradually becoming weaker until their legs started to give way under them. In this condition, camels would fall down, once, twice, three times maybe, and each time their owners would manage to get them up and moving again, perhaps for another day or two, in the hope of reaching pasture before it was too late. But then they would go down once more, and this time nothing that a man could do would get the camels to their feet again. They would be left to die alone even when, with the bitterest irony, their final collapse had come as they reached the salvation they were seeking. These two beasts had been too weak even to eat by the time they got to the well of Chig.

"*Inshallah*," said Mohamed. "It is the will of God." What a very desolate phrase that could be.

The well was only a few hundred yards further on, a hole in the sand, perhaps four feet wide and twenty deep. It seemed to me that if such a well were situated among sand dunes or even on an open plain, one might easily, with the best navigation in the world, pass within half a mile and never see it, and that was not a comforting thought. The only clues here were a crisscross of tracks leading up to it, which would be blown away by the next sandstorm, and an area immediately around the well which was liberally sprinkled with small dark balls of camel dung. Just that, and the carcass of some long-since-dead camel, a grotesque shape of bone covered by hard and dry leather, with nothing but drifted sand inside. We sloshed water into the cooking pots for our beasts to drink from, and a great deal of it dribbled back into the well each time, taking sand and muck with it. After sucking noisily at three or four gallons, the animals appeared to be satisfied, so we turned to filling our guerbas. We had left Chinguetti with four of these goatskins bulging with water, and two of them were now much more than half empty. I was drinking five or six pints a day, the others a little less, quite apart from the liquid we were taking with tea and cooking. I had been much looking forward to Chig, whose water was promised by young Mahomed to be sweet and good, superior to the brown and musty liquid from the wells of Chinguetti. I raised some straight from the hole, eager to drink copiously. As I lifted it to my lips, I saw four lumps of dung floating towards my open mouth, and dropped the bucket in disgust. Our camels, I decided, were creatures of discrimination to limit themselves to a potful or two of this stuff.

We pressed on into a series of days that became blurred by the thickening haze of our weariness. The most eagerly awaited moments were those at midday and evening when we drank the first glass of sweet and syrupy tea, knowing that there were two more to come, each loaded with properties that would restore energy to our wilting bodies. But then the dragging agony of movement would begin again, for the haze was consistently penetrated by the consciousness of pain in various parts of the anatomy: that searing toe on the right foot which had become blood raw, that scalding blister on the left foot, that grinding ache where the left leg joined the pelvis. My lips had started to crack and blister in the dryness, and I had perversely started a heavy bronchial cold which made my chest jagged and tight inside. There was weariness, there was pain and there was thirst, which never failed to produce the images of a more comfortable and well-irrigated existence: scarcely an hour passed without a dancing vision of the jugful of orange juice which I kept in the refrigerator of my flat.

I began to wonder if I could keep this march up as far as Tidjikja, let alone journey on to Tombouctou, and the idea of reaching the Nile seemed a monstrous piece of fantasy. I found myself swearing vividly as we crossed a series of soft dunes with each footstep sinking ankle deep, needing effort to haul the leg clear. I cursed Allah for creating this bloody landscape, Mohamed for not finding a better route across it, myself for wishing me into such a tormenting situation.

Mohamed was at his best now. When our pace showed signs of slackening, he took the headrope of the leading camel, with the second one hitched behind, and all but hauled the beast along. When it was his turn to march at the back of our small column, he would clap his hands and make yipping noises to encourage both beasts to longer strides. When I lay feebly in a heap at a midday camp, he stoned my share of the dates and handed them to me one by one; then he fell back exhausted himself. Since the day before Chig we had marched in almost total silence, for neither of my companions now had the energy to continue their early chatter. Each day Mohamed had asked me to ride, and each day I had refused. I finally gave way in the middle of a blazing afternoon, when we had already been on the move for twelve hours.

It had been necessary to set off at 3 A.M. in order to reach the well of Mrechet by the next evening. As we walked across a gravel plain which glowed like a snowfield in the moonlight, a cloud drifted over the sky, throwing the earth briefly into darkness except for the bright pinpoints of the stars. Young Mahomed started to sing a chant whose words I could not catch, not unlike the one I had heard in the main street of Nouakchott. What was it about? I asked the older man.

"Oh," he said, "he's asking Allah to keep the moon alight."

And Allah did. At dawn we rested for an hour, and again at noon. Then we topped a line of dunes and saw another great plain before us, which seemed to stretch infinitely, discouragingly far. We stood still for a moment, and I was reeling a little when I stopped.

"You must ride now," said Mohamed.

"No, I mustn't," I replied, "we haven't enough camels."

He suggested that we could take it in turns to ride the pair, two men mounted while one walked alongside.

I climbed up gratefully and experienced the marvellous relief of just sitting as the camels plodded on. Quietly we went along, our bodies swinging in the saddles, heavy with fatigue. There was a new perspective up there. The world was no longer simply an excruciating obstacle, to be attacked and overcome step by step. It was a thing of vistas, which one could absorb thoughtfully again. The camels seemed to move with little effort here, their legs going down with metronomic regularity: left rear, left fore, right rear, right fore, left rear, left fore, right rear, right fore. . . . As I watched the beast in front carefully pacing the gravel, I could feel myself beginning to doze off. We rode for two hours apiece, then clambered down to walk our turn, like old men stiff with disuse, until we reached the well. But after that we walked all the way to Tidjikja.

The days were punctuated and marked by their small incidents. The day after the well of Chig was the day on which I saw my first mirage. In Nouakchott, I had been told spectacular stories of such encounters. A pilot had been coming in to land at a desert airstrip and his wheels were about to touch down when he suddenly saw facing him at the far end of the runway a great range of mountains, with snow-clad peaks, though he knew he was in the middle of almost flat desert, with the nearest mountains a thousand miles to the north. Another yarn concerned an Englishman who was sitting on the beach, when he observed high dunes of sand floating a couple of miles off in the Atlantic.

My own mirage was distinctly inferior to either of these. We were marching across the plain, bearing 165 degrees directly into the sun. Straight ahead, and much more impressively to the west, were two sheets of silvery water, bordered by what looked like trees, which dissolved into gravel and rocks as we came closer: the total effect was not unlike the shimmering light on the rise of a tarmacked highway in England during a sizzling day in June. A man would have been demented to expect drink and shade from this source.

The morning of my forty-first birthday, we had been marching for half an hour or so in the early cool of a low sun when young Mahomed, immediately ahead of me, suddenly swivelled to his left, hauling the camels after him fast to get them away from a clump of dried grass, pointing with excitement as he did so. A snake, a horned viper, was coiled there beautifully camouflaged, its skin matching exactly the colour of the sand and the grass. I would never have noticed it. The young man hit out with his long riding stick and the reptile writhed horribly. Then Mohamed came up and stoned it to bits with large rocks, in a savage reflex of elemental fear. He had already, a day or two before, killed a scorpion he found crawling a couple of feet from my head as I lay asleep after a midday meal. I had found another, between my sleeping bag and ground blanket, when I awoke and shook my things out one morning. It, too, was beautiful, a delicate shade of jade green, almost translucent. But as I bent down to look, its sting arched over with menace; and when I touched its back lightly with my stick, it struck, struck, struck wickedly at the wood.

I was too obsessed with the physical struggle of the march to pay proper attention to the most exciting discovery of all. We were crossing a hollow of sand strewn with rocks when Mohamed pointed to an object a yard or so from our tracks. It was a block of red sandstone rounded across its base, its flat top hollowed ovally towards a beak, the whole shaped crudely like an avocado cut in half and stoned. How very curious, I thought, as I gazed at it blankly. My eye registered its details: about two and a half feet long, perhaps eighteen inches wide, maybe fifty-two pounds in weight. Then I trudged on to catch up with the others. It wasn't until that night, when I was writing in my notebook, that the implications of what I had seen dawned on me. It was a quern, in which food could be pounded and then poured out, and it may have been very old indeed. Any museum in Europe would have grabbed at this piece of bric-a-brac belonging to primitive man, and I almost could not have cared less about it in that great wilderness of sand.

Next morning young Mahomed stopped to pick something from the ground and turned to hand me a perfectly formed arrowhead of flint, its point slim and sharp, its base notched into a V, its sides finely serrated by meticulous knapping. I marvelled at the eyesight that could spot something so minute in a confusion of rubble. The older man, Mohamed, was perpetually searching the ground for flints suitable for tinder with which to light his long, straight Mauritanian pipe.

Once or twice, a day was to be remembered because I was able to take in some moment of natural beauty. Invariably this would be early in the morning, when the sun rose just above the horizon and the earth glowed with a golden light and shadows lay long upon the ground; it promised warmth but did not yet threaten to scorch. Or else the moment came during darkness, when everything was still and I was rested, and I could follow the slow movement of the stars, watch the Great Bear swivelling to the northeast of Polaris, and Cassiopeia rotating opposite. But between dawn and dusk the senses were too dulled by the harsh exertions of our progress to be aware of much more than the sharpest discomfort. Thus we marched across vistas of shattered rock and sand with howling hot winds in our faces, across empty expanses of gravel upon which the sun hammered as upon an anvil.

We came down into the Wadi Rachid across great boiler plates of sun-blackened rock, leading the camels with gingerly care, for the surface of these huge boulders was treacherous, the crevices between them very deep, and an animal that slipped badly would certainly have broken a leg. At the bottom of our steep descent was a new world of living vegetation, the greenest place I had so far seen in Mauritania, with grasses and trees growing thickly out of sand, and a small patch of what looked like an attempt at cultivation. There were half a dozen stalks of corn there, and a kind of melon trailing in profusion along the ground.

As we gained the valley floor, some people came forward from the trees, and Mohamed greeted them confidently, for his own camp was but a few miles further on. Though it was only midmorning, we made camp, and while the men squatted with us and started to prepare tea, a woman came up with two melons, which we began to devour greedily on the spot. I doubt whether I had ever eaten food that was more welcome to me.

Mohamed said that one of the men was injured and asked me to look at his hurt. At once a fellow shuffled over and stuck under my nose a foot whose sole was rough and horny, the skin cracked and fissured like volcanic lava. It was badly festered between two toes, where a thorn had become embedded. As I poked and prodded the wound with tweezers, blood and pus began to flow, while Mohamed continued to ply me with slices of melon on the end of his knife, a combination that was too much for me, greatly as I desired the melon. The thorn, when I retrieved it, was quite an inch long, and thick, but the man never batted an eyelid, though he must have been in considerable pain. I hoped that no one would ask me to attempt more serious doctoring than this, though I could see the purely social advantages of travelling in this country with a medical kit. The smiles, the nods of approval, the general warmth that came off these people were more than enough to outweigh my natural squeamishness. We could be friends in this hostile land, even though the communication gap was still considerable.

That afternoon we reached Mohamed's tent. It was pitched with two others on a small plateau above the wadi, a rather bleak place compared with what we had just seen. Although some effort at cultivation had been made here, too, the melons were pitifully small and the corn was dry and stunted, as though water which had been available in the neighborhood had never found its way up here. A rambling fence of thorns enclosed this dusty growing area, to keep out the sheep and goats that were foraging round the tents. As we approached, I sensed in the little man's swaggering walk yet another mood I had not seen before. It could have been that of a commander returning to base with booty after a successful skirmish abroad. He did, indeed, bring some loot, for in Atar he had asked me to give him an advance of money with which to buy things for his family. After reaching the Wadi Rachid, he had also hinted strongly that it was the custom in his country for a new traveller to present a sheep to the family of his companions, and I had bought one from the first people we met; young Mahomed was now leading it on a length of rope. As soon as we had unloaded our gear and disposed ourselves round the tent, the lord and master of this domain slaughtered the animal, while women made up a fire and started preparations for cooking.

Mohamed's wife was a buck-toothed girl, perhaps five months gone in pregnancy, already the mother of two small children. He was exceedingly brisk in his dealings with her, and with the other two women who were round the camp. I knew well by now his attitude to females, for he had spelt it out one night under the stars after he had been questioning me about England. Was it true, he had asked, that my people were ruled by a queen? When I said yes, it was true, and tried to explain the anaemic complexities of a constitutional monarchy, he had snorted with contempt.

"Me," he said, "I never take orders from a woman. Never. Never." Then he spat in the sand for emphasis. Twice before he had been married, but his earlier wives were, he said, "dispersed." When I asked him why he had got rid of them, his answer was very simple. "They wouldn't accept my orders."

He tossed a length of cloth to his wife almost without a word, but he fondled his small son with great tenderness, gazing at him raptly with the only expression of real softness I ever saw relaxing those hard features. In Atar, Mohamed had discovered that my baggage contained a bag of marbles, brought from Paris to give one by one to any children I might meet. In the truck to Chinguetti he had suddenly announced, with remorse, that he had lost the present intended for his son, and I, taking the hint, had handed over the bagful. He now passed them on without, I noticed, saying where they had originated.

The next few hours passed in almost continuous gorging of food. First the liver and legs of the sheep were brought straight from the fire. Later, most of what was left on the carcass came piled upon a great bowl of rice. Mohamed still tried to press more food than I could eat upon me, but at least he now took no for an answer when I had eaten my fill. He seemed to contain a bottomless pit, though his belly was as neat and hard as ropework. He tore at the legs of lamb greedily, savagely, as though desperately afraid that he might never take another mouthful. There was fierce concentration in his face as his teeth ripped into the flesh, his hands grasping each end of the shinbone, the fat trickling out of the tendons, down his chin and into his beard. When he had pared away every vestige of meat with his knife, he smashed the bones and sucked at the marrow with great gulps. It was a very wild, animal performance.

When I had first seen its like at Mafud's tent, I had been sickened by it. Now I could watch it with more equanimity, though still with European distaste. At Mafud's I had been perpetually irritated by the constant grolching of men and women alike; but now I hawked up my catarrh and spat it out as raspingly as anyone. At Mafud's I was much inhibited by the matter of *le cabinet*—will someone see me? shall I mess my clothes? how terribly undignified —but now I moved away from my companions and squatted without a thought. The surrender of myself to this environment had begun, the abandonment of my civilised veneer was on its way, and I recognised my reluctance to let it happen. I was, simply, very afraid that I might become like these people. I would be trapped here if this should happen, and there would be no going back to my own people. So my haunted imagination told me as it strove to delay the loss of self.

In the morning Mohamed completed a very elaborate toilet by dabbing scent upon his face. Then he announced breezily, "Well, we'll get moving again tonight."

No, we wouldn't, I said, we'd get moving straight away. It was a mean response, but I was anxious to be in Tidjikja to equip us properly with our own camels, I was bored and ill at ease whenever we stopped for more than an hour or two, and I was, above all, paying him back in his own coin. A few nights before, he had chided me patronisingly when I had confessed to missing my woman and my children.

"Look at me," he had said, "I am a man who begins a mission and then veers neither to left nor right, but goes straight on until the end." He was very fond of this self-description and I was to be extremely sick of it by the time we parted. "When we pass my camp, I shall not linger with my family, though it will be weeks before I see them again. You must be the same kind of man."

After that, I was not prepared to allow him self-indulgence at home. He muttered something crossly to himself; but he began to make ready for departure.

An hour away from the tent he came up to me and reported that two enamel dishes had been left behind; we must return for them. Not so, I told him; we could manage without them and buy replacements in Tidjikja. An hour later he said the camels needed a rest. He knew that this drew me onto uncertain ground, and we stopped. Mohamed immediately lay down on his blanket, leaving young Mahomed and me to unload the camels and make the tea. He said he felt ill, and indicated that he had a pain in his guts. I made a few sympathetic noises, told him he shouldn't eat so much meat in future, and handed him a laxative. Half an hour later he crawled off behind some bushes, where I could hear him being very sick indeed. This, alas, gave me a certain amount of satisfaction. While he was gone, young Mahomed suggested that we should return to the camp to collect the dishes, for one of them was his. I reassured him that I would find him a new one in Tidjikja and, after a little while, we began to move again, Mohamed having apparently quite recovered.

That night we had the benefit of a tent once more, for we walked into another encampment just before dusk. Not at all put off by his illness, Mohamed demolished another great dish of meat, which these people had just been butchering as we arrived. It was a cold and stormy night which gusted fragments of glowing wood out of the fire, and everyone in the camp appeared to be streaming with mucus. They periodically shed it, as was the custom of the desert, by pinching their noses between two fingers and blowing the mess straight into the sand, both outside the tent and in.

But I was grateful for the shelter they provided in this weather, even though, I had begun to realise, the hospitality of nomads was by no means a one-way traffic. It made severe inroads into our own provisions, for while they would provide meat and milk, we were expected to respond with precious tea and sugar, Mauritanian tobacco and European cigarettes. It was while everyone was puffing away contentedly after the meal that I became aware of an old familiar sound. Rain was falling on the tent. Very light, wind-tossed rain, no more than an intermittent spattering which lasted for perhaps half an hour, but rain, nonetheless. The curious thing was that no one remarked upon it until I pricked up my ears. Even then, no one showed much interest, certainly no excitement. Yet this was the greatest benison in their lives, and the rarest. I was not to hear it again throughout my time in the desert.

It must have fallen more heavily while we were asleep, for we were a good hour's march away from the tent next morning, under a cloudless sky, when I noticed a small puddle on top of a boulder. It was now ten days since we had left Chinguetti, we had walked the best part of two hundred miles, and this put me two days ahead of Monod's 1934 schedule across approximately the same ground. Just before noon we made camp on a hillside above a valley that was thickly lined with palms. They streamed away towards the distant, eastern horizon in two files, and Tidjikja was somewhere at the far end, hidden behind another hill. We rested in the shade of some thornbushes till mid-afternoon, for Mohamed said one should never arrive at an oasis with camels until darkness had fallen; otherwise they wouldn't settle down for the night. He slept most of his time away, while I wrote my notes and young Mahomed cleaned his beloved rifle. As a weapon it was useless, for it lacked a firing pin; even with one, it would have been much more dangerous to him than to an enemy, for most of its working parts were terribly loose. But it was a symbol of his manhood and he adored the thing, always taking it to bits in idle moments, even removing the bullets from their cartridges, so that he could examine the powder inside.

We did not, eventually, move down the wadi towards Tidjikja between the two lines of palm, by the most direct and apparently most sensible route. We approached the oasis from the left in a wide encircling movement, almost stealthily, as though we were raiding it. We saw no one until we were almost up to the outer dwellings. By then it was pitch black, and I was fully aware of a fresh sensation that had been creeping upon me since our first sight of the palm trees. I felt safe again.

5

THE OASIS OF TIDJIKJA, in many ways, resembled some
place out of Conrad rather than the writings of P. C. Wren.
It straddled the wadi we had seen from afar, with hump-
backed tents pitched among palm trees on the south bank
and rows of mud houses standing back from the north
bank. On the rare occasions when the wadi flowed with
water, there would be a river here, two hundred yards
wide, dividing these two halves of the village. Now, in the
fourth year of the drought, there was an expanse of bare
sand on which camels sat couched in twos and threes, and
across which figures in blue sometimes moved, their heads
swathed up to the eyeballs against the dust and wind that
constantly swept the wadi from end to end. Even so, the
north bank, with its fringe of tiny shops on whose doorsteps
men always lounged aimlessly, felt much like a waterfront.
The steps dropped deeply into the sand and formed a kind
of wharf running the length of a nonexistent water's edge.
When the men moved a few feet to unhobble a camel and
kick it gently into action, it required but a touch of the

imagination to see them untying their canoes before paddling off upstream towards the old French fort on the inward bend of the river, now inhabited by the Mauritanian *préfet* and his handful of soldiery. As at Chinguetti, the previous colonial incumbents of this building had placed a great expanse of open ground between themselves and the native inhabitants of the oasis.

We lodged in a room shared by four other men and a small boy while, outside in a dusty yard, a tent was occupied by the women and girls of the household. The room had once been whitewashed, but now its walls were filthy and flaked, its floor was a rubble of dust and date stones, and the only light came in through the doorway. In Europe one would have described it as a cow shed, but here it was a welcome shelter from heat and cold alike. The men came and went about their business of carrying other people's goods upon a couple of donkeys, while the women cooked and interminably pounded meal in wooden bowls with great staves which were bulbous and smooth at each end. Droves of children came from all the neighbourhood to peer through the doorway at the strange creature within, then rushed off shrieking "Nasrani! Nasrani!" in voices which suggested they had just clapped eyes on the original bogy man.

I sat there, happy at first to be inactive, but with a growing sense of strain as I wrote, read, played chess and acted as host to more flies than I could ever recall having seen in one place. At Sidi Ahmed's house in Atar they had swarmed thickly between the bakery and the adjacent midden; on the march one often shouldered epaulettes of flies which presumably preferred the rhythm of a man to that of a camel; but here there were so many that large patches of the floor were sometimes obscured by their crawling bodies—and I was one day able to count thirty-seven moving up and down my motionless arm.

We had been there for twenty-four hours when young Mahomed rose to his feet, wrapped his howli round his head and announced, "I'm off." We went to help him load the camels in the lane outside and then, with a handshake and a big grin, he set out on the lonely way back to Chinguetti—with no moon, in a high and cold wind, out into the black wilderness as casually as though he were strolling down Tottenham Court Road for the last Tube train to Waterloo. Mohamed ould Moctar ould Hmeida showed no such anxiety to be on his way again, and I began to have grave misgivings about his reliability. The day after young Mahomed had departed, he said he'd found someone who would sell us two camels for £150. When I reminded him that in Atar he had vowed that the very finest beast could be obtained here for a maximum of £60, he said the majority of camels had left only the week before for sale in Atar. Next day he invited me to take a look at a good bull he thought we might purchase.

It was hobbled down on the edge of the wadi and, as we approached, a crowd gathered, sensing an impending sale. A dozen men and boys began to examine the animal knowingly, as though they were of a mind to buy it themselves, pulling down its lower lip to see its teeth and pressing their fists into its hump; one old man lifted its tail offhandedly, then gave it a hard tug, to which the camel paid not the slightest heed. As for Mohamed, he walked round the beast, looked at its teeth, felt its ribs and rubbed the palms of his hands together like a fairground salesman tensely waiting for the first bid in a Dutch auction. It would do, he said, for the £64 its owner wanted. What about the other one? I asked. Ah, that one, he said, was to be found at Rachid and he, Mohamed, would ride this one back there to collect it.

Why the hell, I demanded, had he not taken steps to buy the beast three days before, when we had passed Rachid on the way down from his own tent? Ah, he didn't know then that the camel would be there. For a man on whose doorstep all these animals were variously deployed, this seemed to me a very thin story indeed and I told him so, suspecting that he was now paying me back for my failure to allow him a day longer with his family. Hurt by my bluntness, he accused me of not trusting him. It was half true; my doubts had been growing all the way from Akjoujt. We parted coolly, he taking the remainder of the £150 to complete the transaction.

The next few days were a miserable trial of waiting for him to return. I became irritable with the people around me when I discovered in their yard a sack of sorghum flour which bore the plain inscription "Donated by the people of the United States to the people of Mauritania. NOT to be sold or exchanged in barter." I had seen one similar to it in the marketplace of Akjoujt, another trifle of conscience money from the West which had become somebody's bit of graft in the debilitating corruption of the Third World. This family had paid 3,000 francs, about £6, for their flour to a trader in Tidjikja. When I tried to explain the immorality of this commerce, they roared with laughter at my foolishness.

That evening was the first of a sequence in which I was harangued by a pompous young man on the superiority of Islam over all other faiths, on the clarity of its truths, on the sensuous delights that awaited its believers, on the damnation that was in store for all others. He was genuinely puzzled when he discovered that, although I could recite el Fateha and el Shehahda in his own tongue, I could not honestly subscribe to the beliefs embodied in either.

One morning I heard an aircraft descending and watched a small monoplane land on the oasis airstrip half a mile away. Instantly I longed to take flight on it back to Nouakchott, back to Europe, back home to my own people. I wanted to be away from the appalling filth of these surroundings, from the awfulness of this food, from the loneliness of spirit and the increasing alienation I felt wedging me apart from these primitive human beings. I wanted to fly from children who shouted "Nasrani!" mockingly at every corner, from adults who slithered deviously from one apparent fiction to another as it suited their purpose.

But another predicament prevented me from taking a single step towards the aircraft and the American who was said to pilot it, towards the collection of prefabricated huts where a Frenchman was in charge of a petrol company's base for desert operations. I knew I did not dare visit the petroliers, for already I had become a hybrid creature, fitting neither the patterns of the desert nor those of Europe. If I walked up to the huts, the two Westerners would doubtless offer me a beer and a good wash, both of which I could well use. But their first reaction would be one of repugnance at my scarecrow appearance and my disagreeable smell; it would not be uttered, but it would flicker for an instant across their faces, enough to stultify me and turn my indifferent French into spluttering gibberish.

I never did meet the petroliers. I lurked around the village until the plane took off again for the west, before I strolled up to the airstrip and sat upon a boulder. A half gale was beginning to drum up out of the desert and plumes of dust were streaming down the gravel of the runway, stinging the eyes like cigarette ash. The first week of December was over, and in London the Christmas shopping crowds would have started to plunge and plunder the length of Oxford Street in a different kind of wilderness. Was A in the middle of that lot, as sick at heart as I was here, in this sand-blasted corner of nowhere? At my present rate of progress it would be nearly the end of January before I reached Tombouctou, when all my calculations had assumed I would complete my first stage soon after New Year's Day.

After almost a week in Tidjikja I was pacing down the airstrip at sunset when I saw a rider leading a second camel at the trot round the edge of the oasis. Mohamed had returned, and so great was my relief at the prospect of moving on again that I told him to keep the change from the camel-buying. Swollen thus with 6,000 francs and the

92

memory, I assumed, of two nights in his tent, he held court before the household that evening, cocky as a sparrow. Next afternoon, he promised, we would leave, after he had attended to one or two small matters of his own.

It was with a mixture of excitement and nervousness that I led my two camels up the lane and into open scrub, while Mohamed exchanged farewells with three women who had appeared as we were about to depart. At last I had my own beasts, I was more the master of my situation than before, and somehow this seemed to be the real beginning of the journey. But I was much in the hands, for the next few weeks, of this tough and truculent little man who had made me wary of his conduct. We had not gone more than five hundred yards before he started to complain that his back was bad; I said I would put some embrocation on it when we made camp.

We had been walking for little more than an hour when Mohamed indicated some succulent trees about a mile off our course and said that we must stop there for the night, because the camels needed feeding. It was only four o'clock, and there were a couple of hours' good travelling time left in the day, but I remembered Monod's advice about grazing and did not demur. We set ourselves down by some large thornbushes and I started to make our evening meal while Mohamed warmed his back in the sun. In Tidjikja I had obtained a kilo of onions, and tonight, I said, we would have some boiled as a blessed relief from rice, dates and meat. As they cooked on the fire, I strolled relaxed round the bushes, happy to feel the tensions of the past week beginning to slide out of my body. Mohamed lay prone on his stomach, chewing his teeth-cleaning stick, brooding silently on my movements.

As the sun began to dip over the horizon, I noticed a couple of men walking in our direction, though on a course that would not run through our camp. One of them carried a very ancient-looking rifle, with a long barrel and an enormous stock, but otherwise there was nothing un-

93

usual about them; some time before, three women on donkeys had ridden the same way. The men, deep in conversation and taking not the slightest notice of us, were never within three hundred yards before they disappeared into the dunes behind. Mohamed, however, suddenly became very excited. There was, he said, something odd about the men. Telling me to hide behind a bush, he started to walk back the way we had come, towards a tent which was pitched inside a thorn fence about half a mile away. I stood there, feeling faintly ridiculous, for I could see nothing at all in the men's behaviour that made concealment necessary.

But when Mohamed returned, he was jumpy with agitation. We must get back to Tidjikja at once, he said. The men were going to encircle us behind the dunes and would surely attack us the moment darkness fell. This seemed to me patent nonsense. No one intending attack, I said, would have allowed us to see him, for a start. The men were plainly going to some encampment, as the women had been before them. Not so, said Mohamed; he had checked with the family at the tent and they had vowed that no encampment lay in that direction. I repeated my reasoned argument, but Mohamed dismissed it contemptuously.

"You are a Nasrani, I am a Moslem. You do not understand this country and these people as I do. We must go, quickly. I am not afraid for myself, but I cannot have your blood on my hands."

My ignorance I had to concede, and he knew it. Hastily, in the gathering gloom, he started to pick up a few portable possessions. We must leave everything else, including the camels, which had wandered off hobbled to browse out of sight. Disgracefully we abandoned our camp, including the lovely onions, which were ready for eating, and started to walk rapidly back to the oasis. I had never seen Mohamed move so fast, striding so hurriedly that he soon left me behind. In the darkness I walked into a bush and swore at him to stop. At that moment a gun fired and our rout was complete.

"They're after us," he cried, and took to his heels like a rabbit. It was useless, and there was now no time, to tell him that judging by the sound, the gunshot must have been quite a mile away. This was a man who appeared to be very badly shaken by fear while I, stumbling irritably in his wake, felt oddly detached about the whole affair. It was too much like a caricature for me to take it seriously.

Mohamed had recovered his composure by the time we returned to our cow shed. While we ate more awful stodge, he explained to the household, very steadily, what had happened. In the morning, he told me, we must go to the *préfet* and inform him also of what had happened; the matter would then be his responsibility. Meanwhile, I must treat this place as if it were my own home. He, Mohamed, would now go out into the night and watch carefully who entered and left the oasis during the next few hours.

Sometime after midnight I awoke with a start from a highly unpleasant dream. I had been captured by brigands, who had cut out my tongue and put out my eyes. Some nomads had found me and somehow got me back to Nouakchott, where I had begged Jean Abdellahi to arrange for me to be put to sleep completely, because I could not face returning to England in this ghastly condition. As I regained consciousness, I realised there was something new and curious about the room. The door, which had been open each night throughout the previous week, was now firmly closed. Surreptitiously I felt for my flashlight and switched on a shaded beam. There were five figures sleeping near me, but there was no Mohamed. I lit a cigarette and wondered greatly about the complexities of the evening, especially this last oddity. Having concluded that the door was shut merely to keep the cold out, I went to sleep again.

Mohamed came in while we were making the first round of tea in the morning, his face still stupid with sleep. He sat down by the brazier, his back very deliberately towards me. Where had he been all night? I asked. There was no reply. He sipped a glass of tea silently. I repeated my question sharply, resisting the temptation to haul him round by the shoulder to face me. Thickly, he murmured something about spending the night with a cousin. What cousin? The one who had seen us off the previous afternoon, the woman with her two friends.

"Right," I said. "We're going to the *préfet* now—and you can forget about the other two glasses." I was vicious with resentment, for it had been slowly dawning on me since my awakening in the night that I had been the victim of a confidence trick, carefully acted out after Mohamed had seen an opening presented by the man with the gun, whose whole object had been to let him bed a woman he fancied.

Silently we trudged up the wadi towards the old fort, and this time it was Mohamed who trailed after me. The *préfet* listened while I explained the reason for our interruption of his family breakfast, before I asked Mohamed to give his version of events. When his torrent of Hassaniya had subsided, the *préfet* rose to his feet. He couldn't believe, he told me aside, that there had been any danger, but we'd get a couple of trackers from the barracks and go out to look at the ground.

While he was gone, Mohamed said to me, "The best solution to this problem is for you to hire another man to come with us, for additional protection."

This was too much and I rounded on him, blazing with the fury of my resentment. If he had thought this trip was going to be so dangerous, then why had he not said in Nouakchott that he didn't think he could cope with it alone? He was, after all, I added with bitter sarcasm, supposed to know this country so much better than I.

My anger was not only the product of the night's events; it was stoked heavily with a variety of grudges I had against him. I now thought I had the reason why we had not bought camels in either Akjoujt, Atar or Chinguetti: it was because he had arranged, before he left for Nouakchott, to deal with kinsmen in Tidjikja and Rachid, presumably on the understanding that he would get a cut of any agreed price. I was quite certain he had unloaded much of our foodstuffs at his camp without my knowledge: what we had bought in Atar had been supposed to last us a month, and we had been obliged to replace it almost entirely in Tidjikja within a fortnight.

It seemed to me that the best solution by far would be to dispense with his services forthwith, for I most certainly didn't trust him now. Two things held me back from packing him off home at once. One was that such a radical rearrangement would almost certainly provoke much greater delay, and the thought of this was intolerable. The other was that I was fast running short of money, and to abandon Mohamed now might well run me into an impossible financial position, for there was not another bank until I reached Tombouctou. Although it had been agreed that I would give him 30,000 francs when we reached his camp, he now had half as much again: in Atar, in Chinguetti and here in Tidjikja he had wheedled advances out of me, and he owed me something like forty days of work. I really couldn't afford to let him go.

We drove out to our abortive camp by Land-Rover. Not a thing had been touched in our absence. It took the *préfet* and his trackers only a few moments' scrutiny of the ground for the official to draw me apart from the others.

"It's a nonsense," he said. "Everybody passes this way from the village to the encampment over the dunes. The men were simply returning home last night. The shot was either *joie de vivre*—or a rabbit."

It was as my instinct had told me. I asked him what he thought of Mohamed.

"He's making a mountain out of a molehill," said the *préfet*, "because he's scared stiff about your journey. His reputation around here is as a camel handler; nothing else."

I paused for a moment, then took the plunge. What were the chances, I asked, of getting a good man to accompany us to Tichit, the next oasis, starting without delay. It was easy, the *préfet* replied; he knew just the man—one who could bring his own camel.

The activity of the next hour was little short of the miraculous, given my halting progress thus far across a small corner of Mauritania. We left Mohamed to retrieve the camels and drove back into Tidjikja. We stopped there by a tent and hailed a lanky, aquiline fellow who sat on a blanket, surrounded by women and children. The *préfet* explained my needs to him and the money I was offering. At once the man nodded and, without pausing to do more than fill a tassoufra with some things and pick up a saddle, joined us in the vehicle. By eleven o'clock that morning I was on the march again, striding ahead with the camels while Sidi Mahmoud ould Sheddadi loped beside me on long, spindly legs. Mohamed had to bustle like a spaniel in order to keep up the pace. This wasn't the only difference between the two men that soon became obvious. Sidi Mahmoud, questioning me about the purpose of my journey, threw his head back and let out a great high-pitched laugh; and sometime later he started to sing to himself. I had not known Mohamed to do either of these things.

It was clear that I would have to use all the tact I could muster in my dealings with Mohamed over the next few days. As we rested after our midday meal I noticed that, though he appeared to be asleep, he was in fact watching me closely through half-shut eyes. I had scarcely exchanged a word with him since my explosion at the fort, had spent myself entirely on Sidi Mahmoud since he joined us, and did not doubt that Mohamed was now smouldering with resentments of his own. He had much to resent—above all, his exposure as a coward in front of the *préfet* and his men. I must jolly him out of this as gently as possible, while making it plain that I was no longer the gullible novice he had picked up in Nouakchott. By evening we were talking to each other again, and it was not worry about our relationship that gave me a disturbed sleep that night. The room in Tidjikja, I now discovered, had been filthier than I supposed. I was crawling with lice.

The following day was a horrible one, even though by nightfall we had reached the camp where Sidi Mahmoud's camel was grazing and could start riding from there onwards. It started badly with a freezing wind, which had us shrammed to the bone even while we marched. I was forging ahead of the other two in an effort to warm myself up when I heard a commotion behind me. Turning, I saw the younger of the two bulls bucking with fright, its baggage falling off around it onto stony ground. Mohamed and Sidi Mahmoud quietened the beast down, then stood by its side to examine the broken bellyband that had caused it to bolt. I started to collect the things that had been pitched off . . . then stopped and swore violently. There, lying against a rock, was the sextant. A few feet away was its case, the fastenings burst open, one of the wooden sides partially stove in. The instrument itself appeared to be undamaged; the mirror, at any rate, was unshattered, and as I twirled its various knobs and dials they moved as freely as before. But heaven knew what delicate balance of the interior mechanism had been upset by the violence of such a fall.

I felt a little sick at the possible implications for the rest of the journey. Sidi Mahmoud, I was aware, was familiar with the route to the next oasis of Tichit, but I did not for the moment care to dwell on the navigational problems that might lie beyond. Grimly I banged the case back into shape and repacked the sextant before we continued our march. At the camp that night some women repaired the bellyband, while I went through the baggage to see what else had suffered from its breaking. The thermometer had been smashed, and so had some plastic containers of drugs in the medical kit; a carton of cigarettes was half pulverised into dust, and there was a grievous dent in the hardboard cover of my Arabic dictionary. But none of this mattered compared with the possible destruction of the sextant as a working instrument. There was little point in trying to check its accuracy here, with only an approximate position to go by; that must wait till Tichit, when the chart would tell me precisely where I was.

I was explaining to the others my fears about the sextant when Mohamed showed open hostility for the first time. Whenever I had taken a shot of the sun, during our march from Chinguetti, he had watched with curiosity but without comment while I completed the sight and, at the end of each day, made my calculations in the notebook. Once I had suspected him of making a joke about it, for I had heard him murmur something quietly to young Mahomed, who had giggled in response. But now he told me that it was of no importance if the sextant were broken, as it was a useless toy anyway. Maps, too, were rubbish, constructed by Europeans who knew nothing at all about the region. Why, I had talked of taking a direct route to Tombouctou from the border oasis of Oualata, when everyone knew that there was no such thing, that it was necessary to continue south from Oualata to the oasis of Néma, before turning east for the crossing into Mali. It was true that I had spoken of such a route, for it was clearly marked, on two different charts in my possession, as an ancient camel track.

I held on tightly to my patience and questioned him in detail, as I had not done before, about his knowledge of the country that lay between us and Tombouctou. I discovered that he had never, in fact, been outside Mauritania, even during his service with the French, as I had been led to understand. He knew nothing of the land to either the east or the south of Oualata. Then he dropped his bombshell, and he was insolently casual enough about the dropping of it for me to repress a strong desire to hit him. He didn't have an identity card, he said.

I knew very well this meant that he would be unable to travel out of Mauritania to Tombouctou. I knew, furthermore, that he had been carrying his identity card when first we met, for I had examined it in Atar. He now said that he had left it at his camp; he didn't know it would be required for a passage into Mali. He had taken it to Nouakchott because a country fellow like him never knew when the police around the capital would want to examine your papers. It was the fault of Ahmed ould Die and myself that he did not have it now, for not telling him that it would be necessary for movement from one country to the other. He was no fool, this Mohamed: he had been a *caporal goumier* with the French Army, he could read and write his own language and could also speak a little French, none of them common achievements in Mauritania. It seemed to me that he had never intended to travel with me as far as Tombouctou, that he had quite deliberately deceived Ahmed ould Die as much as myself in Nouakchott.

There was nothing to be done about it, and I was not at all downcast at the prospect of losing Mohamed earlier than I had first anticipated. But I felt badly cheated. From now on, I resolved, everyone in this blasted country would have to demonstrate his honesty before I started to treat him as anything but a potential rogue. And from now on, the pace and the manner of this journey would be regulated by my wishes, insofar as this was compatible with the overriding needs of the camels, and not by any sauntering indolence of my companions.

We rode steadily, that first day out of Sidi Mahmoud's camp, though I scarcely fitted the commanding role that my resolution decreed. Throughout the morning I had trouble keeping my mount at the trot and trailed badly behind the other two. From time to time they glanced back at me, then turned away, grinning to each other. They were, I noticed with little relish, becoming very matey indeed. But then I discovered that if I gave my bull a great belt with the riding stick he would, after a protesting snarl, actually start to gallop and recover the lost ground. What was more, I found that by crossing my feet over his neck, gripping the pommel of the saddle between my thighs, and raising my arms in a balancing movement that looked like a gesture of surrender, I could ride at the gallop without feeling that I was about to fall overboard. The result was that we made exhilarating progress till five o'clock, when we spotted a tent about a mile away to our right.

Sidi Mahmoud turned to me. "Camp?" he asked, with

the question mark distinctly in the air. Mohamed said nothing, but watched me carefully.

"No," I replied firmly, "we go on for another hour."

They both looked exceedingly put out, but we trotted on while Sidi Mahmoud, ranging his beast next to mine, said, "It's important to let the camels start feeding an hour before the cold starts."

This might or might not be true, I thought, though between Chinguetti and Tidjikja .we had never stopped before six each evening. I was, however, much more concerned to impose my own will upon the party this night, and they knew it.

As Sidi Mahmoud drifted away from my side, I heard him grumbling in broadest Hassaniya. At my insistence, Mohamed translated. "He says he wants to stay in a tent for the night, where we can have milk and things." The advice about the camels, in short, was a cock-and-bull story devised to justify Sidi Mahmoud's own preference for comforts.

There were many nomads in the desert between Tidjikja and Tichit. Not a day passed without our seeing at least a man tending his herd of flop-eared brown sheep, which at the start of the journey I had easily confused with goats. We spent almost as many nights in the company of others as we did in solitude. Either a small tent was quickly put up for our benefit, or we slept in the lee of a nomadic humpy tent, upon mats which had been laid on our arrival. We were holding to the ground north of the escarpment which crossed the country, below the desolate sands of El Mreyye, the Place of Mirages. The undulating sands which we crossed ourselves were desolate enough, broken though they were by occasional trees and by clumps of withered grass which stood maybe fifty to a hundred yards apart. It was not until much later in my travels that I realised how comparatively rich this area was in pasture for animals. Sheep, goats and camels alike which we saw here were thin and bony creatures, but in this ground, unbelievably by European standards, there was some substance on which they could feed; elsewhere there would be none at all.

Everything in these nomadic lives was bent towards a preoccupation with food, for man and beast alike. There is a word, *ghudda*, which in Arabic can be translated variously as "lunch" or "vegetables" or "greens," but which in Hassaniya is an omnibus expression for food of any kind, for feeding, for whatever represents the antidote to hunger. Whenever men talked together in this undernourished land, for however long they talked, you could be sure that the word *ghudda* would be uttered by one person or another every few sentences. If they were not arguing about the absence of ghudda for their animals, they were deploring the high cost of ghudda for human beings. Food of every kind was their obsession, in a way that no Westerner has known it for a long time. They were particularly avid for meat, which represented to them the most nourishing as well as the most satisfying form of food. This desperate desire for meat, I soon realised, explained their habit of merely singeing it in the flames of a campfire as soon as they had butchered a piece from the animal: they simply could not wait, by cooking it properly, to get their teeth into it. This was not greed, as a decently fed Westerner understands it. It was the product of an existence perpetually balanced just above the level of famine.

Not all these people were abysmally poor, though. We came one evening upon three small tents, tucked in the shelter of a high dune, where two women and two children sat enjoying the cool of the sunset. Mohamed immediately assumed his swaggering All-Moslem Male role, which I had come to detest. One of the women was very old and withered, and it pleased him to tease her coarsely, making bawdy jokes about her on the side to Sidi Mahmoud, who giggled obediently. The women, nevertheless, by force of habit, began to attend to their unexpected visitors.

It was dark by the time two men and a lad showed up, their coming announced by the shuffling pad of many feet in the sand. By the wavering glow of the fire I saw that they were driving a great mob of camels, perhaps fifty beasts in all, which they painstakingly hobbled before joining us round the teapot. The camel, I well knew, was valued as a considerable possession by any nomad: it represented wealth comparable to that of a motorcar in any European household. A man who owned fifty beasts was really rather rich. Could it be, I asked Mohamed, that a family which dwelt as sparsely as this one, with little about its tents other than cooking pots and blankets, actually owned so many camels, or were the men merely acting as shepherds for some well-landed fellow whose home was a building in one of the oases?

No, he said, this herd was theirs. If they sold it off and got the best price for each animal, they could easily set themselves up in the commercial life of Tidjikja or Nouakchott. But they preferred to enjoy the freedom of the desert. Moreover, though this was a substantial herd, truly, it was not exceptional. Mobs of two or three hundred camels belonging to one family were not out of the ordinary, and a few men in Mauritania owned as many as one or even two thousand camels.

We were beginning to doze off that night, under a brilliant full moon, when a great scuffling occurred among the beasts. Raising my head, I saw that one of the bulls had mounted a cow—a bit unfairly, for she was hobbled and couched, while he was unhindered by ropes. That morning, indeed, I had seen the first sign that the rutting season had started; we had passed a bull trailing a cow, he blowing the same obscene pink bubble that Fred had produced at the London Zoo, she walking disdainfully, her tail flicking up coyly to expose her vent. In the moonlight, I now witnessed the entire operation. The bull lay over the cow's back, his forelegs splayed out level with the base of her neck. At thirty yards' range in that light, it was impossible to see the details of their movement, but there was much grunting, disconcertingly like that of the human male reaching his climax. Then, suddenly, the bull tumbled sideways off the cow, or else he was thrown off, and rolled over on the ground. He picked himself up and ambled away, satisfied. She rose and stood, with her tail rising and flicking. Then, her hind legs braced apart, she pissed copiously. The whole performance had lasted perhaps five minutes.

Just before it finished, some movement from Mohamed caught the corner of my eye. Half turning, I realised that the man was masturbating under his blanket.

I turned away again, until Sidi Mahmoud cackled and called over to me, "He needs a woman badly."

I wasn't at all surprised; Mohamed seemed perpetually to be in need of a woman, and I marvelled at his sexual energy when my own had quite disappeared under the physical demands of the journey; though I thought of A a great deal of the time, not once did I visualise any erotic moment we had shared. There were times when I concluded that, from Mohamed's point of view, this enterprise had been conceived to let him bed every woman we met whose man happened to be away from the tent that night. The evening was still to come when he found the nerve to ask me to vacate a tent for the night so that he could enjoy what he clearly regarded as his divine right, and was much upset when I told him that if he required a woman that badly, he could take her over the dune for an hour or two, where, I promised, I would not disturb them. I asked him now what on earth he did if he met no woman for more than a week or so. Quite coolly he replied that in such circumstances a man could do or, in extremity, a donkey.

I could never reconcile myself to the attitude of these men to women. Every move they made in an encounter with the other sex was a crude assertion of their domineering masculinity. However tired we were towards the end of the day, however slowly we had been ambling through the heat of late afternoon, an abrupt change came over my companions if they noticed a tent on the horizon. At once the camels were whipped into a fast trot and we approached the dwelling like warriors eager for more battle, rather than as the weary journeymen we had truly become. If it happened that women and children were there alone, we rode up and couched our beasts without a word, imperiously dismounting to take possession of their quarters as if by right. We would unhitch our baggage nonchalantly while the women scurried round, laying out mats and placing hassocks upon these so that we might recline more comfortably, bringing bowls of zrig for our immediate refreshment. They really were no more than objects of sexual satisfaction, appliances for the production of children and vassals for the performance of menial tasks in an encampment. Their role was thus ordained at birth.

One evening Mohamed tossed over to me a device lying in the sand outside a tent, a couple of sticks each a foot long, thonged together at one end to form something which resembled a kind of nutcracker. He explained that a woman was no good to a man unless she had much flesh on her, that a girl-child sometimes must be forcibly fed to produce the desired results as she grew up. The sticks were clamped round the child's toes and then squeezed together to make her shout with pain, so that fattening food could be shovelled into her open mouth. It occurred to me then, not for the first time, that Mohamed ould Moctar ould Hmeida ought properly to have been making this journey in the company not of myself, but of Miss Germaine Greer instead; both might, in different ways, have profited by the experience.

If men were at home when we rode up to a tent, the initial procedure was somewhat different. We would arrive as gallantly as ever, but there would be no instant dismounting and unloading of baggage. Instead, there would be the exchange of greetings customary to strangers meeting in the desert. Throughout the Arabic-speaking world, this begins with "*Selehmoo alaikum*—His peace be with you," which is swapped for the responding "*Alaikum wa selehmoo*—Peace to you, too." Thereafter the strangers swiftly proceed to general conversation. But in the Mauritanian Sahara, the opening gambit was much more protracted than elsewhere. The first speaker would continue with "*Le-bass*—No evil," and the second would echo it. The formula would then proceed thus:

1: "*Yak le-bass*—On you no evil."
2: "*Le-bass.*"
1: "*Ash halak?*—How are you?"
2: "*Le-bass Hamdulillah*—No evil, thank God."
1: "*Yaksalmin*—May you and yours be safe."
2: "*Le-bass.*"
1: "*Ash nebtekum?*—How have you been?"
2: "*Yak le-la le-khif*—On you, only light burdens."
1: "*Yak ma tara alaikum shekun lekheer*—May only good happen to you."
2: "*Le-bass.*"

It would go on like this for several minutes, according to whatever was the distinctly local prescription, the speakers meanwhile examining each other closely before committing themselves to the point which one or the other really wished to bring up. It served originally, I imagine, as a very elaborate password between friendly tribes, which aliens were bound to stumble over and so betray themselves; it had become, by usage, simply a way of gaining time in which each could weigh the other up while deciding whether to give and take. More often than not, when the formula had been exhausted (with an exhausted-sounding sigh on the part of the last speaker), the men of the tents would invite us to stay the night with them. Once or twice we were told that there was better pasture for our camels farther on, the hint was taken, and two extremely cast-down Moors would lead their Nasrani companion off to spend the night alone a mile or two away. If we stayed, however, the men would come to our assistance in unloading, before all the males in the camp lay together around the teapot, while the women got on with their inferior roles of service.

For myself, I was happiest when we spent our nights alone, for my nerves became frayed by the uncongenial atmosphere of the camps. The perpetual cadging wore me down, not so much because it was a constant drain upon our provisions as by the manner in which it was conducted. People rarely asked me for something directly and simply, as an expression of need which I could scarcely deny. Almost always a request was served with a hint of collusion by my two companions, or with some devious moral pressure which I resented strongly.

One night we stayed with an engaging fellow who spoke vernacular Arabic as I had learned it and with whom I could talk more easily and comprehensively than ever I managed to in Hassaniya. We got on well together and, when he asked me for a tin of coffee, one of two I had found in Tidjikja, I was pleased to give it to him in gratitude for his friendship. Next morning I heard him whispering in the ear of Mohamed, who then turned to me with the following advice. "This man is the son of a famous marabout. He's a great chief. All the Nasrani who meet him give him something. He wishes you to give him tea and sugar." And I did; but this time it was not such a willing gift.

Invariably I was asked for medicines, and almost every evening when we camped with others, I found myself squeezing ointment into eyes that were inflamed with dust, the first stage on the road to trachoma. Out in the desert, people stoically endured the recurring cycle of this condition and accepted the blindness which eventually followed as the ineluctable will of God; but in the oases I had seen them attempting makeshift medications of their own. They would heat a can of condensed milk mixed with water and then hold their cloaked heads over the bowl so that the steam rose soothingly into their eyes. They seemed to disregard the small dispensaries which the Government set up in the villages, though they had a fine appreciation of the drugs and ointments that I carried.

So did Mohamed. There was scarcely a day after leaving Chinguetti when he had not complained of some malady and demanded the dawa to put it right. More than once I had rubbed his back with embrocation, and this was, in the end, the roundabout cause of a remarkable improvement in his overall health. As I kneaded his muscles one evening, the expression on his face suggested that the randy fellow was getting nothing more nor less than sexual satisfaction out of my doctoring. I told him to put his shirt on again, then I looked at him very seriously.

"Mohamed," I said, "I've just realised what your illness is. You have pains in your back, in your head, in your teeth and in your stomach. Day after day you have these pains. I'm afraid you're really rather ill. I don't know the word for it in French or Arabic, but in English it's called hypochondria. It's a very terrible disease." This was the only time, apart from the occasion of our wretched flight in the night, that I saw alarm cross his face. "Don't worry, though," I reassured him, with a pat on the arm, "I can cure it. I have the right medicine here."

I fetched three salt tablets, large ones, from the medicine bag and handed them over. He must suck them, one after the other, I explained. He must not swallow them, and on no account must he drink any liquid for the next three hours. Obediently he sucked the first two tablets. Surreptitiously, he spat the third one out. Never again did he ask me for medicine.

I was, of course, succumbing to the persecution complex that has visited every lone traveller who finds himself in a totally alien environment, knowing himself to be at a disadvantage in all his dealings with others, without anyone to whom he can turn and rely upon for the comfort his soul craves. I was, in fact, feeling rather ill after we had travelled a week out of Tidjikja. I was still in the grip of my chest-racking cold and the lice were tormenting me abominably. During the day my movements were vigorous enough for me not to notice theirs, but whenever we stopped, and throughout the night, I could feel them crawling incessantly across my body. A great welt of bites encircled my abdomen, becoming raw in places where I scratched at the irritation in my disjointed sleep. And though my feet had now become hardened with calluses and were, in any case, no longer punished as severely as on the march down from Chinguetti, the riding was beginning to take its own toll of my flesh. The perpetual chafing of the saddle against the base of my spine, and of the pommel between my thighs, was producing a different crop of sores to compensate for the loss of those that were easing themselves from my feet. I would have felt sorry for myself in civilised company. In the company of Mohamed and Sidi Mahmoud, self-pity was augmented by the increasing suspicion that they were ganging up against me for their own ends. They had developed a nasty habit of ridiculing me in front of people whose hospitality we had secured at their insistence, not mine. They would make some challenging remark in Hassaniya, and when I struggled to respond in the same dialect, they would collapse in patronising laughter at my footling mistakes, inviting the others to join their merriment at my expense.

I did the only thing open to me in the circumstances. I hit back with their own weapons. Sidi Mahmoud, I had discovered, was fond of singing to himself on the march. We came one morning to the well of Tazazmout and there rested for several hours through the heat of the day. As we lay in the shade of a bush, our guerbas refilled, our camels browsing, I proceeded to instruct him in the first few lines of the British National Anthem.

He took to it rather well, chanting within a few minutes, "Gawd sieve our wobbly kween"—which, if anything, seemed to me something of an improvement upon the original. With less enthusiasm, the unmusical Mohamed was induced to join in and, thereafter, for several days I insisted on a choir practice at our midday camps. Maliciously, I hoped that one day the two would discover that they had been invoking God's blessing upon a despised woman—and the wrong God, at that.

And though I am not proud to record it, I have to report that I coached them assiduously in the art of identifying themselves to any other English-speaking Nasrani who might solicit their assistance in Mauritania. The result, I trust, is that if any such person should ask the lanky Sidi Mahmoud who he is, the reply will come pat: "I am a lawng streak of piss." Mohamed, for his part, will oblige with "I am a cunning little shit."

These were very private satisfactions in the wilderness of Tagannt. But they helped.

It was at Tazazmout that we broke through the escarpment from the north and started to traverse the sandy wastes below its southern edge. For the first time since leaving those steepling sand dunes around Chinguetti, there was real drama in the landscape itself. As we paused before our descent I could see stretching to east and west of me the hard black line of the rocky shelf, no more than five hundred feet high, but arrogant as a bastion and formidable with endurance. The tumbledown boulders of the gully, moreover, quite remarkably resembled the millstone grit structure of the Derbyshire Peak District in my native northern England. As we carefully picked our way down to the floor of the lower plateau, I heard myself humming the last triumphant movement of Beethoven's Fifth Symphony. I felt at home and more at ease in these surroundings than ever I could be among sand dunes and shimmering gravel plains. The weather, too, had done something to lift my heart a little. The past week's skies had been leaden with cloud through which the sun filtered in only feeble rays, creating its own oppressive atmosphere. Now the clouds had gone, and though one paid heavily with one's body for exposure to the unhindered sun, the lightening of the spirit was for the moment more than a compensation.

As we packed up to move away from the well, a gunshot exploded somewhere out in the sands, with a *thumpcrack* that could not have been very far away. We mounted at once and began to trot fast, while Mohamed rode close to me and fed me with stories of lawlessness.

There were men in these parts, he said, who would kill any stray camel they met, to provide themselves with meat, who would if necessary kill anyone who came between them and their quarry: they cared nothing for the President and his sanctions, for these were far away in Nouakchott, remote from their imagination. As we hurried along, he was scanning the horizon with a concentration he usually reserved for tent-finding towards the end of a day. An hour later we came upon the remains of a fire, a day or two old, and beside it the jawbone of a camel whose teeth, said Sidi Mahmoud, were very young. Almost certainly it had been killed for food by someone hard-pressed for meat, for no one in this country would slaughter a five-year-old beast for any other reason; it represented too much potential wealth alive. But we saw no one until late the next day, when we camped again with a nomad family. The evening after that, our ninth since leaving Tidjikja for good, we came to Tichit.

All afternoon we had ridden across glaring sand, then over a range of dunes which the wind had carved into fantastic shapes I associated with Alpine snowfields, full of enormous overhangs which ended elliptically in space, so that one subconsciously searched for the icicles that must surely be growing from them. They were very steep and we were moving across their grain, which taxed both us and the camels. The beasts grunted with the effort of uphill struggle, which they made in jerky bursts, the riders leaning as far forward as possible to put their maximum weight over the shoulders of each camel. Riding downhill was even harder, for the camels, moaning now, ran stiffly in long strides to avoid losing their control while we, leaning backwards, our arms braced against the sides of the saddles, had our spines and shoulders jolted heavily. Beyond this obstacle lay the oasis, crouching near a thicket of palms upon a flat gravel corridor, which ran between the rearing cliffs of the escarpment and a rising wall of high dunes to the south.

Tichit was a very ancient village, founded in the eighth century, celebrated for the style of its buildings, which were constructed of uncemented stone flags piled tightly on top of each other to form box-shaped dwellings. Its mosque had a square tower (there was another at Chinguetti) quite ridiculously like that of an Anglo-Saxon parish church at home. But centuries of warfare, pestilence and neglect had transformed the oasis into a ruin of a place, with dilapidated walls which looked as though they had undergone a systematic bombing attack.

The most substantial dwelling by far, apart from the house occupied by the *préfet*, was that of the village headman, Sharif Ahmedu, to which we made our way at once. People in Nouakchott had extolled his hospitality and assured me that he would be very glad to offer me shelter for the day or two I expected to be in his oasis. In this, they were a little misleading. The Sharif did indeed receive us on his premises, allowing us to sleep and feed in the corridor of his courtyard, much as Mohamed and I had done in the fort at Chinguetti. I would wake in the mornings to find him, a picturesque and elderly figure clad in a gorgeously russet cloak and hood, regarding us enigmatically from a position of semiconcealment behind a pillar on the opposite side of the yard. Later, I came to the conclusion that he had been weighing up how wealthy I was.

Naturally, I expected to pay him for our lodgings. I had done this in Atar, in Chinguetti and at Tidjikja, in each case consulting Mohamed about the amount I ought to offer. As he insisted, on each occasion, on acting as intermediary and handing the cash over, I assumed that our hosts had received at least a fair price for the accommodation. I now made the mistake of dealing directly with the Sharif, offering him 5,000 francs for the two nights of our stay, which was somewhat more than I had paid before; but then, his food was slightly better, the couscous, for the only time in my experience, being garnished with gravy. He refused to accept my money; the price, he said, was

113

9,000 francs. Even Mohamed and Sidi Mahmoud sucked their teeth with disapproval when I told them how much I had been obliged to pay.

Yet within half an hour, the Sharif sidled up to Mohamed and bade him ask me for some medicine to cure a pain in his head. The old ruffian, I decided, should be served in kind. Handing him a couple of codeine tablets, I announced that they would cost him 200 francs apiece. He examined them carefully before giving them back with the news that he could obtain tablets as good as those from the dispensary down in the village.

The avarice of Sharif Ahmedu, however, was the least of my worries in Tichit. That first morning I climbed onto the roof of his house and took a shot of the sun with the sextant; six hours later I repeated the sight and scrambled down to work out the position from the double fix. Miserably, I calculated that I was somewhere just north of Tombouctou. In the darkness that night, I sighted Regulus, Rigel and Capella and worked out from them a more precise three-star fix. The result was just as hopeless as the one from the solar observations. Unquestionably the sextant was useless, even more inaccurate than when I had first acquired it. I could see nothing wrong with it, and its parts still functioned smoothly, but something was disastrously awry; possibly the alignment of the mirror had been crucially shifted by the fall from the camel's back. I wasn't at all sure what the long-term implications of this blow to my navigation might be, but I had already made up my mind in the past few days that I would go on from Tichit towards Tombouctou, even if the sextant should prove to be finished. Since reaching the escarpment I was confident that, if the worst came to the worst, I could myself lead the way to Oualata at least, for the map showed that these rocks now continued distinctly in a curve across the desert, Oualata itself being perched on top of them. As for finding wells, I could probably fix my positions by compass traversing the escarpment, provided we held to the ground beneath it.

Such considerations apart, my pride would not allow me to quit at this stage. I was set upon a journey thirty-six hundred miles long and I had not yet travelled five hundred of them. Failure at this point would have been abject.

Yet at Tichit, more than ever before, I yearned to go home. A drone in the sky as I finished my first sun shot announced the arrival of the weekly aircraft. I walked down to the landing strip to watch it unload grain and rice from Nouakchott, together with a variety of equipment for some French archaeologists who would be following later to set up a base here for their excavations of a site some way along the escarpment. Two or three people were hanging about, waiting to fly back to the capital. I turned back to the Sharif's house long before the engines began to fire again, not daring to see them take off. It was December 19, and if I stepped aboard that plane I should be in England for Christmas, which was the only place I wanted to be on that day.

As the plane left, I was scribbling in my notebook, "Must *not* think of that any more. Close door on home thoughts. Simply matter of butting way through to Tombouctou now, nothing more. Nile doesn't exist, Tamanrasset doesn't exist; only Tombouctou and shedding en route two men on whom I must rely and whom I don't trust."

I made an effort to shed Sidi Mahmoud in Tichit, according to our original agreement, but Mohamed flew into a temper and swore that if I paid off his friend, he too would return home. He was aware, for I had stupidly discussed the matter with him earlier, that this would ruin my whole enterprise. I was now virtually without money, in no position to hire anybody else. I had reached Tichit with a postal note that should have enabled me to recover cash from the post office there, which I had deposited on account in Nouakchott. I was told by the postal assistant that his chief had been flown to hospital in the capital and, without his authority, the note was uncashable.

Once more a Mauritanian *préfet* came to my aid. He

would, he said, take custody of the postal note until Sidi Mahmoud returned from Oualata—to which I had now said he could accompany us—by which time it would be cashable, and the agreed payment could be made to the man. As for my general financial difficulties, if I cared to address some traveller's cheques to Ahmed ould Die in Nouakchott, he would see that they went by the next week's plane. Ahmed could then arrange to have cash waiting for me before I reached the Mali border. But it would be necessary for me to travel south from Oualata to Néma, where there was an airstrip. This would put maybe a hundred miles on my journey, but now I had no choice.

Sidi Mahmoud, for his part, sought to increase his terms outrageously for the extra distance he would travel with me. For something rather more than double the distance we had agreed upon at Tidjikja, he was demanding now more than three times the price we had first settled. The *préfet* refused to adjudicate, just as his colleague at Tidjikja had refused to advise me upon a fair offer in the first place. These people allowed the stranger to make his own mistakes. But in front of him I told Sidi Mahmoud that he would have to accept twice the original price to ride to Oualata with us, or go home at once with his 20,000 francs. He accepted without argument, but went into a sulk for the rest of the day.

6

WE WERE MARCHING OUR BEASTS down the village, towards the edge of the gravel plain, when Mohamed asked me to carry on for a little while alone: he and Sidi Mahmoud had some business in one of the houses, they would catch up with me soon. I walked on placidly, enjoying the declining heat of the day and the sharp angular shadows falling from the escarpment, the gentle tug of the leading camel's headrope upon my shoulder, the rhythmic pad of our feet upon the hard and gritty ground. Above all, I enjoyed the solitude of the moment. I would give much, I thought, to be able to go on like this. But I wondered whether I would have the courage to do so.

This was something quite apart from the practical considerations of travelling alone, which I was beginning to recognise as a possibly insurmountable obstacle: it took so long, even with two men, to find the camels each morning. Though their forelegs were always tightly hobbled together, they could move extraordinary distances with unexpected speed in their search for food, proceeding with the determined shuffle of a sand dancer or a series of comical bunny hops. I had watched one shift three hundred yards in a few minutes. The other morning we had been delayed for two and a half hours in looking for them, and I had not known it to take less than half an hour to bring them in. A solitary rider's energy could be dangerously dissipated by this perpetual need to ramble round the desert without advancing his position, just as it would be heavily taxed by the need to load or unload the baggage of two beasts four times each day.

But even if I could find and afford the single-handed energy for these tasks over a matter of weeks and months, could I also muster the plain gut courage to go on alone in the desert? I was not sure yet, but I had begun to doubt it. Thrice now, sitting in an oasis just before departure, I had experienced a deep primeval fear of the void around. Not quite a quaking sensation; no more than an uneasy, feathery turning of the stomach. But there, distinctly there, as a warning and as a question mark that I could not ignore. Wilfred Thesiger had told me that he would most certainly be crushed by the immensity of the desert if he found himself in it alone. I could see very well what he meant now, as I walked wonderingly between the hard impregnable outline of the escarpment and the blank, blank anonymity of the endless dunes. I was a caterpillar wriggling hopefully across an eternal nothingness from which all other life had been apparently extinguished.

I turned to see if my companions had left the oasis yet. They were about half a mile behind, two tiny dots striding vigorously to catch up. A third figure was with them. I slackened my pace and they joined me without a word, Mohamed immediately taking the headrope and handing it to the newcomer. He was a gap-toothed young man, stockily built as the shepherd lad, Mahomed ould Ely, had been, and he paid no attention to me at all.

"Where's the boy going?" I asked.

"Just down there," said Mohamed, nodding straight ahead. "He's joining some friends in an encampment."

It wasn't until three days later, in the middle of nowhere, that I decided this encampment was a long time in appearing, and broached the subject again. Calmly, Mohamed announced that the lad's destination was near Néma. A week before, I would have blown up in his face. As it was, I simply turned away wearily, shaking my head in bewilderment. I certainly couldn't abandon the youth where we were. At the same time, I seriously wondered whether our supplies would see four of us through the next ten days. or so. The only solution was to push on as hard as possible and get this growing nightmare of a passage over.

By then, however, it had become clear that our movement would be retarded by this latest recruit to the caravan. Although for a few hours each day young Erbah rode bareback behind Sidi Mahmoud, whose camel carried little baggage, we spent ourselves much more than we would otherwise have done in marching on foot, and even when we rode, it was impossible for a camel to trot very far with two men up. We plodded on through bitterly cold mornings that had no warmth in them at all until past ten o'clock, though by noon the wind that had been storming with sub-Arctic penetration was transformed into a scorching torrent that flushed the bare skin even where it had tanned deeply after weeks of exposure. We left the wide corridor of gravel. We crossed more dunes. We came to the well of Touijinit, and paused to water our beasts.

Touijinit was a much more ambitious affair than anything I had yet seen outside an oasis, with a deep shaft and a high concrete rim that prevented the muck from flowing back into the water, and troughs running fanwise from the shafthead so that many camels could drink simultaneously. A mob of perhaps twenty beasts was there before us, brought down from the pastures above the escarpment by two herdsmen, and we exchanged news and information with them. There was, they said, a little ghudda for beasts up there. But down here there was nothing, nothing at all, for as far as a man might ride strongly in a week. A few yards from the well lay the withered carcass of a camel, bearing witness to the desperate aridity of this area.

We climbed the escarpment again, so that our camels might find their precious ghudda, into a region scarcely less impoverished, for we were once more hemmed in tightly by the sands of El Mreyye. But between the sands and the rocks, a narrow strip of ground that was a mixture of both bore a scattering of yellowed grasses and even, from time to time, a tree on which the animals could browse.

This was the setting for my Christmas, which barely existed outside my imagination. By the half light of dawn I was attempting to delouse my garments, appalled by the numbers which had now attached themselves to me: they were secreted in scores within the huge ingathering at the waist of my serwal, and they infested the sweater which I had started to pull on at night and during the early cold of the day. The string vest which I habitually wore under my boubou might be a useful insulation against both cold and heat, but it also, I noted with dismay, provided an excellent refuge for these creatures in almost every one of its many joints.

It was so cold, this morning, that I had difficulty in getting the others on the move before nine-thirty. They seemed to be even wearier than I was, inquiring more than once during the morning whether we might not ride now. There was no question of doing so, for we were in dunes again, all of them steep and soft enough to have the camels in trouble without the added burden of riders. Mohamed's five-year-old jibbed so fiercely at one prolonged descent that, tethered as he was to the saddle of the big bull in front, he had his nose ring yanked out, which tore his nostril and left him with a very bloody face. For four hours we kept up a floundering, scrambling pace before our midday halt; then we went on as before until sunset. We had picked up a few small twigs during these hours for our evening fire, but in the end we had to augment them with camel dung. On this I managed to heat the small Christmas pudding I had brought from England. It would have just about capped a solid meal for two men, as I had originally assumed. Four of us enjoyed no more than a mouthful apiece, although the other three, after their initial suspicions were allayed, expressed great satisfaction.

Periodically during the day, I took flight to J and the children, and the ritual whose measured steps I knew so well and loved so much. In spite of my resolve to banish all thoughts of home, I had for days past followed the rising Christmas tide of tree-planting, decorating, cooking and hubbub in that house, which I had always shared so far, and it was strangely a comfort rather than a sadness—some promise of continuity, I supposed. As I paused in my lice-hunting at dawn, I visualised the opening of the presents I had left behind me, a series of cameos that were so vivid I could have reached out and touched them. They were rehearsed throughout the day, when I was not concentrated upon some purely tactical struggle up and down the dunes, for I was loath to leave them behind. In the darkness, with the pudding at last gone, I wondered whether it had been wise or upsetting to leave for the family my tape-recorded reading of *A Child's Christmas in Wales*, for my elder daughter Jane, I knew, had gone through spasms of worrying whether I would safely return. But I had wanted to share their Christmas, and it had seemed gentlest to do it by way of Dylan Thomas. Sentimentality could the better be passed off as fun and games that way.

Sentimentality was rudely interrupted by Mohamed, who rolled over in his blanket and addressed himself to our future together. Perhaps the best way out of the financial difficulties that awaited us in Néma, he said—and I marked well the "us"—would be for me to give him a camel, instead of buying him a plane ticket back to Tidjikja. If I were prepared to do this, Sidi Mahmoud would continue beyond Oualata to Néma and ride his camel home with Mohamed for company.

As a disinterested proposition, it would have had much to commend it. But nothing that Mohamed did, particularly in relation to me, was remotely disinterested. He gave away his true intent by telling me that the cost of a flight from Néma would be about 60,000 francs, which I knew to be rubbish; I could have flown from Nouakchott to London for that. What Mohamed was after, my nerve ends immediately said, was a camel on top of his wages. I did not doubt that he would pursue this objective with all the guile and determination of which he was capable. The rest of our journey, I foresaw, was going to be a wearing one. I must try to counter his strategy with opaque noncommitments of my own.

"It's a possibility," I told him, and indicated that I wished to sleep. But in my notebook next morning, I added a postscript to the entry for the day: "Woke after midnight, worrying about it all, while Orion swivelled overhead and the lice crawled across my belly and up my spine. Happy Christmas to all our readers."

As we worked our way slowly towards the eastern limit of the escarpment before turning south, I wrestled almost step by step with the financial permutations that might be possible at Néma. At least once every day Mohamed again brought up the subject of the camel, and Sidi Mahmoud now joined in the effort to press this course upon me. Only Erbah, the young man, stood outside my dilemma; indeed, he had very little to say to anyone, and I realised very well by now why he had become attached to my party. He had been recruited by the other two simply to take as much of the drudgery off their hands as was possible, in exchange for our food and our company. Whenever we camped it was Erbah who was told by Mohamed to start looking for firewood or dung; in the mornings it was he who was expected to go searching for the camels first. Mohamed and Sidi Mahmoud, meanwhile, would lie like dead things until he returned, while I wrote up my notes.

I found it curious that both seemed to be tiring much more than I was. Mentally I often felt played out, but my body seemed now to have taken a second wind, so that for the first two hours of our daily march I would stride on ahead while they trailed far behind, walking slowly as though to execution, their bodies bent against the furious head winds, the camels hanging heavily on the ropes. It occurred to me that I had much greater reserves of energy than they, doubtless the result of forty years' consistently high nourishment. And they felt the cold cruelly, wrapping their headcloths tightly around their faces, so that only their eyes were visible between the swathes. Halfway through one night I awoke to see Mohamed stoking up the embers of our fire, huddling over its wretched glow, then scraping the warm sand under his blanket before lying down again. Even in a sleeping bag, the cold continually wakened me at night. If it were not the cold that interrupted sleep, it would be the lice, or the moon shining stridently into my face. I doubt whether I had enjoyed more than two hours' unbroken repose since Tidjikja.

We traversed more dunes, and again I felt the deepest fears nudging me. In the hollows between the dunes. It was as though one were very close to the edge of the earth. There was no vista beyond that undulating ridge just ahead, nothing but flawlessly blue sky; gain it, and one would drop off into eternal space. But at the crest of the ridge a vista did appear, and it was even more intimidating than the illusion of space. Move off alone into the endless sequence of sandy hills that now stretched ahead, across the khaki colours of the foreground and into the whiteness that glared forever from afar, and one would become dazed by the sameness of those beautiful elliptical shapes, become mindless, lose the power of concentration, ultimately lose all the senses one by one. How could anyone navigate with certainty for long across such a barrier, when the compass bearing swept through 20 degrees every five minutes, the sun first burning the left shoulder, then the right shoulder, then appearing dead ahead, before turning to the left again?

We came out of the dunes and started to move across a flat pancake of pulverised gravel, maybe a mile and a half in diameter, encircled by sandy scrub. In the middle of it was a huge circle made up of stones, and in the centre of the circle, again with stones, the large lettering of the words Bou Zib. It was an old French airfield, abandoned for some twenty years, with not the slightest trace of any buildings that might have been raised during its construction. Had I paused there, had we camped for the night on its perimeter, it might have seemed spooky in its absolute dereliction, for apart from those carefully laid stones and the fact that the ground had obviously been cleared meticulously of boulders, possibly being levelled mechanically as well, there was nothing to suggest that man had ever visited this spot before. We had seen no one for three full days. Yet there it mysteriously was, shimmering with mirage, stamped with the hallmark of ultimate civilisation. It was indicated, interestingly, on my American military chart, but not on the French maps I had brought from Paris. As we tramped across its surface, I wondered what colonial strategy had been responsible for its appearance in the first place, and whether, in due course, another one might find some aggressive use for it. And this was, for a moment in time, the justification of Bou Zib's existence: to provide me with a tiny mental exercise in the clogging tedium of my journey —that and a navigational beacon from which I might plot my further course.

I went back to take my turn on the camel ropes. As Mohamed handed them over, he announced that in two days we should pass the end of the wadi which eventually led to Oualata. What were we going to do about Sidi Mahmoud? He, I said, should return home as planned. As for Mohamed himself, when we reached Néma I would put him on a plane for Nouakchott with some traveller's cheques; he would take these to Ahmed ould Die, who would settle his account and give him a plane ticket to Tidjikja. I regretted that I would not be able to present him with a camel, but there would be so little money to spare after I had reprovisioned for the next stage of the journey, and paid an advance to whoever would accompany me to Tombouctou, that this was the only solution I could manage, and, indeed, I believed that it was. Though I was now quite capable of bloody-mindedness in my dealings with Mohamed, I exonerated myself on this occasion, while I had the malicious satisfaction of knowing that his disappointment would be essentially of his own making, for it was he who had induced the financial crisis by involving me in much greater expenditure that I had bargained for when I deployed my monies before leaving the capital.

When I told him my decision, he broke into an aggrieved bickering. It would take him a long time to get home by flying this roundabout way, he shouted, and his wife was pregnant. I don't think I managed to avoid a grin when I pointed out that it would take him a lot longer to ride home by camel, if that was what he'd had in mind.

Then something in the tone of his response—"You have decided, then?"—wiped the grin from my face. I watched him join Sidi Mahmoud, speaking quietly and sourly, and uneasily wondered what might happen next. I couldn't imagine that Mohamed would turn to violence, for he had a healthy respect for the law, and I doubted whether he would have the guts to risk falling foul of it. But would he possibly dare to leave me in the lurch here, trusting, in his huge contempt for European navigation, that I would never find my way to either Oualata or Néma? I suddenly recalled the room in Nouakchott where I had imagined him, whom I had not then met, abandoning me in some such wilderness as this one. It was probably just as well, I concluded, that I was sleeping very lightly these days.

We started riding a little later, and Mohamed began officiously to correct my mannerisms. I should place my foot thus, when mounting, and hold the headrope so when in the saddle, and on no account rest both legs on the same side of the animal's neck, as one did from time to time to relieve stiffness in the limbs. The fellow invariably turned pompous teacher whenever he felt put down. As often as not, he made mealtimes the excuse for a lecture on how to roll rice into a ball with one hand before eating it, a trick which I never tidily performed. On other occasions he had fussily rebuked me for my habit of leaving empty eating bowls the right way up on the ground. They should be turned over, he advised, or the Devil would come and sup from them. I was in no mood for his patronage now, though, and irritably waved him away.

We jogged on slowly, with a great space between us. Somewhere behind, Sidi Mahmoud followed, with young Erbah clinging to his camel's rump. For maybe half an hour not a word was exchanged by any of us, Mohamed moodily watching the ground just ahead of his beast, chewing a piece of stick as he so often did. Then he drifted over to me, one arm arrogantly resting on his hip, the headrope dangling casually from his other fingers. He looked up at me, with a wicked half grin on his face.

"Why won't you," he demanded, and there was no mistaking the truculence of his tone or his manner, "why won't you buy me a camel, then?"

It was an ultimatum, a challenge, and in a fury I rose to it, heedless of the consequences. My riding stick came up and I levelled it at his head menacingly; had he been a foot or so nearer, I believe I might have slugged him with it on the spot.

"Listen," I shouted, "and listen well, little corporal. The subject is closed. Do you understand? It's closed. Finished!" And I brought the stick down with a thump on the wing of his saddle. I was shaking with a rage which obliterated everything but a desire to smash this source of torment.

He glared at me for an instant, openmouthed with shock. Then he uttered something between a grunt and a sneer, grinned again secretly to himself, and dragged his camel away from mine, to resume his moody passage across the sands.

Mohamed did not mention the camel again, but next day he pursued a new tactic. We had descended the escarpment now, moving due south across a gravel plain, almost as though we were coasting down the English Channel close inshore to the cliffs. At our midday camp, Mohamed very deliberately made tea, cut up some meat and put it into the cooking pot, then lay back as though nothing else would happen till this food was ready. Up to now, our drill had always been to break open the dates and share them as soon as the fire was made up, while waiting for the first glass of tea. As Mohamed lay down, he said something to the other two, and Erbah giggled.

I waited a few moments, then said "Dates?"

Uproarious laughter from Sidi Mahmoud and Erbah, and a sly grin from Mohamed. I took no notice, but repeated my question, and Mohamed languidly brought them from the tassoufra, then dished them out. The tension passed. We finished our meal and rode on.

That afternoon my camel stumbled four times, always as his left foreleg went down. I wondered whether he was going lame. But Mohamed said that it was no matter, just a tripping over larger stones, and I could see nothing wrong with the beast's leg myself.

Our food situation was, as I had expected, becoming poor. Our flour had been finished three or four days ago, and there was little left of either dates, rice or meat. On December 30 it became serious. We had trekked to refill our almost empty guerbas at Hassi Fouini, a miserable hole flush with the ground, whose water contained much camel dung and was sour with diluted piss. In the hour or two before our arrival, Mohamed had started to lobby me on behalf of his comrade-in-chief. The entrance of the wadi leading to Oualata stretched wide open to the east of us. Sidi Mahmoud, said Mohamed, was prepared to continue to Néma, but there I would have to provision him for his return journey; otherwise he would now ride to Oualata, but would need money to buy food there. I said that I had no wish for Sidi Mahmoud to prolong his journey with us, that I would give him 1,000 francs, which was all that I had left apart from small change, if he desired to make for Oualata.

We had idled by the water hole for an hour or so when Sidi Mahmoud got up and announced that he was going home now. I handed him 1,000 francs and wished him well. Then Mohamed turned to the tassoufra and began to divide the contents. It appeared that Sidi Mahmoud was not going to Oualata after all, but had decided to return home direct, without making a detour to the oasis above the escarpment.

I was beyond arguing about the small deception which had winkled more money out of me; I was too content to be rid of Sidi Mahmoud. His presence had never been satisfactory after the first few days, for he had been too ready to lie around and leave others to do the work, his idleness occasionally causing Mohamed to chastise him resentfully. Above all, from my point of view, he had been an accomplice, essentially a weak yes-man to Mohamed's various ploys, and thus some threat to my security. But as he turned away and mounted his camel without a word to any of us, without a backward glance, I could not help being moved by the bravery of his going back alone, even though he would have our tracks to follow. It would be three weeks before he regained his own tent across some of the most awful travelling country in the world. I recognised that I could not have done what he was undertaking.

His departure was a relief to me, but it left us with little to eat before Néma, which was still three days away. On impulse, I had decided to ride directly there. We had enough rice for two meals, and thirty-three dates—all of them withered, some of them so hard and dessicated as to be virtually inedible. On New Year's Day, we used the last of our precious, restorative tea and sugar, which was a far greater blow than the lack of meat, flour or rice. We were moving now, as we had been ever since Tichit, across ground that was unpeopled by nomads who might give us food if we could find their tents at the end of the day. Had one felt fit and well, the landscape would have been exciting here, for the plain now and then erupted into huge rocky hills that reminded me of photographs I had seen of the buttes of Arizona, gaunt and stratified and lonely, with half a day's journey in between each. We came past four upstanding slabs of rock, too carefully arranged in a rectangle to have happened naturally, which Mohamed said were graves, and which, if that were so, must have been as ancient as the four arrowheads I had now collected; for many centuries would have passed since there was enough life in this ground to support a family long enough for them to have settled and died there.

One took scant notice of such things, however, for hunger was beginning to deaden all the senses. I had long since become accustomed to its daily advance, to those tentacles of discomfort that slowly crawled up the belly and into the mind. On the march I had habitually been less aware of them than when lying inert at an oasis, for the pre-occupying sensations of travel were those of pain and physical exhaustion; a conscious weakness as the moment approached for more food was almost the only signal that one needed food. In an oasis, where there was small pain and no exhaustion, attention shifted to the stomach, to the windy emptiness within, to the growing ache. At all times, food had been reduced to a necessity, quite devoid of its emotional pleasure. One devoured the gritty evening couscous avidly, as an animal among others. One stuffed down the plain boiled rice at midday, no longer caring much, scarcely realising that it had no taste at all. Emotion attended only the meat, rationing the amount one consumed quite as much as the sheer common sense that warned of potential disease, ranging from dreadful hydatids to wasting dysentery, which could reside in this half-cooked flesh.

But now, with no food to revive the body, the body's failures became the focal points of existence. One noted much less the perpetually bitter taste in the mouth than the increasing stupor of giddiness. I began to weave uncertainly when I was walking. It became difficult to climb into the saddle for riding. I found that my chin tended to loll on my chest, my shoulders sagging, when I mounted, and I rolled around the saddle inertly as a sack of potatoes. At noon on that first day of 1973, we drank water, ate nothing and collapsed into sleep. I was astonished that such a transformation had overtaken me in such a short time; only a few days before, I had been surging ahead of my party on the march, feeling much the strongest person in it. Now a curious detachment had set in. Lying there on the ground, nothing mattered but sleep. I wanted nothing but the peace that would let me sink into sleep and forget.

We dragged ourselves on slowly, taking turns to share the two camels between the three of us. Though we exchanged no words on the subject, spoke scarcely at all, it was implicit in our situation when dusk came that we would not stop to make camp, but would continue our sluggish movement through the darkness. By then we should normally have been fed and ready for sleep, but now we had no food. For the first time I was peering ahead and around as keenly as my companions had always done, in the hope of finding a sign of other human life on this desolate plain, which might mean sanctuary and a chance to fill our bellies on someone else's good nature. Instinct said that there must be people in the country just ahead; there always were nomads camped in country immediately around an oasis, and Néma was not too far off now.

It was young Erbah on foot who spotted the faint flicker in the black night. Then Mohamed, then I focused it in our blurring vision from the superior heights of our camels. A campfire was burning in the distance. There was no commanding gallop towards our prey this time. We just stumbled on quietly through the darkness. It took us half an hour to draw close enough to see, in the occulting glow of several fires, that here were no tents, but the mud walls of houses. We got down drunkenly beside the nearest dwelling and began to unhitch our gear. Faces appeared, but no one stepped forward to help until Mohamed burst out angrily at a man who stood watching. He started to berate the fellow for lack of welcome and, as the man listened stolidly, Mohamed addressed his words to include a gathering audience of half a dozen or so. Grudgingly they moved to our assistance when we had done all but hobble the beasts, grudgingly they put down mats in the lee of a wall. Then they left us.

"*Ma marhaba*—Not welcome," I said to Mohamed wearily.

He did not reply, and for the first time in several

weeks I warmed to the man. He was, I realised, ashamed of these people and their failure to offer hospitality to a Nasrani.

It was an hour before anyone visited us, while we lay slumped upon the mats. A woman then brought a bowl of milk, which we sucked noisily in turn. That was all we received from this settlement. It was very strange, I reflected next morning, that the wealthiest group of people we had met outside an oasis—people who had fowls and the first cattle I had seen, as well as sheep, goats and houses—should also be the stingiest.

The bowl of milk, little though it was, had put some life in us again. It kept us going through a hot and windless morning, until we came to a small encampment of tents among trees. There, with the last few coins in my possession, we bought a piece of sugar and some tea, the leaves being carefully measured out and handed over in a small drinking glass. So many times on this journey, we had given tea in this fashion to satisfy the perpetual craving of nomads. But now, for once, I found myself the supplicant. We moved on a little, to camp alone and brew a pot of this blessed infusion. It revived us enough to face the last few miles to Néma in good heart. The plain, which since the previous night had been thickly garnished with trees, now became positively fertile. There were more cattle here, corn was being grown in quantity, and many rough fences had been constructed out of thorny branches; the ground was also increasingly strewn with the wretched cram-cram grass and its scratching, hooked burrs.

We overtook a small family, a man, his wife and their son, and they were the most attractive people I had seen since returning to Africa. The parents laughed and joked together, amiably and affectionately, and looked as if they cared to be in each other's company. There was not a hint of dominance in him, or of subservience in her. I had not before seen a nomad man and woman who appeared to be living together on the basis of what I could recognise as friendship and equality. They shared some food with us and

131

we pottered on comfortably together towards the last range of hills before the oasis. These were no more than five hundred feet high, but my coming to them was both healing and unforgettable. A field of corn was being worked by some women underneath these hills, a warm and declining light glowed upon everything, and the earth's stillness was only heightened by the distant shouts of people across fields, by the movement of some women on donkeys, by the trilling of a few birds.

I remembered those beautiful opening lines of Alan Paton's: "There is a lovely road that runs from Ixopo into the hills. These hills are grass-covered and rolling, and they are lovely beyond any singing of it . . . and from there, if there is no mist, you look down on one of the fairest valleys of Africa." For the first time in my life, I felt touched by the magic of Africa.

It was long after nightfall when we came to Néma and found lodgings with some kinsmen of young Erbah. Next morning, disconsolately, I discovered at the post office that there had been no word from Ahmed ould Die in Nouakchott, though it was now nearly a fortnight since I had dispatched my cheques to him from Tichit, with the urgent plea for cash to be awaiting me here.

Once more I turned to the official residence for help, seeking the provincial Governor who controlled Mauritania's southeastern boundaries with Mali from this place. The Governor himself was away, but I secured an interview with his deputy, a formidable-looking man whose headcloth concealed much of his face, giving what was visible a slightly forbidding air. He questioned me sharply about the purpose of my arrival in Néma and asked me some detailed questions about my journey as a whole, revealing rather more knowledge than I had expected of the geography of Egypt.

All this time he had been doodling moodily on a pad in front of him and now, without looking up, he uttered a sigh and said, "Well, you've a long way still to go, haven't you?"

I gaped with amazement, for he had just spoken impeccable English, the first words I had heard in my own language for the best part of two months. He put his head back, his headcloth slipping down to his chin, and laughed marvellously at my surprise. We swung our hands into a delighted clasp of greeting. We were friends at once.

This man, Abdellahi ould Erebih, was to offer me much comfort as well as kindness over the next few days. He had been his country's ambassador in Cairo and Bonn, as well as a member of its delegation to the United Nations, and I found it very odd indeed that someone of his experience, intelligence, and sophistication should now be dumped somewhat less than grandly in an insignificant township on the edge of the Sahara desert. He was about my own age, and in the West he would most certainly have occupied some senior post in the capital or in one of its most prestigious embassies abroad; or, in some countries, he might have been banished to some obscure and remote place as a potential threat to the ambitions of the leadership.

I did not once detect in Abdellahi a trace of bitterness at this apparent waste of his considerable talents. He had much natural dignity, a piety that he wore very lightly, and he seemed totally at peace with himself in this environment. There was something splendidly innocent and wondering about him as he showed me some curious stones he had found a little while before, during a visit to another oasis. What was the meaning of those whorling marks on them, clearly man-made? His brow furrowed with perplexity as we bent over them together—the look of a small boy who thinks he may have found his first fossil, but still isn't quite sure. Yet he had the gentle wit of the man who is poised enough to be at ease in any world. Once, he told me, he had officially visited Luxembourg, to be shown some steel mill by people who were anxious that this man of Africa should be impressed. What did he think of the tremendous power at work in the building, of this astonishing spectacle of molten metal, they asked?

"I just told them 'It seems very hot to me'"; and he

shrugged apologetically, with a comedian's twinkle, at the memory of it.

Abdellahi did three things at once to raise my spirits even more. He promised to telegraph a message directly to Nouakchott about my money, he asked an assistant to find someone to travel to Tombouctou with me, and he suggested that I might like to move into what was euphemistically called the Government rest house, across the road from his administrative offices. It was rather ramshackle, he said, and more than a little grubby, but at least it would give me peace and quiet.

The rest house was all these things, but it enabled me, after a rusty water tank had been laboriously filled from the well outside, to wash for the first time since Nouakchott; and that alone was good enough. I found a mirror and was dismayed at my appearance. My face was scorched and windblasted, the nose cracked wide open along the bone, the lips badly swollen and blistered, and there were an old man's wrinkles puckering the skin around bloodshot eyes. The eyes themselves held me, much more than the rest of my bedraggled, whiskery Rumpelstiltskin of a face. They were staring, too strained by far, the eyes of someone who looked as if he felt hunted and on the run. This was not the passable Moorhouse of England, home and beauty, but some decrepit saddle tramp discovered in desolation. Would I return to Europe looking as I had done when I left? Would my own people recognise and own me? Could my body survive this elemental treatment intact? The nervous questions tumbled after each other as I gazed upon this relic of myself. "Read next week's instalment of . . . Dick Barton, Special Agent," a boyhood memory mocked me.

Next day I returned from some errand to find Mohamed sharing tea on the floor of our room with a newcomer. He was introduced as Sid' Ahmed ould Eli ould Simmad, and the man who would travel with me beyond Néma. He was of much the same build as Mohamed, but he had a wider face which flashed its teeth frequently, and an ingratiating manner which I did not take to. Sid' Ahmed, I noticed, tipped his head on one side when requesting something, rather like a cocker spaniel attending to master's whistle. I was not at all pleased that the two had struck up an acquaintance, for I could imagine that Mohamed would conceive it as at least a tribal loyalty to inform his successor of every detectable weakness in the Nasrani, particularly those which laid me open to exploitation.

I was very sharp with both, in my attempt to convey the message that the easy meat Mohamed had discovered in Nouakchott was no longer being served up on a platter in Néma. I was not gratified, in these few days, to find Sid' Ahmed lying in wait for me near the post office on my frequent excursions to see if my money had arrived; he, too, wanted a substantial advance of cash before we set out. A couple of times I was stopped by strangers, who promptly burst into eulogies about the fellow, telling me how lucky I was to secure his services, how I must be sure to buy him some cartridges, for he was one of the best shots in Mauritania, and many other praiseworthy things. At which point Sid' Ahmed himself would invariably appear like a genie from the crowd, beaming with pleasure and cocking his head in emphatic expectation.

I found myself with another crisis on my hands, apart from the one involving money. My camels had been taken to some pasture a couple of miles outside the oasis on the morning after our arrival, and in the afternoon young Erbah was told by Mohamed to go and check on their safety. On the second evening he returned to our room when it had been dark for several hours, looking very gloomy and sullen. The animals, he announced, were nowhere to be found. Mohamed became agitated and said that someone must have stolen them, that we must report the matter to the Governor at once.

Unwillingly, for it was late, I went over to Abdellahi, feeling sick at heart in the face of this new reverse. I had already noticed that there were scarcely any beasts about Néma, none apparently for sale. If my camels had indeed been taken, my journey was in jeopardy. Although part of me would by now have been very happy to board the next weekly flight to Nouakchott and have done with the thing at last, the prize of Tombouctou was so very nearly in my grasp, no more than another fortnight away. Reach Tombouctou, I told myself, and I could retire from this awful endurance test with at least a smattering of self-respect.

Abdellahi, when I told him, was inclined to agree with Mohamed that the beasts must have been stolen. Indeed, after questioning both men closely, he took me aside and suggested that Erbah might not be above suspicion of abetting the theft. This I found hard to believe, for the young fellow had never shown me the slightest ill will, and had seemed to me a trifle dull-witted into the bargain. I doubted very much whether he would have had the initiative to take part in such a coup. But once I realised the deputy Governor's suspicions were pointed at Erbah, the thought crossed my mind that, in view of all that had happened before, Mohamed was a much more likely candidate for camel-rustling. I would, by now, have been surprised at such boldness on his part; but I wondered, for he surely had the cunning to appear concerned about a matter for which he was responsible.

Next day, the two were dispatched very early in the morning to accompany a pair of trackers in a Land-Rover. In addition, Abdellahi commandeered a couple of Army *goumiers* mounted on camels themselves, to follow the party in the Land-Rover. Their orders were not to return to Néma without my camels and the men who had stolen them.

"I will not have this happening round here," he said. "Particularly to a stranger. It would be a disgrace to our people."

Then, swiftly, all the crises dissolved. That afternoon the camels were found, and they had not been stolen. They had merely wandered off in search of forage much farther than we had known them to go before. At almost the same moment, I found myself embarrassed by a superabundance of money. Abdellahi, impatient for a reply from Nouakchott, had privately arranged for a wealthy tradér to give me cash in exchange for some traveller's cheques. No sooner had this transaction been completed than a man came running from the post office to announce that Ahmed's money had arrived. I now had just about twice as much as I had hoped for.

In this glow of affluence I summoned Mohamed into my confidence for the last time. I explained what had just happened and said I was now in a position to let him choose how our contract should end. Either I would buy his air ticket to Tidjikja and give him in cash what I owed him, or else, in addition to his outstanding wages, I would simply hand him the 20,000 francs of the fare, and he could use it as he pleased. I had no doubt at all, beforehand, which course he would fancy most. He could cheaply buy himself a place in a truck that would go down the dirt road linking Mauritania's southern villages below the desert until he came to Kiffa, and there he could doubtless board another vehicle that would take him on to Tidjikja and his coveted camel.

That night I awoke to see him doing something secretively by the shaded light of a flashlight. He had his back turned to both Erbah and me, and he was murmuring quietly to himself, over and over again, *"Ilhamdu Lillah—* In the name of God."* He was counting out the notes of the 56,000 francs I had given him. He could never have handled so much money in his life before. If he was careful, he might just be able to buy two camels with it. Even though I disliked the man intensely by now, I could not for the life of me begrudge him this fortune. He was, after all, very poor and I was very rich.

Next morning we parted, and it was a shame that two men who had travelled so far together left each other with so much relief on both sides.

"Well," I said, "buy yourself a good camel, Mohamed."

He barely touched my outstretched hand, muttered a tight-lipped "Good luck," and turned quickly away, scurrying down the street with Erbah like a small boy heading for the sweet shop with his new spending money.

7

IN BETTER SPIRITS than I could remember for a long time, I led the way up the steep hill behind Néma. The little town spread out below, doped with heat, dusty, lying between the throbbing gravel plain to the north and the parched scrublands to the south, had given me great relief in the past three days. Much of this had been Abdellahi's doing, but I had also been conscious of more concerted warmth flowing towards me than ever before in Africa. After Mohamed and Erbah had returned with the vagrant camels, men had hailed me in the streets with cries of "They've been found!" nodding their heads and smiling broadly with genuine pleasure. A youth in the shop where I reprovisioned informed me cheerfully that he had heard about my coming on the radio and wished me good luck and safe journey ahead. My morale was enormously raised by this feeling that I had been surrounded by friends; so many people had shown so much concern for my well-being that it was as though I had become an adopted kinsman of the community. All this, and solvency again, set me on my last stage to Tombouctou eagerly and in good heart.

The one setback I had received in Néma was doubtless no more than a passing nuisance. For the first time I was in the throes of chronic diarrhoeia and acute stomach cramps whenever I took food. I was, if anything, merely astonished that I had not been attacked by such a tummy bug much earlier, considering what I had been eating and drinking since mid-November.

I was also coming to the conclusion that in Sid' Ahmed I might have a companion more suited to my temperament and needs. True, he had cadged a little from me over and above his agreed wages and the advances I had given him. Watching me rearranging my kit in the room one evening, he had dropped a heavy hint that the weather was sometimes cold in the desert and that he would welcome a shirt I kept against the day of my return to civilisation. *"Ana meskeen*—I'm a poor thing," he had declared, with that awful, wheedling tilt of his head. And I'd handed the garment over brusquely, rich man morally trapped by the irresistible blackmail of poverty. After much more than one heavy hint, I had given him another 1,000 francs so that he could buy ten cartridges with which, he said, he would shoot us some meat.

We were to travel armed, then, and I wondered whether this was entirely in order to supply our cooking pots. Mohamed had been full of foreboding about the tribesmen I might meet once I was over the border and into Mali; they were, he said, rapacious and vicious, unlike the Moors of his own country. But Mohamed, I well knew, besides being patriotic, was also alarmist, either born that way or bent by trying when he saw some opportunity to gain from it.

Yet in spite of those mannerisms which had put me on my guard and the cadging that followed them up, one thing in Sid' Ahmed had already impressed me a lot. Alone with me after our contract had been made, he had asked what exactly it was that I required of him on this journey. My reply was that essentially I wanted him to do the heavy physical work of handling the camels and baggage, for I had become worn out by the hard riding and marching across

Mauritania, whereas he would be fresh. The route-finding, I said, I was prepared to tackle myself.

"Ah, good," said Sid' Ahmed, "for I can lead you to Nbeiket el Ouahch"—a well almost on the border with Mali —"but after that I don't know the way to Tombouctou."

If the man could be as open and straightforward as that before we set off, I thought, he had something that I prized and had missed badly in Mohamed ould Moctar ould Hmeida. Sid' Ahmed, I discovered, had been to Tombouctou just once, many years before, when he was a soldier with the French, but on that occasion he had come to it from Araouane in the north, and had travelled to Néma in a truck by a dirt road far to the south of the direct route across the desert.

So although, as we crested the hill, we walked straight into a fiercely hot head wind that swept across clinging soft sand thickly carpeted with cram-cram, the worst possible combination of conditions, I was buoyant. One year ago to the day, almost to the hour, A and I had been sitting in a café in dear old Harrogate, surrounded by tweedy landladies discussing their winter holidays in the Canaries and Majorca; and then we had gone up Wharfedale, walking from Buckden to Hubberholme on a misty and very still winter's morning. Strange that this blistering season should be called winter, too; without the thermometer I could not be sure of the heat, but my body told me it was probably over 100 degrees F. I could not imagine how any human being might endure the superheat of a summer in the Sahara, yet thousands always did, and even Europeans had been known to travel through the worst of it. When René Caillié joined a caravan of six hundred camels moving north from Tombouctou in 1828, it was May; and when they reached Morocco across the desperate Tanezrouft it had become September. How softened, how enfeebled, I wondered, had Western man been made by his civilisation in the meantime? A European would be thought a suicidal maniac to attempt such a journey today; even great Thesiger and glorious Monod had said as much to me bluntly, when I had canvassed them about crossing Libya after March.

We were moving almost due north ourselves for a couple of days, heading for the tent of Sid' Ahmed, where he could deposit his advanced wages and collect his own camel for the return journey. At the midday halt, two men rode up to share our food and afterwards asked if they might continue with us, for they were travelling to an encampment near Oualata and would need to turn aside from our track only a little way before Sid' Ahmed's tent. We all remounted and rode on at a spanking trot, unbroken for three hours, which left me numb from knees to navel, but fairly shifted some ground beneath our camels' pads.

That night we made a huge fire, for there were many trees and bushes around; and, though it seemed to me much less cold than sometimes on the passage to Néma, I woke once or twice to see somebody or other crouched round the embers, blowing them up into leaping flames, with a blanket round his shoulders to hold the warmth. For a little while I would lie awake before slipping into sleep again, aware of a contentment that had been scarce before. It seemed to me just possible that I might actually enjoy the road to Tombouctou, if this day was something to go by. I had dared eat nothing but a couple of potatoes, part of a few kilos I had bought in Néma to vary the diet of dreary rice, for my bowels had been churning madly. But otherwise there had been little but pleasure so far.

Sid' Ahmed had shown eagerness in everything he did, and that, too, had been foreign to Mohamed's nature. The moment we stopped at midday, my new companion had scrambled like a monkey up the nearest tree with an axe, to chop down the tastiest high branches for the camels. He had been anxious to get going again after the break; it was the shortest halt for food I could remember. He had, most importantly, not attempted to belittle things European in general and me in particular. When the others joined us he clearly did not try to raise a laugh at my still stumbling effort to speak Hassaniya.

In the evening, before we slept, he had asked me if my charts marked all the wells he knew in the region. I reeled off the names one by one . . . Achmim, Tingarn, Tiferguig and the rest. And he, looking concentrated as my finger traced the place of each, replied, "Yes, yes, yes—no, don't know that one—yes, yes—no; ah, yes, but we call it. . . ." This was an excellent beginning. If we continued together like this, it should be a good journey.

We rode hard and fast again next day, bade farewell to our fellow travellers at the midday camp, and reached Sid' Ahmed's tent as the heat was going out of the afternoon. It stood with half a dozen others in a gently rolling landscape of sand and occasional scrub perhaps a day's ride southeast of Oualata, which I had now almost circumnavigated but never seen.

No sooner had we taken tea than Sid' Ahmed lay down, complaining of pain in his back. He had done this twice already since leaving Néma and I had been very cool in my sympathy, fearing that once again I might have picked up a man who made hypochondria the excuse for laziness. I had, in any case, nothing but codeine left to offer him, for the embrocation had long since been rubbed away upon a variety of nomadic aches and pains from one end of Mauritania to the other. Here, however, it was evidently not in demand. Sid' Ahmed summoned his young son, who massaged the father's back with fat. He then took two of the small tea glasses, lit a match in each, and smartly upturned them upon Sid' Ahmed's spine, pressing the rims hard into the flesh. As the flames swiftly died, the vacuum inside each glass clamped it strongly to the body. The boy then moved them up and down the greasy skin, while Sid' Ahmed groaned and winced histrionically; but afterwards he declared that his pain had been much relieved.

Later, in the lambent glow that followed sunset, the people of the encampment said prayers together outside their tents, the men shoulder to shoulder, the women standing a little to one side, the small boys behind their fathers and elder brothers, the girls mixed in with the womenfolk. In that brief space when the lingering blue of the desert sky is swiftly overtaken by shadow and then by darkness, lending every shape a softness and substance that it never knows by the harsh outlining light of day, the people gradually went through the motions of their worship. They bowed deeply, then knelt and submitted their heads to the dust; then rose again for an interval before kneeling once more and kissing the earth.

All this time the senior man at each tent intoned the words of adoration and obeisance . . . *"Bismelleh er Rahman er 'aDheem*—In the name of Allah, the compassionate and merciful . . . *Mahlik yaw medeen*—King of the Day of Judgement . . . *er Deen esseraht el mustaqeem*—lead us into the straight way . . . *walla Dahleen*—and not those who have gone astray . . . *Ahmeen."* But when these people knelt for the last time, it was in silence, and silently they sat there for a while, their faces turned to the eastern darkness, blankly wondering. I had watched this expression on the faces of Italian peasants kneeling before gimcrack statues of the Virgin Mary, and I had seen it stamped upon Mongolian comrades as they stood for hours contemplating the marble blockhouse that shelters Lenin's corpse in Moscow.

I had never known any of my companions in the desert to miss a prayer time, in the morning, at midday, in late afternoon or at nightfall. On such occasions I would wait quietly on one side until they had done, and I had never failed to be moved by their piety and their devotion, which was something far removed from raging fanaticism. Even the truculent Mohamed had been transformed at these moments into a helplessly obedient child-man, who kissed the earth with the same greedy noise that I had once heard from the lips of an old woman after she had crawled with very clumsy dignity to lower her face upon the gaudy star which marks the birthplace of Christ in Bethlehem. There

143

was a verse which A had found for me in the Hebrew of her prayer book among the Psalms that said something of what these people and I together sensed in the tranquillity of the desert prayer times; "*Lo tira mippahad lay'lah, mehetz ya-uf yoman.* . . . You shall not fear the terror of the night, nor the arrow that flies by day: Because you have made the Lord your refuge, the Most High your habitation. . . ."

I could see very well how the devotion of simple Moslems had turned Charles de Foucauld back to the Catholicism of his youth after years of separation from any faith at all. However repugnant some of Islam's philosophies might seem, like some of Christianity and others of Judaism, the devotion itself was clearly so central to the life of these people and so fortifying in circumstances that were otherwise almost wholly bleak as to incite whatever form of imitation one might manage in good conscience.

I had known the same feeling myself when staying in Christian monasteries, much of whose life was quite intolerable to me, yet containing a central activity and mood with which part of me very strongly wished to identify. Christian monks and Moslem nomads alike were in these postures sharing that proximity to vitality, to truth, to holiness, which I had fleetingly experienced on my visits to the Russian Orthodox in Paris. A prolonged encounter with this mood in the Sahara had made de Foucauld into a hermit-monk himself in the end, a not improbable translation after a swashbuckling life in the cavalry. God alone knew what it would do to me. But on this journey so far, I had found myself frequently wondering a great deal about de Foucauld and about that other deeply faithful but unorthodox Frenchman, Pierre Teilhard de Chardin.

In the months before leaving England, it had occurred to me that I might have to take refuge in fantasies in order to survive moments of impending crisis, or even the merely uncomfortable humdrum of the almost day-to-day. I might have to pretend that I was a second El Aurens (in reality,

144

Mohamed ould Moctar ould Hmeida.

Mahomed ould Ely.

Sidi Mahmoud ould Sheddadi.

Sid' Ahmed ould Eli ould Simmad.

Sid' Ahmed ould Mohammed with young nomad.

Sandstorm blowing up at the oasis of Tidjikja, Mauritania.

Oasis of Tichit, Central Mauritania.

Street scene, Tombouctou.

The sheep slaughtered near the well of Anechag. Ould Mohammed on the left.

Ould Mohammed on the trans-Saharan highway, moving towards Tessalit.

Ibrahim examining loads on the first day out of Tessalit. Tamanrasset, and journey's end, is three weeks away. Two camels will have died in this time.

Approaching the almost dry water hole of In Azaoua.

On the edge of the Tanezrouft, and a rare chance for the camels to feed. The two animals in the middle will be dead within the week.

The white, broken-toothed bull from Tessalit goes down for the last time, and Ibrahim leads on the remaining two towards Tamanrasset.

of course, a second Peter O'Toole portraying Lawrence of Arabia) or another Sir Richard Burton, who had long stood higher than most heroes in my private and wistful pantheon. It would not have been foreign to the nature of someone who, at the age of fourteen, had fondly imagined himself into the position of Nat Lofthouse, centre forward of Bolton and England, and who, in his mid-thirties, was to be found filing dispatches from Czechoslovakia, blissfully aware that he was now as much of a foreign correspondent as any of the fictionalised figures who had so frequently before swirled attractively in the foreground of his ambitions.

I had not, so far in the desert, caught myself wearing such fanciful camouflage as might have been provided by the images of Lawrence or Burton. But my attention had become fixed from time to time upon de Foucauld and Teilhard de Chardin. If I was identifying with them at all, it was because they were both men who had made long interior journeys of their own, as well as travelling the hard way across rough parts of the world, as I was myself. I was eager to see civilisation again at the end of my travels for many reasons: one of the smaller, but gradually more pressing, reasons was my desire to reread Teilhard's letters from China and to discover what I could for the first time in de Foucauld's journals of that period when he wandered the northern Sahara before at last finding his anchor-hold near Tamanrasset. Could either of them possibly have experienced within themselves any of the things I felt out here? How did they submit, in what terms precisely, to what they and their Church called the will of God?

And then, with a furtive genuflection towards the greatest traveller of them all, I wondered whether, if Isabel had not made that wretched bonfire of diaries, I might have found that Burton, too, could descend to the trivia which constantly adorned my own notebooks: "As I write that, I watch a louse, drugged with my blood, lumber slowly up the leg of my infested serwal. I am not outraged any longer, merely interested; maybe I'll squash him, maybe not (What's the point when there are so many more where he came from?). Is this the beginning of surrender to Inshallah?"

At the end of the family worship, with the light now almost vanished from the sky, Sid' Ahmed ould Eli ould Simmad laid a hand upon the outermost pole of his tent and fairly bellowed into the night the information that prayers had just been said in this household, in the name of Allah, the compassionate and merciful. I liked this man. He was upstanding and he had gusto.

In the morning, he half hinted that we might stay another night in his tent, and my very firm no made me feel guilty for a moment. But he seemed to accept the decision as though he expected no other, and dispatched his two sons to find his camel out in the pastures. They were gone for hours, for so long that I began to wonder suspiciously if they had been told to lose themselves and the beasts until it was too late to start the day. Sid' Ahmed himself rubbed his face with the contents of a tin labelled Tarzan's Mustard Ointment (Made in Ghana) and then disappeared to gossip with the men of the other tents. His wife and another woman bent over pieces of hide with knives in their hands, fashioning a fresh pair of sandals for him. I examined his aged and double-barrelled shotgun, and the cartridges that went with it. In Néma he had implied that unless I provided some, he would have no ammunition at all, but here in his tent was a bag containing about 50 cartridges, a remarkable assortment of colours and balls, manufactured variously in Mali, France, Italy and Poland. I hoped that he would be carrying the new ones I had bought, for some of these looked very old and insecure.

By the time the boys returned it was past noon and, a lamb having been slaughtered for our journey, everyone gobbled at its entrails almost steaming from the carcass. I picked cautiously at a small piece of liver and wondered how long it would be before my ailment cleared up. I was

146

loath to use the drugs I was carrying except in case of dire need, but, the way things were shaping, that point might not be far off.

We got away at three o'clock, and I had not known such warmth in a desert farewell. At Mafud's camp and throughout my time with Mohamed, I had often reflected how curious it was that, although people fairly flocked to greet someone arriving, they paid scarcely any attention when he departed. It was not so here, however. As I led the camels away from the tents, Sid' Ahmed walked slowly some distance behind, surrounded by his kinsmen and their women. The men pressed their hands upon his and put their arms round him. A woman, walking alongside, carefully made signs across the palm of his hand with her rosary. Children danced and waved, shouting his name over and over. Sid' Ahmed himself responded to all this affection with wide-eyed pleasure, flashing his smile like a boy after collecting his prize at the school speech day. Yes, I did like this man. I was very glad to be travelling with him.

We rode for two hours and then, seeing a tent just ahead, Sid' Ahmed suggested that we might camp here for the night. His style was much different from Mohamed's. There was no riding arrogantly up to this dwelling, as of right. We stopped two hundred yards away and unloaded our baggage. After a while a woman and a small boy appeared, bringing a mat and some milk. We arranged our possessions round the mat for a windbreak, made a fire and, while the teapot was brewing, I medicated a baby which the woman brought from her tent, its crotch badly chafed and blistered. Later a man joined us for our evening meal. The other day, he said, not far away, a "lion" had killed seven goats in one night. Certainly it could not have been a proper lion, and the presence of any predatory cat in this part of the world, so far north of the Niger River system, seemed most unlikely to me. But just before we slept, Sid' Ahmed vowed that he had himself shot a "lion" only a month before. He described it as a brown creature about four feet long and

147

maybe two and a half feet high, with a smooth and un-ruffled fur, which made it sound like some puma or cougar. I had no idea whether it was theoretically possible to find such animals even in the scrub which grows profusely on this southern edge of the Sahara. This was so thick in the area of our camp as to put me in mind of an everlasting and abandoned golf course, devoid of greens and fairways, but overendowed with thousands of sandy bunkers.

The next day was unpleasant. I had never really shaken off the bronchial cold that had attacked me on leaving Chinguetti, and we now found ourselves riding directly into a strong wind from the east, which seemed to drive straight through my nostrils, setting them aflame. My inabil-ity to eat much was beginning to take the stuffing out of me, so that I was riding like a sack of potatoes again, barely able to sit straight in the saddle after an hour or so. Walking, too, was a penance, for the cram-cram was thick upon the ground and the burrs were a perpetual irritation upon the legs. By the time we were ready to mount, both in the morning and the afternoon, we spent about twenty minutes picking them from our garments, taking anything up to fifty from my serwal alone.

We had one mishap after another. First, a tin mug, which I had inadequately secured, disappeared. Then a bag, tied on by Sid' Ahmed, plunged to the ground, smashing more cigarettes and leaving an awful mess of bits and pieces inside its battered canvas. Finally, and much worse, there was a sudden gusher below the left flank of my camel, and as I struggled to control the startled beast, I looked down to see the water pouring out of a guerba and onto the sand. It was the only skin we had jointly heaved up into place, and we exchanged exasperated looks without a word. With three others still well filled, the loss was not serious, for Nbeiket el Ouahch was no more than three days ahead. But I made a decisive mental note that such a thing must never happen again.

We camped again with nomads, and I was glad to crawl

into someone's tent without the need to set up our own refuge for the night. I was somewhere beyond mere weariness and approaching real exhaustion, for several parts of my body were not functioning as they ought to. I found myself blinking rapidly to bring things into focus, and my limbs were trembling with excessive fatigue. As I lay limply on a mat I fervently hoped that the weakening of my flesh would not seep into my spirit, enfeebling it so much that I would give up and go home at the next opportunity. That evening and night was one of intermittent sleep, sporadic awareness, haphazard thoughts. I emerged from a doze to perceive the movements of people eating food which I had refused, to avoid the scalding pains which would instantly have followed digestion. In my hunger, I had dwelt much on my stomach during the day, my imagination floundering towards oases of European cooking. Once, before Néma, I had been dazzled by a vision of gooseberry pie; now I began seriously to consider the respective merits of bread and cheese, rich French stews and sticky Danish pastries (I knew the very shop in Hampstead where I would buy some the moment I reached home).

Sleep again, then consciousness once more at 11 P.M. As I looked at my watch, with its tiny calendar, I reflected on the different time scales of existence. At home it was based upon the hour: "In an hour I must be . . . a couple of hours ago I was . . ." Everything was immediate there. Here, one went by the month: "It is now ten days past the beginning of January . . . at twenty-three days towards the end of the month I shall be . . ." The immensity of everything here, including time. Sleep yet again until just after two o'clock. The sound, unmistakably, of an owl hunting. Well, why not? There were other birds about. There were hares, too, for we had started three or four from their hiding places during the day. As always, there had also been small khaki lizards scuttling over the ground, leaving their foot-dappled, tail-trailing marks in the sand. Plenty of food for an owl.

Halfway through the next morning, we were jogging gently along when an enormous bird rose cumbersomely into the air from behind a nearby bush. It was brown, white and black, and its wingspan looked greater than the distance I could have stretched with both arms extended. Sid' Ahmed shouted "Bustard!" and reached for the gun lodged in the wing of his saddle. The bird had cruised through the air a little way and gone to ground again, though just where I could not see. Still riding, we began to circle the area, and I was searching the bushes as keenly as my companion. In Europe I would have been horrified at the idea of killing a wild bird, but now I was beginning to smack my lips at the prospect of roasting over a fire something that resembled a large turkey; it was yet another small fall from civilisation. Suddenly, Sid' Ahmed threw the gun to his shoulder and fired—and the bustard rose from the ground, unhurt, no more than ten yards in front of us, and flapped heavily away over the trees. Without question, I was disappointed, and Sid' Ahmed was sucking his teeth ruefully. Only the camels were unmoved by the encounter. Not one of them had shown the slightest reaction to the gunshot.

By the time we reached Nbeiket el Ouahch, the drugs seemed to have taken some effect, stanching a little the flow of my bowels. But I was still feeling so wasted that an hour or two of riding had me reeling in the saddle, and I almost fell over when I dismounted. We had pushed on east through a succession of mornings more bitterly cold than any I could remember, the wind howling into our faces till almost midday, freezing and slashing even through the headcloths we wound tightly round everything but our eyes. We had suffered another mishap. Twice in one day, when riding too close together, the legs of the cooking pot lashed behind Sid' Ahmed's saddle had snagged in my baggage, threatening to tear something adrift, and I had warned him to keep a distance. When we stopped for his afternoon prayers, I found that one of my sandals had vanished from where the pair normally dangled when riding; almost certainly it had been wrenched off in one of our collisions. I groaned at the loss but could not be angry, for Sid' Ahmed immediately volunteered to ride back the way we had come, to look for it—a pointless exercise in that scrubby ground, like searching for the needle in the haystack.

The well itself was much more sophisticated than any I had seen so far, including Touijinit. It not only had a deep concrete shaft, with four outlying troughs for watering many beasts, but was equipped with a wooden pulley at the angle of each trough. A camel was hitched to the rope running over each pulley and driven away from the well to haul the bucket up. Judging by the distance each went before the bucket reached the surface and the animal was turned and brought back to the shaft head, the well must have been about 150 feet deep. It had been bored, what's more, through the top of a hillock, so that the liquefied muck which surrounded any watering place would tend to drain away and reduce the chances of pollution almost to nil. As we came up to it, half a dozen men were drawing water for a herd of camels, the ones standing by the shaft shouting loudly to those leading the haulage beasts as the buckets surfaced, squirting jets in all directions from their leaky leather sides. As well as warning their mates to turn back again, they seemed to be enjoying the shrieking echoes they were producing from deep inside the shaft.

We made camp with these men, and once more I found myself warming to Sid' Ahmed for his attitude towards me in front of others. Far from inflicting the petty humiliations that I had occasionally experienced before, he seemed actually to be proud of his relationship with me.

"When this Nasrani," he told them, "flew from England to Africa he was sitting in the sky for six hours!"

And they all shook their heads and clicked their tongues at the fantastic nature of this feat; aeroplanes they seemed to understand, but to stay in the sky for six whole hours was obviously regarded as some unconnected form of the miraculous.

151

I then heard my companion extolling my excellence as a navigator, which at that stage was more than a large assumption on his part, for I had done nothing but keep a compass check over ground that he knew well enough by heart. "Tell them," he said with massive confidence, "tell them which way it is to Tombouctou."

I drew the chart from its case, fiddled with the protractor, found the bearing with my compass and flung an arm out decisively across the sand and scrub that surrounded us monotonously.

"Eeehhh!" they all said, with definite approval.

Sid' Ahmed beamed like a man whose favourite poodle has just won the dog show against most of the popular odds. I seemed, *Ilhamdu Lillah*, to have got it right. I noticed, nonetheless, that before we moved away, Sid' Ahmed was careful to inquire about the route to the well of In Kerchouf, two days over the border.

We probably crossed the frontier sometime during the next morning, January 12, two men and three camels simply moving from one arbitrary longitude to another with an uncertainty that mocked territorial possessions and international politics. There was nothing at all to tell us at any given hour whether we were still in Mauritania's share of the wilderness or Mali's. Yet some things were beginning to change. The camels we had seen at Nbeiket el Ouahch seemed stockier than those I had encountered in the past two months. Their humps were indisputably firmer and more upright with fat; they looked better fed than most I had seen so far.

At the well I had also discovered a different kind of saddle for the first time. The Mauritanian rahhla was large and rather cumbersome, with high side wings and a backpiece to match, as well as a sturdy pommel in front, the whole usually much decorated on a basically yellow ground. Riding in one of these was a bit like sitting in a bucket. The saddle used in southern Mali, on the other hand, was comparatively light, without sides, with a very slender piece

Mauritanian   Mali   Tuareg

of wood to hold onto in front and an equally high panel to rest against at the back. Without the pommel it was basically a legless chair mounted on the camel's back, quite without decoration. I was later to see that it involved a different method of mounting, the rider invariably twisting the beast's head round so that he could hold it firmly by its lower lip, while he cocked his leg into the saddle without the acrobatic leap that the Mauritanian rahhla demanded. And because of the structural difference, as much as anything, men in this part of the Sahara tended to ride with their feet resting on the nape of the camel's neck, which consequently acquired a bald patch there as often as not.

The days now telescoped into a sequence of pain, of hunger and of blinding exhaustion. Only thirst was missing from the perpetual agonies of travel, for our supply of water was secure. From Nbeiket el Ouahch we dragged on to In Kerchouf, then to El Basriye, then to Tin Fata, and there were never more than a couple of days between any of these wells. One never suffered more than the bitter and gummy dryness of the mouth that invariably began within half an hour or so of drinking deeply from the canteen I had slung from my saddle. Otherwise, I was rapidly sinking into something close to a physical wreck, compared with the lusty individual who had left Nouakchott in the middle

153

of November. There were raw and weeping patches of flesh spreading everywhere from my ribs to my thighs. A network of sores had broken out upon my face. Curious blisters had started to appear upon the backs of my fingers and hands, oozing pus instead of fluid.

Resentfully I scrutinised this damage, contemplating my body with growing distaste. The anticipated, dramatic nightmares about this journey had not so far materialised, but now all manner of sublimated fears rose to the surface. Not only were precious possessions slowly falling to bits —the kit bags worn into holes through constant friction, the map case unstitched and coming apart, the books badly tattered and torn—but my body, cared for and enjoyed so much over the years, was becoming unrecognisable as a source of vanity. Oh, yes, one feared these things very much: the loss of possessions and the loss of beauty.

The drugs no longer seemed capable of holding my sickness in check. When I had gone without food for a day before Néma, I had realised how slender my resources of energy had become. Unless the body could receive some nourishment every few hours, it wilted alarmingly in these conditions. Now, nothing that I ate remained in the body for more than a quarter of an hour or so; it was evacuated long before it could do me any good. I was existing on liquids alone and the almost wholly emotional comfort of masticating a few dates, a boiled potato, a handful of rice or a fragment of meat. I could only guess what my condition would have been without the invigorating refreshment of highly sweetened tea and coffee. As it was, by the time we were half way to Tombouctou, I knew that I was in deep trouble.

A succession of brief but vivid cameos lodged in my consciousness during these days. There was a night when we camped with nomads whose tents had been pitched in a deep basin of sand. A great fire had been built up in the ground between them. Every time I woke, a group of sheep was huddled motionless, sitting or standing, around this fire,

154

their glass-eyed, slightly anxious faces glowing in the yellow light. There was something instantly recognisable in the posture of the sheep, in the light upon their bodies, in the tranquillity of the moment. Dozily my mind groped for the origin of the painting in which I had seen it all before, but I drifted away again before deciding whether it was something in the National Gallery at home, or one of the Le Nains in the Louvre.

There was an afternoon when we rode up to a small camp where three men lounged and a woman sat apart, nursing a baby so new that it was still pink. We paused to exchange a greeting before riding on, but the men seemed anxious that we should stay and talk. Supposing that they wanted tea and sugar, we dismounted, Sid' Ahmed murmuring that it would be a good chance to obtain information about the lie of the land ahead. One of the men was wearing a European coat over his boubou, and this strangeness made me uneasy. All three continued to stare at me, while they talked with Sid' Ahmed about the lack of ghudda to the north, the plenty to the south. As Sid' Ahmed handed the first glass to the man in the coat, asking him to pass it to his mate, the fellow made an insolent gesture to my companion with his mouth, which Sid' Ahmed appeared not to notice. But as the third round of glasses was being poured out, I sensed that he was suddenly intent on getting away quickly. We had done nothing but remove the kettle and tea things from our baggage, leaving the camels couched and loaded, so we were off with little delay. As we mounted, out of earshot, Sid' Ahmed muttered that it was dangerous to stay; one of the men had asked him whether the Nasrani was carrying much money. We must ride fast, to get away from this camp, he said. And we did ride fast, at an appalling gallop for the best part of two hours, until the sun was almost set and I all but unconscious in the saddle.

There was another evening when we rested with some friendly people who put up a small tent of hides for our benefit, and then produced a great stream of children and old men, all suffering from eye infections. I was squeezing tetracycline across the lids of the prettiest child I had seen for months, a slim and delicate girl with pigtails hanging to her waist, when I suddenly fell over, half swooning away. Dizzily, I staggered behind some bushes to be ill again. It was the first time since reaching the desert that I could remember being drenched with sweat, which sprang out of every pore in my body in an almighty rush.

Then my camel, the twelve-year-old bull I had ridden down from Tidjikja, started to founder. After stumbling a little one day before Néma, he had carried on as well as before. But since leaving Sid' Ahmed's tent, he had begun to show signs of growing tiredness. Once or twice, after being unloaded, he had seemed reluctant to rise again and start browsing. After our furious gallop away from the camp of the sinister three, he had been limping in the left foreleg, which had troubled him before Néma. Sid' Ahmed suggested cutting the leg above or below the knee joint and letting out some blood, which, he said, was a well-known remedy for lameness. I had refused to allow this at first. Next day, we travelled very softly, but even so my bull and I were trailing badly. Sid' Ahmed, leading the spare camel by its headrope, kept looking back anxiously to see how the two sick creatures behind were doing. When he asked my permission to bleed the bull, I agreed, telling myself that perhaps there was pus on the leg that ought to be drained.

We couched the beast and I held down its lower lip with one hand, covering its right eye with the other, hauling its head round parallel with its neck so that it would be unable to see out of the other eye, too. Sid' Ahmed slashed it above both knee caps, then cut it deeply at the shoulder of its right foreleg. The poor creature scarcely struggled at all when this happened; it really had very little energy left. But it got to its feet without much trouble, blood streaming everywhere. There was no question of riding it now; the question seemed to be whether we could get it to Tombouctou, which was at least five days away.

An hour later the bull fell down, his forelegs giving way beneath him. With Sid' Ahmed hauling on his headrope and with me kicking him hard behind, we got him up. We put him between the other two camels, fastened headropes to saddles, and led them in line ahead for half an hour. Then the rope which Sid' Ahmed was hauling pulled taut with sudden strain, the rope behind broke in two, and the sick bull was down on his knees again before settling on all fours. We got him up once more, spliced the broken headrope and started off. Almost immediately, the same thing happened again. Again we got him moving, and this time he kept going until we made camp for the night.

I was badly spent myself by now. I had drunk a mug of coffee before starting the day's march, I had eaten a boiled potato at noon, which had gone straight through me, and I had sipped a round of tea. Sid' Ahmed ordered me to lie down while he unloaded and hobbled the camels single-handed. I lay like a log while this splendid, bandy-legged fellow arranged our camp, collected wood for a fire, made it up, brewed tea, did everything himself.

I raised myself on an elbow as he offered me the first glass. "You're a good man, Sid' Ahmed," I said.

His head tilted to one side in that mannerism I had associated with wheedling. I realised now that essentially it betrayed embarrassment. "You're a good man yourself, *sayyid*," he replied.

Quickly, I turned my head away from him. I could feel the tears springing into my eyes, starting to roll down my scarecrow cheeks. There had been something terrible but very beautiful in that gesture of his. It was as though the thought that he was a decent human being had never crossed his mind before.

The next day, January 16, we marched for almost two hours, much longer than usual, having some vague intention of sparing the sick bull with a reduced pace. After a mile or so I stumbled and fell. For a fraction of a moment, as I collected my breath on hands and knees, I was of two minds whether to get to my feet again or lie down properly and

157

rest for a little while. I hauled myself up and carried on walking. Some time later I fell again. This happened two or three times, until Sid' Ahmed insisted that I mount his own stocky bull, on which he would return to his camp from Tombouctou, while he walked with the other two. I scarcely noticed the relief from marching, for the pain from my body sores was now intensified by the rubbing jerks of the saddle. I realised, in a moment of coherence between the blurring waves of torment, that I was holding onto the pommel, as I had not done since my prentice days of riding, in an effort to reduce the strain upon my body. My hands were clutching it as fiercely, as weakly, as an infant holds onto a security when it is learning the first spastic movements of walking.

I tried to think of my children setting off to school, of J dashing round the house to get them away on time, of A walking down a hill to catch a bus for work. Normally, the vacuum hours of a day's journey were much relieved by such thoughts. I would linger over them fondly to make them last, and sometimes I would start talking audibly, asking these two women in my life what they were doing this day, explaining to the children something that I was seeing for them and wished to convey at once. It was my lifeline, without which I would be lost, and it was a promise that the dreariness and discomfort of this journey would not go on forever, that one day I would have done with it and return, that what I cared for most deeply went on without me and would be there awaiting me at the end. It was assurance and insurance, both.

But now I could not even focus the images of home for more than a split second. They flicked into my consciousness and were gone again, and I had neither the strength nor the will to hold them to me, to retrieve them from the blankness that encircled me. They seemed to have lost their power and their hold upon me. They had no meaning in this blinding struggle to go on. They were irrelevant. Even food was irrelevant now. I could no longer identify my stomach-empty pain. Body was pain and it had no separate parts. I wanted release, nothing more. I wanted to sleep, nothing beyond.

I reined in the bull and made him couch. I got myself out of the saddle and began my tottering walk forward again. If I stumbled and fell now, I would go to sleep. I knew it. I desired it. I think I almost willed it. But we then walked over a low dune and saw two tents in the hollow beneath. It was hardly past midmorning but Sid' Ahmed, I saw, was already couching the other two beasts and removing their gear. We stayed there all day and I lay without moving for hours at a time, with my boubou billowed about me like a tent to ward off the great heat that had now overcome the days of glacial cold. This was the only distinct advantage in what was otherwise a quite impossible garment. The people in the camp gave me some milk, and towards the evening I was revived a little, though otherwise I ate nothing.

On January 17 we marched again. I fell down once, the sick bull twice. At some stage in the day we reached the well of Tin Fata and I, sitting dazed under a tree, could hear Sid' Ahmed asking three men if they had a camel they could sell. But he returned from the wellhead without a word, and we marched on to the southeast.

Next day, we lost the sick bull. We had walked for three hours when, without warning, he fell down again. This time we couldn't get him up. After we had hauled on his nose ring, as always, and offered him kicks from behind, as we had done before, Sid' Ahmed unhitched a guerba and brought it over to the beast. Then he poured water into its nostrils in a rushing jet, while the bull strained laboriously to get its head out of the way. More hauling and kicking, and still he wouldn't budge. Sid' Ahmed drew his knife and, before I realised what he intended, he had jabbed it into the animal's side. I sharply ordered him to stop, as the blood began to flow, the bull having merely uttered a grunt and twitched along the flank. Sid' Ahmed turned away and began to cast around the area for wood. I supposed he had decided that we should make camp, to see if a rest might revive the camel enough to go on. But when he returned with an armful of firewood, he dumped it alongside the sitting beast and asked me for the matches. What, I asked, was he going to do? Sid' Ahmed replied that sometimes a fire would make an exhausted animal rise when everything else failed; it hurt more than a knife.

I shook my head. "No," I said, "we're not going to do that."

Sid' Ahmed gestured impatiently. "Then he's finished," he said.

"Then we must leave him," I replied. I was remembering the two camels I had seen—how long ago it seemed —which had been abandoned on the brink of the well of Chig.

Sid' Ahmed removed the animal's headrope and the few small things it had been carrying. I could see that he was very cross with me. How long would it be, I asked, before the bull died? Sid' Ahmed shrugged. Perhaps the bull would sit there for two days, manage to get up and browse a bit, then slowly regain his strength. But probably not. "He's finished, that one," he said.

We mounted the other two camels and slowly rode away. I did not look back. I was blank about this, too.

We were now heading for the northern shore of Lac Faguibine, which had seemed in prospect a pretty implausible thing to find anywhere within the limits of the Sahara desert. But every chart clearly marked this wedge-shaped sheet of water, about fifty miles long and ten miles across at its wider end. I knew it to be of comparatively recent origin, for the German explorer Heinrich Barth, who travelled in this area in the 1850s, observed only that the village of Ras-el-Ma lay at the head of a creek connected to the Niger River system; and Ras-el-Ma now evidently looked down the full extent of the lake from its westernmost end. The question in my mind had been whether the lake would be dried up when I reached it, but the men Sid' Ahmed had talked to at Tin Fata said that this was not so. They called it "the sea."

Almost as soon as we left the dying bull, we entered a region quite unlike anything I had seen before. The ground was still basically one of extremely shallow, undulating sand dunes. But now it became thickly forested with thorn trees. They were set so close together that, mounted, we found ourselves swerving sharply to avoid being swept off by the branches. They were pitifully poor in green leaves, but it seemed to me that, given a week's heavy rain in these parts, they would have had something as lush as the Forest of Arden here. As it was, the place was eery with a blessed gloom which protected us from the sun's burning. I was but dimly aware of gratitude, for my mind was clamped ferociously on the twenty yards immediately ahead of my camel and the need to hang onto my seat.

We had almost trampled into a small encampment before we knew it lay there in a clearing. Here were dwellings which spoke of Black Africa, not the desert: tipsy hutments made of rattan sheets and bundles of thorn. A girl stood naked to the waist, motionless after she had turned her back on us. Sid' Ahmed ignored her completely, but addressed the hutments with *"Selehmoo alaikum,"* though there was no one else in sight. Nothing stirred, and there was no response. We rode on, twisting and turning around the trees again, the thorny branches scratching our arms and plucking at our garments.

Then it lay before us, this miracle of water. We trotted towards a dense belt of shade, like many we had already passed, but on the farther side, instead of dappled light, there was dazzling, glinting glare. Immediately ahead was a flat, white, sandy shore, maybe five hundred yards deep. Beyond that, utterly smooth, the water. Here and there were tiny islands, covered in green vegetation. Two dugouts were fishing a few hundred yards offshore. To the west, the lake evaporated in a shimmering haze of heat.

161

To the east, a few miles away, was a ridge of low rocky hills, and the lake at that end so much reminded me of a Scottish loch that I wanted to embrace everything I could see in one great enveloping hug.

Slowly our camels walked up the shore towards those hills, and there we came upon a marvellous thing. At the foot of the hills was a tiny bay, fringed with green trees and rushes. On its farther shore some children were bathing, scuttering the water up into each other's faces and squealing with laughter. A heron was standing up to his knees, peering steadily at the surface. An egret stood quietly some way off, on the edge of the rushes.

Sid' Ahmed wanted to refill the guerbas, but we already had enough water to last us four or five days at a pinch, and Tombouctou should be only a couple of days away now, so I forbade him to. I suspected that Lac Faguibine might breed the flukes of bilharzia; otherwise I would have stripped off and bathed myself. So we sat there for a little while, while the camels drank deeply, and then we walked quietly past the hills to make our camp for the night among the lushest trees I had seen since Europe.

That night I wrote in my notebook; "'I will lift up mine eyes unto the hills, from whence cometh my help.' It's always been one of the loveliest Psalms. Tonight it perfectly expresses what I've felt this past hour or two. The last few days have been so awful, we're not out of the wood yet, I'm a half wreck of an exhausted man but, by God, my spirits have come up off the deck again. My thanks."

I wrote that too soon. I should not have been so enthusiastic about the hills. Next morning I decided that we must cross them, to shorten the time to Tombouctou, though Sid' Ahmed was in favour of taking a longer but easier way round the back. At a distance I had thought them to consist of nothing but rock. Now, on their flank, it was obvious that we were facing a six-hundred-foot dune of sand extending between two proper cliffs of stone. Almost as soon as we started, the incline became something like one in three. The sand was soft, the beasts were in difficulty from the beginning and, though we were not really hauling them up the slope, the strain on the headropes felt like it most of the time. Sid' Ahmed, reaching the top before I was even halfway up, came slithering down to help me bring my camel up to his.

We mounted for the descent down the other side, which was hardly less steep, but the flaming agony of my sores with the rub, rub, rub of the saddle and the jolting of the gait was such that I couched my camel and dismounted before reaching the bottom. I had walked no more than a few hundred yards when I pitched forward and lay there, shaken, without the energy to rise again, not even wanting to make the effort. I raised my head. Sid' Ahmed was some distance away, riding slowly, waiting for me to catch up. Foolish man, he didn't know that I wasn't going to this time. Sleep was what I wanted, what I would have now. My head went down on my arms again and I could feel my body relaxing beautifully. Then a voice somewhere above me was curtly saying that I must get up and move on. I paid no attention. I was supremely uninterested. The voice insisted and began to irritate me. It would not stop haranguing me; it was breaking my wonderful peace.

I heard Sid' Ahmed hissing his camel to couch. Murderously my head came up. How dare this little shit take it upon himself to disturb me when I wished to be left alone? Then I was on all fours, hurling obscenities at him in English, hauling myself to my feet in mid-flow of my shrieking invective. The little bastard now had a half grin of superiority on his rotten wheedling face; he was in the saddle again, waving his arms forward imperiously and shouting, "Come on, advance, advance!" as though he were talking to a dog. Still shouting my oaths, I dragged my camel up so that I could mount and pursue this appalling little tick to tell him what I really thought of him and his God-awful self-inflated image of himself.

At midday, camped beside some bushes, I wondered whether I would have lain in the sand for good if I had been travelling alone. Sid' Ahmed, who had conceivably just saved my life, paused before downing the third glass of tea. "Tomorrow night, *Inshallah*, Tombouctou." Then he grinned at me with God's face.

We had just crossed a desolate plain, which had followed the steep ridge of rock and sand, in a high wind that was laced with dust from the open desert. There were blackened stalks of corn standing in long files, the useless remnant of a crop which either drought or disease had wiped out. There were humpy tents made of grasses bundled across sapling frameworks and, as we rode past one of them, three small boys looked up from a game they were playing. The largest urchin, his black and naked body almost whitened by the dust, rose and laughed at us. Then he broke into a loose-limbed dance on the spot, his legs dangling from side to side like a marionette's, perfectly mimicking the swinging and lopsided gait of the camels.

Occasionally we passed men riding beasts which were much more richly decorated than those of Mauritania; they were geared with halters tricked out with woolly tufts, tiny bells and brasswork. The men themselves wore broadswords at their belts, their scabbards gaudily coloured green and scarlet. Two or three carried long spears as well. We passed one man on foot who had a bow and some arrows slung across his back. There was not a flicker of hostility from these people, but there was almost complete indifference to our presence. No one altered course to come and speak with us, which was the unvarying rule in the open desert; if we met by chance, we exchanged a "*Selehmoo alaikum*" and nothing more, without stopping. Sid' Ahmed, I noticed, had no inclination to converse with them. I sensed that he, wholly of the desert, was ill at ease among these people who lived on its edge and who belonged, even more, to the Black Africa of the savannah away to the south.

We left the plain and people behind, we made our midday camp alone, and we continued our way across shallow sand dunes well covered in scrub. At first we walked for a while, Sid' Ahmed soon outstripping my pedestrian meander, which had become so slow that the camel I was supposed to be leading was padding close behind me, his neck looming over my head. In an effort to jerk some morale into my fading spirit and some vitality into my tired body, I began to hum "The British Grenadier."

It was exactly the wrong choice of music. Among other things, it had been the regimental marching tune of the old Lancashire Fusiliers, in which my grandfather had been an undistinguished but very proud lance-corporal long before I was born. More times than I could remember, when I was a child and the tune had been played on the radio, Grandad would stiffen a little at the sound and announce, with a gleam in his damp old eyes, "I've marched thousands of miles across the desert to that tune," by which he probably meant a number of ceremonial parades upon the South African veldt in the Boer War. As I hummed the first few bars, I remembered all this again and burst into tears, weeping uncontrollably for several minutes, very thankful for once that Sid' Ahmed was so far ahead that he couldn't possibly see what was going on. I was crying for so many things. For my present abysmal state, for my loneliness, for the memory of that gentle old man, with his obvious jokes and his dogged loyalty to the Fusiliers and the six VCs which, I must never forget, they had won before breakfast in the assault on Gallipoli.

I was crying, too, I think, from a sense of shame, for he had come home from two wars to support a blind wife, a divorced daughter and a small grandson and had not failed one of them at any time, while I, who had not been to any war, had failed so many people. I wished, through this mixture of tears, that Grandad were still alive to know that I was slogging through the desert; I wanted to be told that he might have been proud of that, too.

We made camp that night in the sandy scrub. Sid'

Ahmed sniffed the air and said that there were people camping nearby, but we saw no one. In the desert, he said, a man could smell a campfire anything up to three miles away. He began to put henna on the fingertips of his left hand, to restore the red stain that was almost faded away. It was his preparation for our arrival in Tombouctou. He was the only man I had seen decorating himself thus, and when I asked him why he painted his left hand, but not his right, he said it was because he was left-handed.

We cooked our last piece of meat in the embers of the fire, such a gritty, dried-up lump of gristle as I would not have thrown to a pet animal in England—it looked like something dropped behind the stove while cooking, to be discovered weeks later and pitched rapidly, with much distaste, into the rubbish bin. But I was very hungry, I needed anything that would nourish and I wolfed it down greedily, hoping that the after-effects would not be more than usually unpleasant.

Next day, January 20, we rode into thorn trees again. They were not as close-set as in the forest before Lac Faguibine, but they reduced the visibility ahead to no more than a few hundred yards. After the midday camp, we came upon the first wheel tracks since Néma and began to watch eagerly for the first sign of habitation. Tombouctou, one of the world's fabulous place-names, was close at hand, and I ought to have been tingling with the excitement of this landfall. But my eagerness had nothing to do with the fable; I was looking hard for a refuge from the desert, a place where I could rest and repair my body. It could have borne the dullest name on earth and I would have ridden into it with boundless gratitude.

Uncharacteristically, I was the first to spot it. A pale flash above the treeline caught my eye, and I realised I was looking at a tall cylinder of corrugated iron, possibly a water tower, maybe a mile away. It was probably part of the local airstrip, for we rode another hour along the wheel tracks before we saw anything else. Then gradually the trees around us parted and Tombouctou came into full view. In the diminishing light of late afternoon it seemed to be a grey place, not white as I had somehow imagined it. Nor was it walled, as I had expected, though the strong horizontal lines of the buildings suggested something of fortification. Only the conical tower of the mosque stood vertically above this lateral sweep. In the foreground, before the buildings began, was a great hollow in the sand, and here many men were busy making stacks of muddy grey bricks.

We reined in our camels and paused a moment before dismounting. I looked across at my companion, who was studying the walls beyond the brickworkers. "Well," I said, "we got there."

"*Inshallah*," said Sid' Ahmed, still looking to his front. He tilted his head, more dramatically than usual. "*Ilhamdu Lillah! Ilhamdu Lillah!*"

8

THEODORE MONOD HAD ONCE described Tombouctou to me as "a dreadful place," but in the time I spent there I could not see why. Given my condition when I arrived, no town could possibly have seemed dreadful, yet I found in Tombouctou something more than a welcome refuge. It was, above all, a tantalising mixture of styles and derivations. It was something between a small French provincial town, any town in Black Africa, and a rather grand oasis, which owed the deepest strains in its personality to the overwhelming vastness of desert that drifted up to its doorstep.

The French strain was the slightest, but clearly marked all the same. It was represented by the methodical placing of traffic signs in a community that didn't have much traffic, by the battered Renault runabouts which you occasionally saw parked up some sandy alley, by the basketball court in front of the *lycée*; above all, by the Place de l'Indépendence. Not so much by the municipal and Government offices that were ranged, one after the other, on all four sides, as by the war memorial. This commanded all roads into the square from its position in the middle, a curious wedge-shaped edifice, with a Pegasus emblazoned in concrete high relief along one surface; only in the case of this Pegasus, on close inspection, his rider Bellerophon could be seen wearing a desert headcloth, half veiling the face. Something out of Medusa, by the Sahara, under the auspices of Gaul.

The Black African strain most clearly succeeded the French in the cry *"Donnez-moi un cadeau,"* which was upon the lips of every child in town the moment he spotted a Westerner; sometimes it was to be heard from adults as well, though neither they nor the children seemed to have learned the additive *"s'il vous plaît."* Black Africa was also the great pit behind the solitary hotel, with muddy water swilling in the bottom, into which all day long great processions of people climbed with buckets and plastic jerry cans. This they did with much laughter and merriment, for fun and games and social intercourse as much as for drinking supplies and the washing of clothes, which was something that never happened at a well in the desert. People out there drew water deliberately and confined their shouts to animals harnessed to the haulage of buckets; having done this, they would sit and talk quietly, as though afraid to challenge the gaping silence that surrounded them. Black Africa in Tombouctou was the arrangement of the marketplace, with mammies sitting by piles of vegetables in the open and with a large functional shed of mud brick and corrugated asbestos, in which the more privileged salesmen and women could set up shop in the shade.

The rest was of the desert. It was more colourfully of the desert than any place I had visited, with the billowing robes of the camel men running through a whole spectrum of shades that included deep royal blues, lime and avocado greens, gorgeous oranges and yellows. Here was Tuareg as well as other Berber blood, quite apart from the smattering of tribes that had drifted up the Niger River from the Negro lands in the southern bush. Men here strode about with headcloths concealing most of their faces as a vocation, rather than as the necessity which the searing desert winds sometimes imposed. The trappings of the camels were now invariably as ornate as those I had encountered in that ride across the plain after Faguibine. The beasts themselves were more splendid than any I had seen before. Most of them were white, they were woollier than the brown camels of Mauritania, they looked bigger-boned and firmer-humped, and such was the combination of their breeding and the Tuareg spirit that they seemed always to be ridden at a roistering gallop.

The desert was not only encroaching upon the outskirts of the town. It had drifted into every street, none of which was tarmacked, so that the sound of everything in Tombouctou was muted into crunching sibilants. It was a town without an echo. The sand was ankle-deep alongside the main mosque, which René Caillié had once sketched covertly under the guise of prayer, just as Richard Burton had daringly made drawings inside the very Ka'aba at Mecca. Not having the courage for impersonations similar to theirs, and since entrance to a Nasrani was still discouraged, I contented myself with a stroll round its walls, past the tower whose extruding wooden pegs Caillié had identified as a means of holding the mud cone together. It was a mysterious building, half fort, half temple, crude and indigenous.

Yet there was another mosque, all angles and apexes, which quite preposterously suggested a Gothic priory in Christian Europe. For that matter, the buildings in the street where René Caillié lodged looked like reach-me-downs from Florence, with copings at the roofline, lintels at the foursquare windows and pilasters projecting from the walls. His old house had a heavy and studded wooden door to it, surmounted by a bronze commemorative plaque which tactlessly told the curious that here was a *"Souvenir Colonial Français."* Just around the corner was a ruder dwelling, totally sub-Saharan, with another plaque in slate, this one put up by the British. Here was where Gordon Laing stayed in 1826, the first white man to reach Tombouctou but not, alas, the first to take the news home again, being murdered by his Tuareg guides somewhere among those thorn trees through which I had ridden on my way into town. White men now were lobbied rather fiercely outside that house to buy all manner of baubles. But people were still making bread in the communal ovens shaped like beehives which stood at most street corners, just as they would have been making it when Laing was here.

The houses in the street where Caillié rested were also equipped with great projecting rainwater heads. The Niger itself might have been swirling muddily in a great curve past the Government hotel if it had not been for the years of drought. As it was, the waters stopped short of Tombouctou by many miles, and the river bed now was merely a sandy basin in which men and camels lounged picturesquely for hours each day in the hope of being hired for short rides by the tourists. There was a medley of French, Germans and Americans in that hotel, most of whom seemed to find the sanitation unspeakable, the catering inadequate and the service slatternly bad. There were also four Swiss, who befriended me, slipping me extra portions of *crème caramel* which the two ladies found inedible, eventually taking my notebooks and films with them back to the safety of Europe.

To me the hotel was a luxurious haven. Sid' Ahmed had declined to stay there with me, and I had almost been thrown out before I even got to the reception desk. A policeman whose permanent duty was either to protect the guests from harassment or to keep an eye open for their subversive intent, told me later in the week that he had observed two filthy Arabs approaching the terrace, one of whom had insolently continued to march towards the door. On getting up to fling the fellow off the premises he had realised only just in time that this intruder was, in fact, a European and therefore entitled to enter the hotel, however disgusting his appearance.

I changed much of my appearance very quickly. I shed my desert clothes and sent them to be deloused and washed, donning jeans and shirt instead. The effect on morale of this alone—of being in clean clothes which fitted close to the body, instead of grimy wrappings which hampered every movement—was enormously uplifting. Not that my European dress fitted as closely as it had done. I had already lost much weight. I was a dismal sight when I looked at myself naked in a mirror: all ribs and pelvis, and terribly messed up with sores. As soon as I was clean I reached for antibiotics and took some monumental doses of tetracycline, smearing it in ointment upon my wounds, digesting it in horse pills for my sickness.

Somehow, I must eat well in Tombouctou and keep the food inside me, if I was to continue this journey. I must also rest, and restore some of the wastage that had already taken place. For three or four days I did little else, lying on my bed for hours, drifting between consciousness and sleep, rising only at mealtimes to shovel in the most welcome food I had ever tasted; bread, pasta, fish, decently stewed mutton, *crème caramel* and more bread, all devoured with the most appalling table manners that a dining room full of tourists can have experienced in a fellow Westerner. Evian water I drank by the litre, hideously expensive though it was, staring at its perfect clarity as though I were regarding a Holy Grail. And, wonderfully, after a day or two I began to retain all this nourishment.

The finest thing in Tombouctou, however, was the mail awaiting me there. Before leaving England, I had instructed everyone not to write to me, believing that only by shutting out all thoughts of those I loved and liked could I strengthen myself enough to face isolation. But I had long since discovered that home thoughts, far from weakening my resolve, were a vital means of endurance. Only at the lowest ebb of all, in the days before Tombouctou, did the people I most wanted to be with mean nothing at all to me, having apparently been wiped out of my consciousness by exhaustion and the overpowering desire to sleep.

At Néma I had managed to write some letters home, and at Tombouctou I received a whole bundle in reply. A wrote of sitting on a beach in Cornwall and gazing for a long time across the great expanse between us. J said she was sending posthaste some substance to rid me of lice. Andrew had carefully copied out the leading positions in the English football leagues, and Jane told how at Christmas they had listened to my reading of Dylan Thomas, surprised that I had managed some sort of Welsh accent. A Benedictine monk I had known for years had dragooned half a dozen convents into praying for me, and the sisters were wondering about the theological niceties of praying for my camels, too. One of my oldest friends, who had been on the Annapurna expedition and had a better idea than most of hard going, advised me to "remember the trick with the bricks." Was that merely a way of saying take care? Or was Alan obliquely offering me a get-out, the trick being to know when to stop?

I would not stop now, not now that I had achieved the first objective. As mind and body slowly surfaced from the bog of weariness, I rose to a subdued form of elation and began to plot the way ahead. Two things were already settled in my mind. One was that, as I had been advised by both Monod and Thesiger, it was indeed impossible to travel entirely alone. I must have a companion to share the hard work of loading and handling the camels, and I needed the insurance of another man against the possibility of disaster. I was very acutely aware that if Sid' Ahmed had not been with me I might just have foundered, like the unfortunate camel, a couple of days short of Tombouctou; on the other hand, my collapsing into the sand, and my wish to stay there and drift fatally into sleep, might have been a deeply subconscious abdication of responsibility for myself, something the life force in me would have resisted had I been alone. Nevertheless, there was an unreasonable risk in travelling alone, and I dared not take it now.

My other decision was that, if I were to reach the Nile, it would now have to be the result of a continuous movement. I simply did not have the resources, spiritual much more than physical, to spend months in a Libyan oasis, awaiting not just the end of summer but the passing of Ramadan which followed it. Given that I needed a companion, I would not find anyone willing to move until the fast was over, which meant the middle of November. I would thus be sitting at Murzuk, in conditions I basically disliked, for something like seven months, and I knew I couldn't do it. The moment I stopped moving for more than a few days, I would head for home by the fastest means available. It had been something of an effort to start off again after Néma, and here again, in Tombouctou, I was conscious of the intimidating emptiness around, which I was reluctant to face now even more than at the start of my journey.

The question was whether it would be possible to drive straight through to the Nile before the start of summer made movement suicidal. I had ridden something over eleven hundred miles in two months. The odds seemed much against adding another twenty-five hundred or so in the time available, but it might be done if I could keep my present pace at its highest level and if I could risk riding into the edge of summer. I reckoned that, with the best luck going, I might just reach the Nile by my chosen route early in June. This would expose me to a few weeks of the heat that everyone seemed to think impossible for travel in the open desert, but I reasoned that if I got so close to a triumphant ending by the time the heat became desperate, the intoxication of achieving the record would see me through. The immediate priority was to lay a course to Tamanrasset and, after I consulted the deployment of wells on the chart, it seemed possible to ride almost all the way along something much closer to a straight line than in my traverse of Mauritania, crossing the Algerian border after the oases of Kidal and Tin Zouatan. If I could do this, it should certainly speed things up.

I had by now been lulled into complacency about territorial jealousies and official prohibitions. At Bamako in October, I had been made well aware of the purely political hazards of travelling across Mali. I had been told, among other things, of a young American who had tried to ride camels down from Morocco to Tombouctou and who had been clapped into prison at the salt-mining oasis of Taoudenni, a legendary hellhole of a place in the middle of the terrible Tanezrouft. Only when he had become seriously ill after several weeks there, had he been flown out to the more salubrious climate of Bamako. But, with a costly and indefinite visa in my passport, I had settled in Tombouctou without difficulty. As advised by a notice in the hotel, I had gone down to the police bureau the morning after my arrival, filled in a form which was placed among those of other Western visitors, and had my precious passport restored to me.

A few days later, however, when I felt well enough to take a look at the town, I was walking towards the great mosque when a Jeep drew up beside me. Two policemen ordered me to get in and I was driven to the bureau. It was a scruffy place, with a framed photograph of the President on one wall facing a lottery poster on the other. The striped and pipped members of the constabulary were fairly smart in khaki denims, but the rankers were a sloppy crowd who had grubby blue overcoats dragged over their uniforms to ward off the early-morning chill. The bureau didn't quite suggest nasty happenings in the cells, but I could see how it might, given the wrong answers to questioning. My nerves tautened as I was told to sit on a bench and await the commissioner's pleasure.

When I was led into a dusty room full of filing cabinets and a desk, I found myself facing a very smart and slicked individual, with a thin moustache and a skin which was several shades lighter than that of the lieutenant next to him, or of any other policeman on the premises. He wore a red turtleneck sweater under a khaki drill shirt and he dangled, even when sitting, a fly whisk from his fingers. He looked as though interrogation was his bread and butter. He was very hostile to start with, in a controlled way that hinted at the coiled power of a snake. Where was my Mauritanian companion? he asked. Why was I travelling by camel and why had I not declared this on the form filled in for the security services when I arrived? At a pause in the questions, I heard a sergeant outside ordering the Jeep driver to "go and collect this man's effects," and wondered uneasily how long I would be lodged in the brig. I tried to answer the questions calmly. I had, in fact, declared my means of transport and my intentions on the form, if *m'sieur le commissaire* would trouble himself to look again.

Then I played my trump card and blessed the instinct that had given it to me during my last weekend in Paris. For in the Champs-Elysées I had, on a sudden whim, photocopied the letter of recommendation from the Mali Embassy to the Director-general of the Security Services in Bamako. Handing the photostat over to the commissioner now, I artfully dropped the name of M. Bagayoko into the conversation, as though he had personally guaranteed my safe-conduct across the republic. Maybe he had, though I had never met the gentleman.

At once the hostility was replaced by level correctness. I offered a cigarette and was glad to be a smoker. The commissioner wasn't, but his lieutenant accepted politely. The commissioner, twitching his fly whisk and still reading the photostat as though he hoped he might spot forgery, gave me what he called advice. I was absolutely forbidden to go anywhere near the oases of Kidal and Tin Zouatan, which were areas of the highest military security. I must not even travel across the desert outside Tombouctou. Instead, I must take the dirt road that ran parallel to the Niger, due east, as far as the village of Bourem; there I must switch to the trans-Saharan highway running north from Gao into Algeria and ride up it to the border oasis of Tessalit. After that, it was up to the Algerians to decide whether I could proceed as I wished. As long as I understood all this clearly, I was free to leave Tombouctou.

By this time, Sid' Ahmed had made arrangements for his return home. Within a week, a small caravan would be leaving Tombouctou for the Mauritanian border, and he proposed to ride with it. He had bought himself a new camel with the money I had given him, but he had been mindful of my interests, too. He suggested that he should take the camel I had brought down from Tidjikja in exchange for the one he had brought from his camp. Slyly, he added that as his beast was fairly fresh, having travelled for scarcely more than a fortnight and having been ridden for only two or three days, he would want some more money in addition. We smacked hands on the deal at once, and there was no man I would more willingly have wished to make a decent profit out of me. He had found someone prepared to sell me a new camel, so that I should be able to continue with a pair of beasts, and the owner brought it from his encampment the next day. It was a handsome white animal, a seven-year-old more solidly built than the brown six-year-old that Sid' Ahmed had transferred to me. Fancying it on sight, I bought it there and then. This was the one, I decided, that I would ride up to the Algerian border.

As soon as the transaction was completed, Sid' Ahmed said that I must brand it with my mark, for there was much camel-thieving in Mali. I drew a large M in the sand and asked if that would do for the mark. No, it resembled a brand already used in the district. The same went for the letter A. In the end, the beast was branded with a clumsy version of 41, for my desert birthday. We made up a fire and couched and hobbled the bull, with a lashing of rope around its jaw. While its last owner hauled on this, to bring the animal's head hard round into its flank, Sid' Ahmed burnt the mark halfway down the right side of its neck. As the grey smoke arose from the scorched hide and the acrid fumes of burning wool watered everyone's eyes, the bull roared and struggled for a moment. Released again, he struggled to his feet and stood quietly, uttering a series of aggrieved grunts.

He was not nearly as well marked as some camels. The twelve-year-old that I had lost before Faguibine had borne the brands of four different owners, on both sides of his neck, on his buttocks and on one haunch. The animal I now had from Sid' Ahmed was scarred in all these places, as well as on his cheeks and a shoulder. Apart from my own

41, the new white had only one other brand, on the other side of his neck.

I had asked Sid' Ahmed if he could find someone to go with me up to the Algerian border. A few days later he introduced me to a man whom he identified as his "cousin," though I knew well enough that the word did not express the relationship of that name understood in the Western world, merely reflecting a trace of shared blood that had probably flowed in different mainstreams for a dozen generations or more. This man was a Berber of the Ledaeesh tribe, whereas my old companion was of the ouled Bille. It is possible, indeed, that the title "cousin" was bestowed simply because the two had the same given names, the newcomer being called Sid' Ahmed ould Mohammed.

He was a good deal older than anyone I had travelled with before, probably nearer sixty than the forty-five he claimed, though I was not to see his bald head until we were well away from Tombouctou. But he seemed amiable and he spoke a little French as well as Hassaniya, so I engaged him after discovering that he, too, had done time in the colonial camel corps many years before. Yet I soon realised, before ever we set off, that he was as craftily intent on extracting much more than he bargained for as Mohamed ould Moctar ould Hmeida had been in Mauritania. First he agreed on a price which would include the cost of his fare home by truck down the trans-Saharan highway from Tessalit to Gao and west on the dirt road from Gao to Tombouctou.

No sooner had this been accepted and an advance paid than he attempted to renegotiate for the price of the truck fare to be added on when we reached our destination together. And in the next few days there were various supplementary payments to be handed over, of dubious validity, for a man who had allegedly been guarding some rice for us in the marketplace, for a bag to be made for the rice (I already had plenty), for a long pole with which to pull down high branches for fodder and for a boy to carry

178

CAMEL MARKS

Mali	Mauritanian

Mali

7-year-old bull—2 owners

right neck   left neck
(author's mark)

6-year-old bull—2 owners

left shoulder   right haunch

right cheek

base of right neck   buttocks

Mauritanian

8-year-old bull—2 owners

left haunch   right neck

12-year-old bull—4 owners

right haunch   right neck

right buttock
under tail   left neck

5-year-old bull—2 owners

right neck   right foreleg

provisions from the market to our loading place (he turned out to be ould Mohammed's son).

When Sid' Ahmed formally handed over my two camels to ould Mohammed, this new man seemed exceedingly wooden to me. It was not just that he was meekly accepting orders from my established factotum. This, I knew, was well in the established custom of things. Over the past few months I had realised that in this part of the world, perhaps throughout Islam, it was virtually impossible for two men to have a relationship based upon equality. There must always be hierarchy and, at a first encounter, there would always be a form of combat to decide which of the two would assume the position of superior, which would fall into the role of subordinate. The stronger character having emerged from what was usually no more than a verbal tussle, with a great deal of peremptory gesture, the two would settle to a perfectly amicable relationship, sharing everything they had and performing most tasks together. But they seemed incapable of starting off without knowing who was top dog and who was underdog. Always they seemed to be searching for someone to whom they, on the receiving end of orders, could issue their own orders if they felt like it. I was convinced that this philosophy partly explained Mohamed ould Moctar ould Hmeida's need to have a travelling companion from among his own people and why, when Sidi Mahmoud had been recruited for this position, young Erbah had then been enlisted so that Sidi Mahmoud should not feel he was lowest in a chain of command that theoretically began with me.

Sid' Ahmed, who since reaching Tombouctou had taken to greeting me by coming to attention and offering a kind of military salute, was thus merely fulfilling an expected role by ordering ould Mohammed about and briskly explaining our baggage. He was the senior native around, and this must be demonstrated. Yet even allowing for the new man's complaisance, there was something about ould Mohammed's attitude that made me wonder just how effective he might be in the desert. He claimed to have been acting as a guide

180

to some American petroliers in recent months. But as he stood by the two camels, with Sid' Ahmed bustling round, showing where certain things fitted into place, he looked more than anything like the raw rookie to whom the sergeant's revelations are bewilderingly foreign. It seemed to me, even then, that I would probably have to handle him firmly from the start; I only hoped that I would not also have to check up on every commonplace thing he did.

In the courtyard outside my hotel room, provisions slowly mounted beside the heap of my equipment. For a journey that should in theory take us no more than three weeks before we were in a position to replenish our stores, we amassed 15 kilos of dates, 10 kilos of rice, 1½ kilos of tea, 8 packets of lump sugar, 3 kilos of potatoes, 3 kilos of onions, 2 pieces of rock salt, 1 kilo of peanuts, 5 tins of Nescafé, 4 tins of evaporated milk and 4 cartons of cigarettes. I was thus much better provisioned than before, with greater variety, appreciating fully by now the need to feed well, unwilling to risk more dangerous hardship by confining myself to a diet of rice, dates and meat. I was also allowing for the undoubted fact that a proportion of our stores would find its way into stomachs other than our own.

After six days in Tombouctou I felt well enough to go on. Indeed, I must go on without more delay if I was to have an outside chance of reaching the Nile by the beginning of June. I was still walking slowly, and walking little at all if I could avoid it, but it seemed to me that I could manage again even though, when my mind dwelt on immediate prospects rather than ultimate goals, I had very little relish for committing myself once more to the wilderness beyond these comforting walls. I spent a restless last night in my room, my nerves jangling me awake every hour or two. At Nouakchott, at Chinguetti, at Tidjikja, at Tichit and at Néma, the restlessness had been spiced with eagerness to be away and getting on towards journey's end, but this time the feeling was absent. My thoughts twirled, instead, round my anxieties concerning ould Mohammed, round the possibility of conflict with Mali soldiers, round the state of my health.

I took comfort this time by dwelling exclusively on my own world, which was so alien to this one, switching on the light in order to reread letters from home, pondering the public changes that had occurred since last I heard news in mid-November. I had learned that the war in Vietnam was finished at last, that Harry Truman and LBJ were dead, that Ezra Pound had gone, too. Of England there was no news at all that anyone else in Tombouctou was aware of, and my letters made it plain that the nation was still lumbering, as I had left it, through strikes and wage freezes and general discontent, still accursed by the internecine warfare of the Irish. How very insignificant the British Isles were, to all but a Briton, when seen at this range.

It was January 26 when ould Mohammed and I led the two camels through the back lanes of Tombouctou towards open country again. An hour or two before, I had said farewell to Sid' Ahmed, feeling sad to see the last of such a good companion and decent man. We had already exchanged final salutes the day before, but I had met him on the street again, as he was leading the new camel he would be taking home with my old one. I examined the beast with him, feeling its hump, looking at its teeth, tugging its tail, and we agreed that it was a fine animal, a bargain at the price, which was approximately equal to the money I had handed over to supplement the exchange of my camel for his. He had neatly rogued me on the deal, and we both knew it. As I admired the proceeds of his superior commercial acumen, the sly old twinkle came into his eye, and he asked me if I'd now like to buy the camel from him. I reached out and pulled his nose gently, telling him he was an old cutthroat, at which we burst out laughing in each other's faces. Then we said at last "*Marra selehm*" and walked off in opposite directions. He made me feel warm, and I wished he were still riding with me.

9

WE LEFT THE TOWN by its northeastern edge, where great
caravans of camels are still mustered twice each winter for
the long journey to the interior of the Sahara to bring salt to
Black Africa from the mines of Taoudenni. Towards the
end of January, however, there were only a few beasts hobbled and couched on the outskirts, waiting to take part in
more local traffic along the southern rim of the desert.
Mud buildings had here given way to a scattering of humpy
tents, with wide spaces between each group, and the municipal boundary of Tombouctou was signalled by a great iron
water tank raised on stilts. By its side was the collapsed
skeleton of a wind-driven pump, blown over in some storm
and never repaired. Ould Mohammed's young son was with
us, and the two camels were much overloaded with goods.
Besides the baggage and provisions for our journey up to
Algeria, they were carrying bulk foodstuffs to be deposited,
with the boy, at the family's tent. Ould Mohammed had told
me that this was "only an hour" outside the town.

He was an artful deceiver. After three hours' march
through the blistering afternoon, he declared that his camp

must have been removed, though we continued to walk on the same bearing, ould Mohammed showing not the slightest uncertainty concerning the whereabouts of his family. It was almost noon the next day before we reached his tent, and I in a filthy temper. Ould Mohammed had vowed that, after unloading the foodstuffs and taking a meal, we would continue our journey without delay. By the time we arrived I was being nagged on a variety of pretexts to linger until the following day.

I could never reconcile myself to the deviousness of these people, which even Sid' Ahmed shared to a degree. Why was it, I continually asked myself, that a man in ould Mohammed's position could not straightforwardly say, "Look, I haven't seen my family for a fortnight; do you mind if we stay a day with them before going on?" It would have been impossible to resist such a plea. As it was, their slithering methods only made me cantankerous and sometimes unreasonable, doubtless leaving them with the grudge of being ill used.

On this occasion, however, I gave in without much argument. The long walk in the heat had tired me. I was, moreover, beginning to feel a little ill again. My sores had almost healed under the anointment of tetracycline. My desert clothes were clean again, though at the tent I found that they were not immaculately deloused, for I spotted two prime adults on the move and correctly assumed that eggs must still be somewhere in my garments and would soon hatch to infest me as badly as before. Worse than this, though, was the ominous churning within that said my intestinal sickness was on the way back. As long as I took drugs, all was tolerably well; the moment I came to the end of the prescribed dosage, my bowels opened up and food dropped from one end of my body almost as soon as it had been shovelled into the other. This was a pattern that would now stay with me until the end of the journey.

As I lounged away the afternoon in the shade of a thorn tree, I had much on my mind. I was worried by ould Mohammed's evident incompetence in the role I desired of him. He seemed much more sophisticated than anyone I had travelled with before. Many people had cadged my cigarettes since I had left Nouakchott, but they used them awkwardly, being generally accustomed to taking their tobacco tamped into the end of short brass pipes. Ould Mohammed, on the other hand, had bought himself in Tombouctou several packets of Gauloises, which he smoked with a flourish that would have seemed effeminately affected at home. At our first night's camp, he had brought from his tassoufra a spoon and eaten his rice with that. I had seen no man do this before (though I was to learn later that it was common among the Tuareg), and I assumed he had picked up the habit in imitation of his old French superiors in the army, or possibly of the American petroliers. We had been joined at that camp by another man and, when I made coffee in my tin mug, I offered them both some in a bowl they could share by drinking turn and turn about, according to the custom of the desert. But ould Mohammed had waited till I finished drinking, whereupon he crawled crabwise over to the tin mug, poured his share of the coffee into it and drank European-fashion, apart from the other man.

He fancied himself, I think, as a cut above the generality of his people. Yet it was already clear that he was abysmally deficient as a camel handler by anybody's standards, even including my own. He had stood around uttering words of command while I and his small son together loaded the beasts, until I had curtly ordered him to join in and haul on this rope or that. We had been obliged to stop every hour or so to readjust the loads, and on each occasion it was because ould Mohammed had failed to secure something properly. I had come to the conclusion that it must have been years since he had travelled with camels, possibly not since his days with the French Army nearly a couple of decades before, though there seemed little point in pressing him about this, for I doubted whether he would answer truthfully. Even Mohamed ould Moctar ould Hmeida would have been an improvement as a travelling companion in this respect; he at least was efficient in his work when he chose to be.

My other worries concerned what lay ahead. At the previous night's camp, ould Mohammed had asked me whether I carried a gun and grunted with disapproval when he found that I didn't. In the months of my preparation for the desert, I had at first wondered whether perhaps I ought to, particularly after Wilfred Thesiger's gloomy prognostications about the tendencies of the Tuareg. But I had not fired a rifle since my days in the school cadet corps, and I had no taste at all for arming myself in any circumstances I could think of, taking the view that an armed man is much more likely to provoke hostility than not and that, even where this might not be so, I would stand no chance at all if it came to a gunfight with men well accustomed to shooting. Ould Mohammed seemed to think that this was a grievous error. There had been many killings in Mali of late, he said, because people were going hungry as a result of the drought. In the past few months, he knew of half a dozen instances where men travelling with much food in their baggage had been set upon and murdered.

Maybe this was a genuine warning, or maybe it was a ploy similar to the one Mohamed had mounted so elaborately during our flight in the night after Tidjikja. If it were genuine, there was nothing I could do about it but hope for the best. I was much more concerned with falling foul of the republic's security forces than with being attacked by starving brigands. For our prolonged march to ould Mohammed's tent had taken us almost exactly along the bearing I had originally chosen for my route across the desert to the Algerian border. I had already put myself in peril of imprisonment by being where I was, and I had an uncomfortable feeling that if either military or police discovered me here they would not deal gently with me. Yet to get to the dirt road which I had been ordered to take would now mean turning at right angles to my course and travelling at least a day in the process, losing two and a half days of real advance. Nor did I wish to travel along that road, or up the trans-Saharan highway that followed it, like a country tinker; this would be entirely against the spirit and purpose of my journey, besides adding days to it that I could ill afford to spend if I were to get to the Nile in time.

I scrutinised the charts again, as I lay there pondering the future, and concluded that it was possible to cross the desert and strike the trans-Saharan highway just below the border oasis of Tessalit. If I rode this course, along a bearing slightly north of my original choice, I would avoid the two sternly proscribed oases of Kidal and Tin Zouatan, which it would obviously be folly to visit, and I could trot up the highway to Tessalit for a couple of days as though I had been following the police commissioner's orders from the start. It seemed to me that with care—and not too much openhandedness to nomads we might meet—our provisions might just see us through the extra distance to a place where we could replenish them.

That night, I awoke to the most marvellous display of stars I could remember. Everything that hangs in the heavens must have been there, with throbbing clarity, Orion hemmed in as never before by hundreds of small fry, the Great Bear well up in the sky. In the middle of Mauritania, this constellation had never started to poke over the northern horizon much before 2 A.M., but here it was fully visible by midnight. I was as excited as a child at the display, wished A were there to share it with me, and in my elation made the decision that had been shaping up for hours. I was going to continue across the desert and risk being found by a military patrol.

We had, in fact, crossed some wheel tracks on the way to ould Mohammed's tent and he had given me severe palpitations by saying that they were made by army vehicles travelling to a military camp in the desert. After questioning him closely, I had been satisfied that this was, as he asserted, "*bareed, bareed*—far away." Judging by his outflung arm, it was somewhere to the northwest, at almost 45 degrees to the course I wanted to take. After telling ould Mohammed most emphatically that we must avoid any area where we might hear of soldiers operating, it seemed to me that the danger from that direction would be slight.

We made an early start from his tent, with ould Mohammed in excellent spirits, as he should have been—he had extracted another 1000 francs from me in order to buy a sheep for our journey from a family living nearby, a sheep which never materialised. Half a mile down the track he had demanded a big *cadeau* as bonus if we reached Tessalit within fifteen days, to which I, seeing no reason why I shouldn't play this old ruffian at his own game, said airily that he would get some sort of present if we managed such excellent time. This so pleased the fellow that as soon as we were riding he broke into song. He was quite the best singer I had yet heard, skirling a very wild, warlike chant with great nasal verve, plunging through interminable verses that challenged any enemies we might jointly have to come and do their worst, but warning them to take care, for we, we of the righteous, had Allah most compassionately on our side. It must have been a bit like this, I thought, in spirit if not quite in tonic scale, when Cromwell's cavalry chanted metrical Psalms on their way to Naseby and Marston Moor.

Having exhausted the verses, and presumably finding the day's heat a trial to his throat, ould Mohammed lapsed into silence for a while. Then he turned to me and shouted, "Tessalit isn't far now; Tombouctou is very far. Always say that to yourself when you put a bit of distance behind you."

For all his jauntiness, he was still at odds with the camels. He complained that the Mauritanian rahhla was an impossible thing, that no one would ride such a saddle after Tessalit, and I would do well to get rid of it there. The young brown bull, Sid' Ahmed's old beast, had almost thrown him when he was mounting, at which he thrashed it with his stick and told me it was a bad one. It was also, he said, very ill, for he had seen it pissing blood;

something I most certainly hadn't noticed myself. The white, too, was sick in the region of its nose and eyes; something else I couldn't see. I thought it moved much better than my earlier mount, though occasionally it tripped a little, and ould Mohammed said its toenails were too long, as indeed they probably were. The nails of every camel I had seen so far were worn almost to stumps flush with the pads, whereas these were like claws. But, having become wary of such observations about saddles and camels, I took it that ould Mohammed was carefully trying to undermine my confidence in both, with an eye to his own profit later on.

He was quite hopelessly inept when it came to loading the animals. The case containing the broken sextant was left hanging like a bell against the brown bull's side, where it would have created a sore patch before long, with its bumping and bouncing. After I had told ould Mohammed to secure it firmly, I found that he had lashed it tightly against the animal's hide, where its hard edges would have rubbed open a wound in no time.

If I had entertained any doubts about my initial impressions of him, they were dispelled on that first day out of his tent. A young man caught up with us and we rode until nightfall together. At some stage in the afternoon, when ould Mohammed was trailing some hundred yards or so behind, the lad drew my attention to the fact that he had fallen asleep in the saddle, his head lolling tipsily on his chest, and added, for good measure, that the old fellow was pretty ill and had no brains, either. That night I awoke to watch ould Mohammed surreptitiously raiding the tassoufra for a handful of dates, very stealthily tying up the mouth of the bag when he was done, and glancing over his shoulder to see if I still slept. He was the only man I had known to break the great unwritten rule of desert travel, that companions share everything and do not steal from the common store.

Next day, we encountered the midden smell of putrefying flesh which had been sickeningly in the air for the

189

first time when Sid' Ahmed and I crossed the dusty plain after Faguibine. Only once in Mauritania, at the well of Chig, had I seen an animal that was newly dead. Many other times I had passed carcasses which years of exposure to the mummifying heat of the desert had withered into grotesque shapes of bone and leather. But from Faguibine onwards, the most recent effects of the long drought had been apparent—first a sheep with green guts coiled along its flank, later a donkey with its teeth drawn in a dying bray of abandoned hope. Here, a cow and three goats were scattered across a few hundred square yards, puffed up with gases and stinking so horribly that ould Mohammed lit a Gauloise as he rode and I wound my headcloth tightly round my nose.

As at Chig, it seemed especially unfair that these animals should perish where there was vegetation, though I knew well enough by now that not all of it was edible. There were succulent-looking cactus bushes out in the bleakest parts of the desert that tne camels would not touch, though they would tackle the thorniest of tamarisk trees, ingesting the long spikes and spitting them out at leisure sometime later. Nor would they have anything to do with the plant bearing wild gourds, though I was told that goats would eat this bitter and purgative fruit. All these things had been growing along our route from Tombouctou though by the afternoon of the third day out from ould Mohammed's tent the distance between the trees had opened up to half a mile or so, the ground plants very thinly trailing upon the sand. Happily, from my point of view, this meant that I would soon have done once and for all with the wretched cram-cram that had plagued me severely from the start of my ride with Sid' Ahmed some four weeks before. I was sick and tired of the incessant scratching upon my legs as I walked, weary with the labour of picking the burrs off my serwal each time I prepared to mount.

And then, as we trotted down a low dune which seemed to mark the northern limit of plenty for the camels,

I saw the wheel tracks again, running along the level ground at right angles to our course. Instinctively, I cut my beast into a gallop to get over the tracks and out of sight across the dune opposite. As soon as I had put them well behind me, I paused and waited for ould Mohammed to catch up. Again I asked him about the military camp in the desert, and again he gave me the reply that it was far away, nowhere near where we were heading. A little later, ambling over the undulating sands, I heard a growing hum and jerked my head round. A Land-Rover, about a mile away, was driving to the northwest along the tracks we had just crossed. I had scarcely got over the shock of it, thanking my lucky stars for a narrow escape, when I topped another dune and there, almost beneath me, no more than half a mile away, was the military camp itself.

My heart thumped once, like the beat of a big drum, as I took it all in on the instant—the long range of mud buildings, the Land-Rover, now speeding towards the gateway in the middle across hard, flat sand, the sentry boxes set one on either side of the gate, the handful of soldiers moving inside and outside the fortified square, the neat arrangement of tents pegged out around the perimeter. Then savagely I swivelled my camel below the concealing edge of the dune and beat it into a gallop to get us away from this place as fast as possible. For three days I had been warning ould Mohammed against this danger, and the imbecile had, either from ignorance or incompetence, allowed us to ride almost up to the front door. I roared at him to follow me, and when he had drawn alongside I blazed at him with anger that was fuelled by fear. When he could get a word in edgeways, he said, "But we did avoid it; it's a long way away," gasping out the words with the effort of trying to hold on to his bucketing seat. At which I viciously belted his camel on the rump with my stick to make it go even faster.

For an hour I kept us at this gallop, my heart thumping erratically with the fear of what might happen if we had been spotted and were pursued. I could visualize all sorts of undesirable consequences if the military found me here, against the express orders of the security forces, equipped as I was not only with a compass and navigational manuals that could be mistaken for code books by any illiterate, but with charts issued by the United States Department of Defense. They ranged from an unpleasant journey back to Tombouctou under escort and on to Marxist Bamako, where I would be put on a plane for England, to the positively awful prospect of several months in a Mali prison. We had to get away from this area rapidly, which meant much hard riding not only now but for the next couple of days. I did not allow us to dwindle to a walk until the camp was well out of sight, but in the meantime we had bypassed a couple of nomadic tents at a distance, and I saw a further danger in the possibility of someone mentioning to the military that a Nasrani had been seen riding past, in which case, even with a twenty-four-hour handicap, troops sent out to search by Land-Rover wouldn't have much trouble in picking up our tracks and overtaking us.

The moment we slackened our beasts to a less punishing pace, ould Mohammed dismounted and squatted to piss. I had already noted that he was uncommonly incontinent, pausing every hour or so to relieve himself. This time, when I turned to see if he were about to catch me up, I saw that he was examining himself with delicate care. On a sudden thought, as he came up to me, I asked him whether he was pissing blood. He looked a bit shifty, but admitted that he was. I guessed then that I should hear no more of the brown camel's imaginary ailment. At the same time, I could much more do without ould Mohammed being sick. Not being able to rely on the certainty of my own fitness and good health any more, I was perturbed by the possibility that the two of us might break down together. This would be disastrous. For the moment, I decided, I would dose him with tetracycline, hope that it would do more good than harm, then wait and see how he fared over the next few days.

We spent that night near a couple of tents pitched among a group of thorns. It was almost the last thing I wanted in the circumstances, but it was my own fault that we had to stop near other people. I had not yet accustomed myself to the idea that I was in charge of this expedition, that everything about it was my responsibility, that every single decision, however trivial the matter, must be taken by me. I had not yet shed the assumption with which I had started my journey—that any man travelling with me patently knew much more than I about the ways of the desert and everything relating to it. I had thus left the filling of our guerbas to ould Mohammed in Tombouctou, had paid no attention to the amount of our water that he had left at his tent and now faced the price of my negligence: we had run out of water and must beg some from the people of the two tents. We had had so little to drink all day that we were both drying up with thirst.

Two youths and a woman gave us half a guerba, enough to see us through to the next watering place, and joined us for tea when we had made camp and hobbled the camels. After the customary opening exchanges, their conversation with ould Mohammed became heated, warming up to such a pace that I could not follow it clearly, though the words "government," "soldiers" and "prison" were tossed about from mouth to mouth like hot pancakes. I wasn't at all sure what position ould Mohammed had taken up in what was obviously a discussion of the day's events. But then the idiot described me to the three as an Arab; and only someone of his outstanding foolishness, it seemed to me, could possibly expect anybody to believe that of someone who looked, behaved and spoke Arabic as I did.

After a while, the talk softened into quieter generalisations, and the three departed to their tents with casual farewells. I slept badly that night, waking every hour or so, while the Great Bear and Cassiopeia pinwheeled slowly round Polaris, and Orion glided gently from south to west, rotating as it went. I gazed at the stars for long periods between bouts of sleep, but what I was really doing, I realised after a while, was keeping an ear cocked for sounds, then peering into the lighter shadows between the trees. In the morning, before we moved off, I very carefully burnt the remains of a cigarette packet and half a dozen stubs in the embers of our fire.

At midday we reached the well of Irtek, where some Tuareg were drawing water, stripped to the waist in the shimmering heat. It was the first time I had seen such men unencumbered by their insulating robes, which normally left only the eyes and the nose bridge visible. Now I could see the peculiarity of their hair style, their foreheads shaven at the top and the sides so that the free growth began in a tuft at the crown. They were a friendly gang and helped to refill our guerbas—from what was the deepest well I had seen. Two donkeys were trotted one hundred yards from the concrete head before the buckets surfaced, the haulage rope running over a pulley mounted on makeshift gantries, forked timbers that were deeply grooved with friction and looked as though they were models for the crutches in a Dali painting. So deep was the well that, when the buckets hit the water at the bottom with a splash, the echo was translated into a sound resembling the hollow *boom-clang* of a dungeon door being slammed.

We made our midday camp with the Tuareg and, resting afterwards, I noticed the first signs of exhaustion setting into my body again. It was nothing more than a listlessness, an inclination to linger for another ten minutes rather than to be up and away, but it suggested that the stoking up I had enjoyed at Tombouctou was beginning to play itself out. Idly, I constructed an equation of camel-riding, which held that after ten weeks of travel, six days of good food and rest would sustain a man in decent condition for four and a half subsequent days of travel, after which a decline began. The listlessness was partially explained, perhaps, as a reaction from the excitement of the previous twenty-four hours. We had by now, I reckoned,

194

put something like twenty miles between us and the military camp, and unless an alarm was raised as a result of rumour, it seemed unlikely that the soldiers would happen upon us here.

My tension of the previous evening had dissipated enough that afternoon, at any rate, for my mind to wander haphazardly away from the immediate preoccupations of the journey, except for the perpetual need to make compass checks. In such circumstances, apart from recurring thoughts of A and everyone else at home, I was likely to be visited by notions of the utmost inconsequence. I had one day been riding slowly across the Mauritanian desert when, without warning, I decided that on my return home I must investigate the British Museum Reading Room catalogue for the titles of two books I had relished far back in my childhood: the first concerned the adventures of one Trooper Ouless of the British South Africa Police, the second the public-school days of Jack, Sid, and Stan, good chaps all of Altonbury—and it must have been the first time in thirty years that either book had entered my mind.

On this afternoon, however, I found my imagination playing more pleasurably with the memory of music that I loved. In the manner of a radio programme that the BBC had been running for as long as I could remember, what ten records, I asked myself, would I choose if I were cast away on a desert island? Could I afford the luxury of something from both *Boris Godunov* and *Fidelio*? If I picked the quadruple harpsichord concerto of Bach, would there also be room for his concerto for violin, oboe and strings? I wouldn't want to be without Simon and Garfunkel, but if I also chose a piece for the bouzouki by Theodorakis, could I then plunge on through bagpipe music and Maori chant, for both of which I have longstanding weaknesses? Could I accommodate Dvorak's cello concerto and Allegri's *Miserere* (with the boy hitting that crystal note high above top C)? Not to mention Vollenweider (or Walcha) on the organ, the choral movement from Beethoven's Ninth, the Taizé monks chanting *psaumes chorales*, and so much more besides.

I would also want to take the Vaughan Williams *Wasps* overture, though it is scarcely a favourite of mine, something I never listen to except by accident. But for some reason which escapes me, it is forever associated in my mind with Chaucer's Canterbury Pilgrims and their progress across medieval England; these are the images that form whenever I hear a particular passage in *The Wasps*. And that romantic, bucolic, completely lopsided concept of my homeland was something that stirred me deeply at my roots, however much I might try to be level-headed and unsentimental about my nationality and its historical heritage.

My instinct in packing Wavell's anthology of verse for this journey had not failed me. I had not dipped into it very often, for I was usually too tired to read, or else I needed all the available daylight to write my notes by. But when I did, I invariably found myself turning for comfort to the poems of place, the poems expressing British nationality and glory. Anything of Kipling's, which at home I generally disdained, I fairly wallowed in now. Bits of Macaulay, coded with words like "sheriff," "market cross" and "yeomen," were tonics in this savage wilderness. So was an epic called "The Red Thread of Honour," a regular Gunga Din of a poem by Sir Francis Hastings Doyle that outdid even Kipling in its heightened view of British fighting qualities. Nothing at all moved me more than an unsuspected thing by Dorothy Sayers, "The English War," which read like all the most militant Churchill speeches rolled into one rhythmic form, but which, safe in London, I might have found more emetic than inspiring.

Well dosed with music, I enjoyed that evening, which seemed one of the most beautiful I had known in the desert. As I lay inert, while the water boiled for tea, the sun slid down between my outstretched legs out of a paling sky, its edges trembling for a moment, as though liquid, before it disappeared. The camels, browsing among a bit of scrub, were outlined against its glow, darkening into mere shapes as they rapidly lost all hint of substance. We had set up camp beside the only tree for miles, and a cricket was singing somewhere deep within its thorny branches. Apart from that noise and the sputtering of the flames, the world was soundless, without even a wisp of wind; it seethed with silence. Apart from the slow, ponderous shuffle of the hobbled beasts, it was entirely still. In this stillness, I could see, lay the fruitfulness of the desert that mystics had found across many ages. It calmed the soul and made it possible to fix the attention at any point one chose without distraction. I wished, that evening, I could remain in that spot, motionless, until I had so absorbed the desert's balm that something unknown to me dawned upon my understanding. Lying there at peace, one felt so close to a brink of revelation that it seemed almost within willpower. But not quite. Not on this journey. One could never rest long enough to receive the vision of the small thing that might lighten the darkness. Always there must be movement, the hasty passage from oasis to oasis, from water hole to water hole, the anxious transit from one sanctuary to another. To delay overmuch was to die out here.

Next day, I spotted a movement ahead of us, a tiny disturbance against the dazzling white glare of the sand, that was translated into a spreading pattern almost at once. Half a dozen gazelles were leaping off to avoid our coming, flying as fast as the desert hares we sprang from time to time, bounding and galloping in springing arcs, their white rumps flicking with the motions of fear. Ever since Mafud's camp below Nouakchott I had heard of these creatures, and several times in Mauritania Mohamed had pointed out their tracks, but not until now had I sighted the animals.

Within the hour, ould Mohammed reined in his camel

197

and pointed excitedly to some marks in the sand with the long pole which he had brought to pull high branches to earth and which he carried in the saddle as though it were a lance. I turned back to look at tracks which were new to me, each one a triangle of blobs about six inches apart. Ould Mohammed assured me they belonged to ostrich, but we never saw anything of the birds themselves. That afternoon we passed a small area of thornbushes and around each was a palpitating cloud of white butterflies, such an astonishing display of fragile beauty that for the next mile or so, I kept turning my head to mark and linger over the place where they had been.

For the rest of the day my curiosity fed on ecological balances. What on earth was it about those bushes that attracted the first butterflies I could recall seeing on this journey? And why was it that I had seen no sign of lizards for the past few days, though—apart from the squadrons of flies that were perpetually attached to camels and riders alike—lizards had been my only constant companions from the outset? The sudden appearance of the gazelles and the first trace of ostrich were more easily explained by the lack of human beings to hunt them. For the desert had become more barren than anything I had experienced except in sporadic patches, just after Chinguetti, and on the ride from Tichit to Néma. There was nothing now but rolling sand, with occasional clumps of dried grass and, two or three times a day, the sight of a tree.

January turned into February and, in spite of the intermittent sickness and the lousy sores that had broken out again on my body, I was buoyant that day. The start of another month helped, for it signified a real inroad into the New Year. There was also something foolishly uplifting about my course and my position. We were bearing 20 degrees, almost exactly north-northeast, which meant that for the first time on the journey I was literally on course for home. February 1, indeed, saw me approximately on the meridian of Oxford. "I like that thought,"

I wrote in my notebook at night. "Go North, young man, and you should strike Carfax—next Pancake Tuesday but one."

The danger from the military was now past, and I would have been well content had it not been for my anxieties about ould Mohammed's health. He was now trying to piss about every half hour, and when he failed to do so—as often as he succeeded—he complained of sharp pains. He didn't think the tetracycline was doing him any good and asked me for "white tablets," which he was sure would make him better.

Next day, he took an alarming turn for the worse. We had reached the well of Chlea, and after drawing water and making a midday camp, I was resting until the worst of the day's heat had passed. I became aware of ould Mohammed sloshing water in quantity behind me and turned to see that he was pouring a basinful over his head. At once he got up and moved away with his usual short, almost mincing steps, his shoulders bobbing up and sideways, his boubou wrapped tightly round his body above the spindly legs. It was a nearly crouching movement that always put me in mind of an elderly spinster coming late to the communion rail from the back of the church, after the rest of the communicants have been served and the priest is ready to consume the last of the bread and wine himself. He had gone to squat again, some distance away, and something made me get up to look at the ground where he had been. There, in the sand, was what looked like a scarlet cowpat, about a handspan across. For a moment it didn't register properly: but it was blood, all right, and a considerable effusion at that. When ould Mohammed returned, he said that it had suddenly poured from his head, though he seemed uncertain whether it had come out of his mouth or his nose. He didn't make a fuss about it. Quietly he gathered our things together, while I went off to catch the camels.

As we began to ride again, I started to work out the new equation confronting me. My companion was obviously a pretty sick man, one way and another, and I wasn't at all sure what I ought to do about it. We were now almost at the point of no return between Tombouctou and Tessalit. In another forty-eight hours or so, it would take us about ten days to obtain help from any direction in an emergency. I was in no mood to turn back to Tombouctou, for if I did so, I could most certainly say goodbye to all chance of reaching the Nile. Even if the authorities didn't detain me, it would be almost the end of February before I could hope to get back to my present position, and by then I must be over the border and into Algeria. Callously, I concluded almost at once that the problem was simply one of deciding what to do if ould Mohammed's condition deteriorated to a point at which he was unable to continue. In that case, I must leave him with food, water, most of the baggage and one camel; I would take the other beast, with one guerba and enough food to keep me going for a week or so. I would then ride like hell due east, where eventually I should strike the trans-Saharan highway and presumably find vehicles that would bring the necessary aid back to ould Mohammed.

I was not so much afraid of the outcome as preoccupied with it. I could feel myself bracing inside, tense enough to watch ould Mohammed consciously for some sign of impending collapse. If I had felt the slightest affection for him, it would have been like watching a small son climbing a big tree for the first time, helplessly willing him through the risk to safety again, with nerve endings pricking the while. We were riding gently, about seventy-five yards apart, when he dismounted again. I assumed he was going to squat but, no, a bag behind his saddle was slipping sideways and the whole load needed adjusting. His method of dealing with it was extremely simple. He emptied a guerba full of water, which was hanging on the overweighted side, straight into the sand.

I watched, fascinated, half excited by the sheer lunacy of this operation. I wasn't even capable of cursing him for it when he had done. Yet I knew that water was now becoming more precious than ever before. The days had suddenly become much hotter, a month or more earlier than I had been led to expect. Gone were the freezing winds that numbed all extremities of the body and pierced our thin garments until midmorning. It was still bitterly cold at night, but it was now warm before eight o'clock, and gaspingly hot by nine. By ten-thirty I was past the customary stages of thirst; the back of my throat was beginning to thicken, my tongue was almost completely dry, and I could sink half the contents of my water bottle, about one pint, almost in a single gulp. The increase in temperatures I could only measure crudely by the amount of water I was consuming each day. Before, I had scarcely ever needed six pints, apart from the tea and coffee I drank when camping. Now I was taking eight pints, and still could not shake off the thirst.

I had come to the conclusion that, whatever the reason for ould Mohammed's sudden haemorrhage, his recurring ailment was the result of venereal disease. He had started to complain of passing white matter as well as blood and conceded that he was suffering from "woman sickness." And whether it was because we had now entered more difficult country, or because he was himself worried about his illness, he was now praying more frequently and fervently than when we had started off. I knew that he was pious enough to have made the journey to Mecca once on a charter flight from Tombouctou, though this was not the highest form of devotion I had heard of; in Nouakchott, Ahmed ould Die had told me that some Mauritanians were so zealous that they actually walked across Africa, to take a boat over the Red Sea to their holy city, the pilgrimage lasting several years and sometimes ending in death. At nighttime now, I could hear ould Mohammed muttering one prayer after another in the darkness, repeating his name over and over after that of Allah himself. He had a prayer ritual that I had not seen in anyone else: pointing the first two fingers of his right hand in a cabalistic sign towards the four corners of the earth, while spitting rapidly in the direction of his chest, his armpits and his shoulders.

Navigation was becoming more of a strain, the landscape being almost without features. It was easy enough to keep a compass bearing when there was a tree, or a prominent outcrop of rock somewhere on the horizon; after checking the instrument, one simply held the object in the corner of the eye as a reference point, to be relinquished when another appeared ahead. But without these aids, with nothing to look at but the same anonymous, sweeping slopes of sand, endlessly, for hour after hour, it needed all my concentration, and very frequent compass checks, to hold a course without swinging 2 or 3 degrees to right or left, as the camels tended to do if left to their own devices. In the absence of natural features, the trick was to hold the shadows of men and beasts in the same quarter for long periods, but I didn't trust my own judgement of this enough yet, preferring to stop every twenty minutes or so to check my course by the instrument. We were aiming for the well of Abelbod, and I needed to bring us pretty close to it by dead reckoning if we were to have a chance of locating it in the shimmering glare.

Like Mohamed ould Moctar ould Hmeida before him, ould Mohammed had a fine contempt for European methods of route-finding. He had sneered at me loudly when I had confessed a small error the day before we reached Chlea, a matter of forgetting to allow for magnetic variation. Now, as I studied the chart, he saw that I was worried about my sense of direction and began to deride the compass anew. I should put the thing away, he said, for he, ould Mohammed, would take me to the well of Abelbod without any of the delays I incurred by stopping to look where I was going; and with a fine repertoire of gestures he mimicked the way I squinted through the compass prism when taking a bearing.

As far as I was aware, he had never been this way before, though I thought it possible that he had at one time been more skilled in finding his way across the desert than any of the other men I had travelled with. He had impressed me one night by giving names to a dozen or so stars I pointed out, some of which were recognisably local variations of the names I knew myself. Contrary to my expectations, neither Mohamed nor Sid' Ahmed had shown the slightest knowledge of the heavens. Mohamed, indeed, had said that stars were useless for finding your way by "because they change places during the night." It seemed to me that most of these nomadic people, far from being the instinctively skilled navigators that Europeans supposed, were utterly lost unless they had already traversed the ground and committed it to an extremely retentive memory, or could ask the way of someone whose locality they were crossing.

But it was in childish petulance rather than from any conviction of his ability that I told ould Mohammed to go ahead and lead us to Abelbod. At once he began to ride much farther to the west than I had done. Late in the afternoon he asked me to look at the compass, and I found that we were a full 40 degrees off the course I had taken. This was so preposterously wide of any conceivable mark that, as we crouched round a miserable fire of dung that night, I told ould Mohammed that from now on we would stick to the compass. To my surprise, he merely nodded.

Next day we rode hard along a course that I hoped would rectify the error we had obviously made, our pace quickened by anxiety, though neither of us said anything to the other about being lost. But the truth was that I had only the vaguest notion where we were, and I could feel myself tightening up with worry. We had ridden until the sun was only just above the horizon when, quite suddenly, I went limp with exhaustion, as though someone had just removed a plug which allowed all life to drain out of my body. For an hour we went on, with me rocking and rolling without much control in the saddle, until just before darkness fell like a slow theatrical curtain. That night we drank tea, but took no other liquid, eating dry dates and nothing else. My water bottle was half full and we had perhaps half a gallon in one guerba; maybe six pints in all. If we didn't find Abelbod within twenty-four hours we should be in a mess. It was pointless to bewail the lack of a working sextant, with which I could have fixed our position, or to berate my companion for his criminal act in throwing away fifteen pints or more of water in order to balance his load. My mind was fairly blank to everything but the immediate reality of our situation.

Ould Mohammed prayed vigorously next morning, as soon as dawn blurred the eastern horizon. It clearly did much for his morale, for he set off confidently almost due east, asserting that we would reach the well within the hour. In spite of my resolution of the previous day, I weakly allowed him to lead again, pacifying my will with the thought that on this course we should at least run towards a range of rocky outcrops that were marked on the chart and might give me a chance of recognising our position. After riding for a couple of hours, I checked our bearing with the compass, whereupon this bewilderingly changeable man asked me if we were going the right way. I suggested we turn to the northeast, and we did. An hour later, a thin dark line appeared distantly to the north. It was no more than a reef, stepped up twenty or thirty feet above the sand, but ould Mohammed hailed it joyfully.

"Ah, the mountains," he shouted. "Abelbod is up there."

There was no sign of the well when we reached the rocks, or of any tracks which were generally to be found within a mile or two of every watering place. But some distance away were three trees, spaced half a mile apart, the first we had seen for a couple of days, and here we made our midday camp. Sheltering beneath the branches of one, I noticed that the camels had sat down in the shade of the other two. They, poor beasts, had nothing to eat in this arid place, for even withered grass had now vanished from the land, and the trees were bare of leaves. Ould Mohammed and I spoke little to each other, sipping our tea carefully, treasuring each glassful for much more than the energy it contained, masticating the dry dates with difficulty. Somewhere below the surface lurked my fear, but above it was the curious assumption that all would eventually be well. I was, I supposed, trusting in Providence this day, merely doing the best I could to give Providence a leg up, as it were, by trying to act intelligently—by rationing the water and by willing away any tendency to panic.

We moved on, silently, at a gentle trot. My head was aching dully and my eyes were pricking with the strain of staring at this lifeless void, but as the afternoon dragged past, I could feel my chin beginning to settle with fatigue upon my chest. And then—there was no mistaking it—dark shapes were on the horizon and they were not rocks. They were bushes, and bushes in leaf. Suddenly, a white flash in the middle of a clump, and it was not the rump of a spring-heeled gazelle. As we drew closer I could see that it was a kid. We were safe again, for where there were goats, there were people, and where there were people there was water. Another movement behind another bush, and we rode up to a woman and two children, sitting in the sand beside a humpy tent. Abelbod, said the woman, was just up there, not far away now.

Within the hour, as the sun was setting again, we were at the well. Two men already there from the tent helped us to draw water, and we camped among some trees a little distance away. We ate well and drank deeply that night. I scraped ten days of beard from my face and felt much restored. In the firelight, I watched ould Mohammed perform the most elaborate ritual of prayers I had seen. He went through the customary pattern and then, standing, he took two paces forward and two paces back before turning a full circle and repeating the sequence thrice. Oddly, he never once faced Mecca, except during a turn. Each obeisance he made was towards the west. Next morning, I asked him why this had been.

He grinned and said, "My head was spinning by then."

It was his only admission that all had not been well that day.

10

WE MADE OUR MIDDAY CAMP below a long reef of rocks which were at times obscured by a haze of scudding grit. All morning the wind had been rising, driving clouds of dust into the sky so that, by noon, the sun glowed indistinctly in a leaden atmosphere. It was much like a misty day at home, except that it was most oppressively hot. With my headcloth wrapped round my face, I was all but suffocated, but the alternative was to have sand driven forcibly through my nose and mouth, coating my throat so that my desire for water became unendurable.

We were cooking our rice when there was a movement nearby. Two women had appeared from the undergrowth by which we sat, though we had seen no sign of life as we rode up. They had taken up position lying propped on their elbows, halfway round a large thornbush, and they would not come any nearer. My presence evidently deterred them, for when I looked in their direction they turned their heads away and drew up the hoods of their black dresses to obstruct my view. But ould Mohammed crawled over to them and talked intently with them for some time. Then he gave them some tea and sugar, and they disappeared as mysteriously as they had come.

He looked severe when he returned to my side. "They say the country behind here, towards Anechag, is bad," he said. "There've been some killings lately."

Anechag was the next well, and we needed to use it, for there was only one other before the trans-Saharan highway, about a week away. The women had asked ould Mohammed whether he carried a gun, and the wily old fox had told them that of course he did; it was stowed away inside his tassoufra. He winked at me as he retailed this small but important deception. He was no surer than I whether the women had given a friendly warning or whether they had been sent to assess potential victims. I began to wish rather badly that I was out of Mali and over the border into Algeria, which represented some form of security, a place where law and order would be maintained with justice. Ever since leaving Mauritania, and particularly since my brush with the police in Tombouctou, I had been uneasily aware that in Mali I was contending with rather more than the hostile desert. Ould Mohammed, too, treated this encounter with the women seriously. We did not, this day, linger to rest after we had eaten. As soon as the rice was consumed, we packed up and made off again.

We climbed the reef and began to cross a table of black gravel, bare of everything but stone. After an hour or so the wind died, and by the middle of the afternoon the unhindered sun was blazing down on us once more, the visibility gradually returning to normal. As we descended into a wide and sandy wadi crammed with scrub, I could see that on the other side a long range of rocks ran from east to west. They were no more than five hundred feet or so in height, but they were distinctly mountainous in outline, the first outstanding natural feature I had met since leaving the great Mauritanian escarpment near Néma a month before. As we moved into the scrub, there was a flash of blue to our right, and for one nervous moment my senses pricked at the prospect of danger. But then a small man wandered into full view and greeted us amiably. He was looking after a flock of sheep and, after a few moments' conversation with ould Mohammed, was persuaded to part with a lamb. The 1000 francs which my companion had taken from me at his tent for this purpose did not, I notice, change hands. The fellow virtually gave us the animal, taking only a little tobacco in return.

It was butchered on the spot. While the man held it on the ground, ould Mohammed, with one hand holding the animal's mouth tightly shut, thrust my sheath knife high into the upper part of its neck and sliced down to the throat. The blood spouted onto the sand in a thick jet, while the limbs thrashed wildly for a moment and a rasping cough of air came out of the almost severed neck. There was not a sound after this, though the legs continued to twitch with nervous spasms and then to kick with dying agony for several minutes.

When the lamb was still at last, its head lying at a broken angle to its stiff-legged body, a deep puddle of blood coagulating in the sand round the wound and a cloud of flies already descending to the feast, the two men began to skin it. This was a meticulous art, for the hide of any animal was a prized object and not to be spoiled in butchery. The knife slit the skin down the inside of the hind legs for a start, and then the entire pelt was eased off the carcass, ould Mohammed and the man punching with their fists to turn it inside out and separate it from the body. As the carcass was revealed, it looked almost like that of a plucked chicken, and as the inside of the skin was exposed, it shone a dull and milky blue, like the sheen on a newly landed mackerel.

I watched all this, the removal of the stomach and guts, with only the faintest stirring of emotion, for I was much changed by the desert. The Englishman in me dimly acknowledged something called cruelty to animals, but the savage much more aggressively relished the prospect of meat for the first time in ten days or more. I was as greedy for it now as any man I had met since coming to the Sahara. I was hungry, and I would have butchered the lamb myself if it had been necessary.

We rode on like a pair of buccaneers, with the gutted corpse lashed to ould Mohammed's saddle as our booty. Any fearful undercurrents that had been running since we met the women had now gone. We had slaughtered, we were triumphant, we were men of the desert. We looked down upon almost all living creatures—literally, for we sat a good six feet off the ground when riding. A man could powerfully imagine himself a lord of creation when mounted on a camel. I slept uneasily that night, but it was more from anxiety that someone would ride up and share our precious lamb than from fear of being attacked. The barely cooked meat, which would have turned my stomach not so long ago, I had torn at like an animal the moment we took it from the fire. It was good, good, good, and I cared not that the fat from the tendons ran down my hands and smeared my face as I stripped the leg bones with my teeth.

We had struggled up and across the range of rock, walking our camels down the steep sides of the wadi that ran into it from the north. We had then turned to the east, with the rolling sand dunes of the Tanezrouft to our left and at our backs, and made our camp among a thicket of trees close under the line of cliffs. Next day we rode steadily along what was virtually a wide valley, with the cliffs forming one side and the gigantic rolling mound of sand, scarcely less steep, forming the other. In the middle of the morning, there appeared over the brow of the sand sea a herd of camels, twenty beasts in all, which were being driven to drink at Anechag. Such was the scale of this landscape that, for almost an hour, they were no more than dots crawling diagonally down the slope of sand to the valley floor. Then, streaming in an untidy line ahead stretching over a mile or more, they followed us sedately to the well. It was noon when we arrived, and men were already busy hauling water from the deep shaft for another mob of beasts.

As never before, I was aware of suspicion at Anechag. It could have been autosuggestion on my part, but ould Mohammed clearly felt it, too, for he was unusually silent as we waited our turn to draw water. Nor did the half-dozen men gathered there seem eager to make conversation. They stared wordlessly at me and at our baggage. They may have been wondering mostly at the nature of our saddlery, which was of a design strange to them, but my imagination said they were more interested in what the tassoufra contained, in the significantly rich decoration of the tassoufra itself, whose newness was only just beginning to wear off—a gaudy object when compared with their own aged possessions. After we had filled two of our guerbas, ould Mohammed motioned me towards our camels, and together we hitched the guerbas into place and mounted. We were both in a hurry to leave. We should have enough water to see us to the well of Asler, which was only three or four days ahead.

We set off at a brisk trot and headed down the valley towards a distant clump of trees, the only vegetation in sight. As we began riding, two men at the well hastily mounted their camels and came fast in pursuit. When they had pulled their beasts into step alongside ours, I saw that one of the men was almost completely blind. His right eye was white with trachoma, his left becoming milky, too, and there was something exceedingly sinister in his way of scrutinising me: he held his hands to the eyes as though they were binoculars, presumably to shut out dazzling and painful light so that he could bring me into some kind of focus. But as he did this only when looking at me, it made me feel as though I were being singled out for some particularly keen and malevolent examination.

It was a forlorn hope that the men would swerve off in some direction other than ours; they were clearly intent on sticking to us. They themselves were heading for a tent pitched under the cliffs some way beyond the trees we could see, and they questioned us persistently about our purpose in these parts. As always in such situations, I left most of the talking to my companion, and ould Mohammed was glibly reciting some cock-and-bull story about a mission for the Government, which was the nearest thing to a joke I'd heard for a long time.

Inevitably, the men unloaded their camels with ours when we camped among the trees late in the afternoon. We had given them a haunch of the lamb to take to their camp, but it was clear that they also intended to share whatever we might cook for ourselves. No sooner had we started the fire than three figures rose from behind a bush and walked over to squat beside us. One of them announced without introduction that we were in the presence of a famous marabout, who desired some tea and sugar. I had encountered this graceless form of begging once before, in Mauritania, resented its arrogant assumptions strongly and handed over the goods very grudgingly indeed. I had already noticed that morning that we had only enough sugar left for another couple of days at the most, with something like five days before we could hope to obtain more. But I was uneasily in no position to deny anything to anyone in these parts; the stories I had heard since Tombouctou of men killing for food were too vividly on my mind. I was feeling very vulnerable, and when the marabout—who had not spoken a word—and his two companions left us, I wondered whether we had seen the last of them.

They had not long been gone when two more men appeared. We shared our meal that night with four people, and each of them demanded tea and sugar to take away. The meal itself was a tense affair. Beneath the superficial talk of pasture for animals and our object in riding across this country (a fiction which had now become remarkably embellished by ould Mohammed), it seemed that the visitors were essentially watching, weighing up, quietly waiting . . . for what?

The blind man's companion, in particular, seemed full of menace. He was, I think, the strongest man I had encountered on my journey, and this was not a matter of physique, though he was very tall and powerfully built. I was well used to people staring at me, but I had generally found that if I was so disturbed by it that I fixed my eyes on theirs in return, they became uneasy at my gaze and swiftly looked elsewhere. This man was different. His very black aquiline face expressed absolute resolution, and his eyes hardly left me from the moment we made camp. Whenever I looked at him, he was gazing at me steadily, without one flicker of an eyelid. He seemed intent on penetrating my soul, and there was no care in this intent; those eyes were empty of all emotion. Perhaps they had become intensified by acting as surrogates for the blind man, but to me they felt like instruments of inquisition.

The blind man himself still disconcerted me, though after a while a memory of my childhood stirred and I realised that it was a distant association which so unnerved me, rather than the present. I had been brought up more accustomed than most children to blindness, for my grandmother, who had lost her eyes before I was born, dominated my life with a purely matriarchal sense that seemed more than compensation for what she called her affliction. But once, just after I had read *Treasure Island* and that haunting passage where Pugh comes tapping along the frosty road with the black spot, I had been scared out of my wits by blindness. Standing outside the house one foggy morning, I heard a sound breaking the stillness of the side street nearby. *Tap-tap-tap* along the ground; there was no mistaking its meaning, and the hairs of my neck felt as if they had become quills. And then, out of the mist, came the ghost of Pugh—a man in a gabardine coat, prodding the pavement's edge with his white stick.

For one horror-stricken moment I watched him coming carefully towards me. Grandma never used a stick and she had no eyes at all, but this man's eyeballs were still in their sockets, opaque and glaring at the sky. It was this, and the sightless, uptilted angle of the head, that finished me off. In a panic, I fled and buried myself in the recesses of the house, where, pottering about the steamy kitchen, that sightless old woman herself represented nothing but comfort and security to me.

It was the ghost of both Pugh and this blind man that now threatened me in the person of the nomad for whom trachoma had almost run its wretched course. But even when I had laid these ghosts, the darkness still seemed full of danger. The blind man's companion suddenly flung more wood onto the fire, making it blaze with light. Then he stole away and disappeared. Reason told me that he had probably gone to relieve himself. Something else told me that this could be the preamble to attack. I peered into the darkness; with that great glare by our side, it was—I had known it would be the moment the wood was flung onto the embers—very difficult to see anything around us. Then the two latecomers rose and left, taking the blind man with them.

I had lately been sleeping naked in my bag, which meant that I was less troubled by lice. But this night I kept my clothes on. I also stuck my knife into the sand by my side, where I could grab it in emergency. As I lay down, there was a small rustling by the tassoufra, and a tiny brown head popped up, twinkling at me for a moment before disappearing again among the baggage. The little rodent was the first jerboa I had seen in the desert. Two or three hours must have passed before I slept, and ould Mohammed didn't even seem inclined to lie down. He sat swathed in his blanket by the fire, nodding off occasionally. I listened tensely for any sound above the spit and crackle of the burning wood and wondered why the camels seemed to be unusually restless in the scrub towards the cliffs. Then I awoke with a jerk and saw that the knife was missing . . . but almost at once realised that ould Mohammed had placed it by his side; he still dozed near the glowing embers of charcoal. Next morning a corpse lay in the sand beyond my feet. Ould Mohammed had killed the jerboa, a creature inoffensive as a mouse, when he saw it coming out of the tassoufra in the middle of the night. But there had been no other visitors.

We got away soon after dawn, eating a few nuts with our tea to avoid delay. Within the hour we approached a hillock cluttered with rock. Ould Mohammed handed the camel ropes to me, removed his sandals and set off towards it at the run. The marabout lived up there, he said, and ould Mohammed was going to pray with him. I must continue marching with the beasts and he would catch up with me in a little while. As I trudged past this hallowed place, I could see that a lean-to shed had been constructed against a rocky buttress and that many possessions were strewn in the sand of the hillock, including a couple of saddles. Holy this marabout may have been, but he was obviously no more of an ascetic than any other inhabitant of the desert. When ould Mohammed rejoined me, he had a thread of red cotton tied round the first finger of his right hand. I asked him whether he had given the marabout money. No, he replied, he had not, for that wouldn't be right, but he had presented the marabout's son with 1,000 francs. The techniques of holy poverty, I reflected, seemed to be much the same in every religion I had known.

We mounted and rode almost due east, holding closer to the towering side of the sand sea than to the cliffs, for there the going was easier for my white bull, who still had a tendency to trip on stony ground. Basically, he just didn't pick up his feet enough to avoid projections; his normal gait was the shuffle of an old man making for the bathroom in his bedroom slippers sometime after midnight. He could get away with this on sand, but on rougher going he was in difficulties.

214

All day we plodded steadily on this course, while a hot wind coming straight off the Tanezrouft scorched us and slung grit into our muffled faces. It drove across the wide valley until it was spent against the cliffs, which sent the heat back at us in great dehydrating waves. Yet the cliffs were a comfort, for I knew where I was with them, with an exactness that I had missed since Mauritania. I could follow each turn and each opening in them on the chart, picking out the occasional conical peaks from what was mostly a long and table-topped range of rock. Riding that day was much like running down a coastline after a long time in the open sea. If it had not been for the terrible heat, it would have been an enjoyable passage, for danger seemed past once more; we saw no one after the marabout's camp. But by midafternoon I was again conscious of energy suddenly drained from my body, and rode slumped in the saddle until we made our evening camp.

Thursday, February 8, began inauspiciously. We finished the sugar with our first round of tea. All our stores were at a low ebb, particularly the dates, our other chief source of energy. As I picked up my sleeping bag to fold it, a green scorpion scuttled away from where it had been resting, between the bag and the ground blanket. It was a salutary encounter. I had not seen a scorpion since that first week's march out of Chinguetti in November, and I had become careless, walking barefoot in the night to relieve myself and forgetting to shake out my canvas shoes—which I had worn since losing my sandals—before putting them on. That, I told myself now, mustn't happen again.

The cliffs dropped away to our right, slowly slipping over the southern horizon, while the bulk of the sand sea which we now entered had flattened into a white plain on which there was scarcely a blade of even withered grass. It was a world without a single reference point, frightening in its vast loneliness, but exhilarating, too, for it represented the essence of the challenge I had set myself to meet on this journey. Ould Mohammed said that the men who shared our food after Anechag had told him that the well of Asler would be reached this evening. Perhaps riders who galloped hard on camels unburdened with baggage might have made such good time, but I knew that at our pace we would be lucky if we got to the well before Saturday. We must keep our beasts at a decent trot and not linger too long over our midday camp.

We had only just started to ride when a strong head wind blew up, turning the blue sky muddy with incredible speed, a white spindrift of sand steaming along the surface of the plain towards us as the visibility was reduced at an alarming rate all round. Several times before, I had experienced these conditions, but only twice had they caught me in the open, and on each of these occasions the dust storms had died not very long after they had started. By eleven-thirty, this one had so intensified that, when we saw a solitary tree looming out of the haze to our right, we made for it and unloaded the camels. A fire was out of the question, so we drank water and ate a few dates, spitting out sand along with the stones. Then we wrapped ourselves tightly in our robes and lay under the lee of the baggage and saddles. The storm by then was raging so fiercely that I put snow goggles on before covering myself completely in clothing. Even so, I could feel particles of sand rasping my skin, penetrating the tightest folds of my garments. I was conscious, beneath the booming of a powerful wind and the lashing of grit, of an urgent desire to reach the oasis of Aguelhok as soon as possible—the nearest inhabited point on the trans-Saharan highway, a village some sixty miles or so south of Tessalit. The strategy for deceiving the authorities about my true passage from Tombouctou no longer mattered. Tessalit was no longer significant and Tamanrasset was laughably far away. My instinct was to reach safety, for here, in this raging sandstorm, I felt in danger and terribly lost.

At three o'clock, the storm had slackened enough for

us to crawl out of our improvised tents. All but our largest possessions were smothered in sand. The blankets on which we were lying had disappeared except where our bodies covered them. There were three or four inches of sand in the cooking pot. The saddles were half submerged. We stood in the middle of a thick fog, and I wondered how on earth we were going to make our way through it to the well of Asler.

Never before had I been forced to concentrate on a compass needle as I did when we started riding again. We had been bearing 84 degrees all day and must hold that course rigorously if we were not to land up in the most appalling mess. With the visibility never more than a quarter of a mile and sometimes down to two hundred and fifty yards, I found myself checking the instrument every ten minutes, reining in my camel for stillness each time I did so. My head began to ache with the effort of concentration.

Paradoxically, it was somewhat like driving fast down a motorway, where you occasionally thought, "One slip and I'm a goner," but where mostly you were so fixed upon the steering, the rear mirror, the dashboard dials, the other traffic and the beat of the engine that you were unable to think about the possible consequences of a skid, a burst tyre or a collision as well. Here, everything was obliterated from the mind but the need to keep the camel steady, until the moment came to stop him, wait until that swinging mark settled at the right number again, then clamp the whole of one's attention once more upon an imaginary point in the blankness just ahead. There was not even shadow by which one might gauge the consistency of direction, for the sun had vanished from the sky.

After a couple of hours, it reappeared as a pale disc, and visibility opened up to something like a mile as the wind died down. Then the worst possible thing happened. Ould Mohammed had been trailing behind me for some time, and I had paid him little attention. He now came riding alongside me and, as I turned to greet him, my eye caught something hanging from his saddle. It was one of the guerbas dangling nose down, the cord which bound the neck now gathered in a loose coil, the lashing which should have supported the whole skin in front undone and swinging uselessly. The guerba had been well over half full of water when we started riding again. There was now not a drop left.

I was so stunned that I could only point to it. Ould Mohammed looked down and made a gesture of astonishment. Then he recovered his poise, swept the emptiness ahead of us with an imperious wave of his arm and announced that the loss didn't matter because we would be at Asler by nightfall. I knew very well that there was not the slightest possibility of this. I also knew that we were now facing a critical day or more because of this incompetent man's negligence. Not only had he failed to secure the guerba properly but, having gone to sleep in the saddle, he had not even noticed when the front of the skin plunged down and emptied its load with what I knew, from my experience with Sid' Ahmed, would have been a mighty gusher.

By six o'clock, fatigue had hit me again like a crippling blow and, with darkness imminent, we stopped for the night. There was nothing but bare sand as far as the eye could see. The camels went without food and we did little better, munching a little raw potato and onion because they contained moisture. We had two pints of water left—virtually liquid mud, black and undrinkable. Its transformation to clarity by the light of my flashlight was the one relief in what had been a bad day. I had brought with me from England a small purifying device for use in such an emergency, a canister in which you could pass the most polluted water through a chemical filter and see it emerge clean. I now fished this from the bottom of a kit bag for the first time and pumped the mud through. It looked like tap water when it trickled down the plastic hose at the bottom, and it tasted as sweet as anything I had drunk in the desert.

218

But it was not going to last very long in the heat of the next day.

I had taken no more than three or four pints in the previous twenty-four hours and was beginning to dehydrate badly. It was this as much as the lack of sugar that had me so blindingly weary now that I could focus my mind only on immediate and necessary tasks. Without intending to, I dropped off to sleep still sitting up in my bag. Some time later I awoke, cut through with cold, and heard a movement a few yards away. Ould Mohammed was squatting by the tassoufra, munching the last of our dates. Resentfully, I tried to curse him for his stealthy greed, but the voice I heard sounded more like a reproachful whine.

We drank half our water neat before facing Friday and ate more raw potato and onion. It was a beautifully clear morning when we set off, but by nine-thirty the sandstorm had blown up again. Visibility dropped to a quarter of a mile, but we could not afford to stop, which would have been the most sensible thing to do if it had not been so vital to find water as soon as possible. We had to keep going through this lacerating void of khaki and white, in which we were beginning to veer from our course alarmingly. Between two checks, taken only twenty minutes apart, I found that we had swerved off the bearing by no fewer than 25 degrees, which by any reckoning and in any conditions was a disastrous amount of error. It would have been much more accurate to adopt the soldier's procedure for night marching, by having one man walk ahead up to the limit of visibility, before setting him on course again. But this would have been a laborious exercise, taking up much more time than we could now spend. We had to move fast to Asler or we might perish. The chart showed that it was set between two reefs and, if only the storm lifted, we would have something to look for.

Just before noon, a line of rock appeared from behind the sheets of driven sand ahead, no more than a low shelf with a few trees standing by it. Jubilantly we settled under a bush and contrived a fire by using the saddles as windbreaks. On this we made unsweetened tea with the last of our water and cooked a piece of meat. Eager as I was for the nourishment it offered, it tasted abominable; it had, after all, been rubbing shoulders with a camel for several days on one side, and on the other it had been crawling with flies in two sandstorms. But I tore into it greedily, mouthfuls of grit and all. As soon as we had eaten we mounted again and began to search the area of the rocks for the well. We found the limits of the reef and rode round them. Then we pushed on along our original course, for this was obviously not the place marked on the chart.

By four-thirty, the storm had died again, and slowly the sun reappeared, the visibility increased, and we could see for several miles around. There was not a rock or a tree in sight—nothing but empty sand again. We went on. The light was almost gone when, feeling myself about to roll out of the saddle, I called a halt. I almost fell over into the sand as I dismounted, and ould Mohammed climbed from his camel like an old man who is afraid of breaking his bones, very carefully and slowly easing himself down on anxious arms. We both moved like old men as we fumbled with the hobbling ropes and couched the beasts by our side. We would have no energy to spare for bringing them in to us in the morning, and there was nothing on which they might browse. The effort of unloading the baggage was enough to prostrate us mutely for a long time before we could muster the strength for more movement. I was conscious, above all, of my dry and throbbing throat, my thumping head, and the need to stave off a deep desire to sleep.

I had to face the fact that we were lost. The well of Asler was somewhere in the vicinity, but whether it was five miles to the north, ten miles to the south or somewhere behind us to the west, I had no idea at all. Nor did there seem much point in trying to find it now, from such a totally uncertain position. The only sensible course,

220

the only way in which we had some chance of saving our lives now, lay to the east. In that direction there was one certainty, and it was the trans-Saharan highway. I estimated that it could not be much more than thirty miles from where we were. It ran directly from north to south and we were bound to strike it by riding east. The question was whether we could get there before we both collapsed and died of thirst and dehydration. Thirty miles would normally be one and a half day's journey, but I had no idea whether, in our weakened condition, we could make such time now.

I recalled reading in some textbook that twenty-four hours without any water in these temperatures was the limit of human endurance. Half a day had already passed since we finished the last of our liquid, and we had drunk far less than the advised requirement during the previous thirty-six hours. We might well fail to reach the highway in time, but if we did get there we should presumably meet a vehicle before long, and that would be our salvation. I saw on the chart that, northeast of Asler and almost alongside the highway, there was another well. If we held a course of 75 degrees, instead of riding due east, we might just find it. This was no more than a rough bearing, but it seemed the most intelligent one to take in the circumstances.

I had brought several packets of emergency rations from England, blocks of highly concentrated glucose and other foods designed originally for Norwegian mountaineers. I decided that we must eat some of this stuff tonight, to gain as much energy as possible while we were still able to get food down. From the way my throat had already swollen, I guessed that it would soon be so blocked that nothing solid would get past my mouth. I broke open the packages, explained what they contained to ould Mohammed, and started to chew some blocks myself. This process was so painful that tears came to my eyes and, wiping them away on the back of my hand, I licked them up with a clumsy tongue.

Ould Mohammed had said almost nothing since we

made our camp for the night, except to murmur prayers, over and over again, where he sat. He had been praying intermittently in the saddle since the storm had died down and we had found ourselves in the middle of nowhere. He ate little of the rations, but sat quietly with a blanket round his shoulders, a look of absolute dejection on his face. There was something so unusually hangdog about his whole posture that it occurred to me he might be resigning himself to death. I crawled over to him after a while and took his limp hand in mine.

"We're not going to die, ould Mohammed," I said quietly. "We're going to find water tomorrow. We are."

He didn't even look up into my face, but continued to stare disconsolately at the night. "*Inshallah*," he replied, nodding very slowly. "*Inshallah*."

I was scarcely aware of my own fear, though this was the crisis that had most racked my imagination in the safety of my home. I was not detached from our situation; my body was too tormented by it already to allow that luxury. But I seemed to be drained of all emotion as well as energy: it was as though I were confronted by some taxing intellectual exercise and nothing more. I saw very clearly what must be done. We must start riding at first light and keep going with all speed until midday. We would then rest until sunset and ride again by the light of the new moon until it set about midnight. I would then take stock of our condition again before deciding on the next move.

Before settling down for the night I wrote in my notebook. "Something has risen above the physical awfulness and keeps the fear down to very brief, sharp spasms. I *do* believe we're going to get through. If this is the product of A's love and J's love and the prayers of all those nuns, and the best wishes of my friends and everyone else who's willing me to safety, then I'm profoundly grateful to them all—even though I don't quite understand how it all works. I *am* going to get through somehow, even though I know damn well that the margin is now very fine indeed. Odd to think that I could be dead by the time the weekend's over. But I'm not going to be." A little later, I remembered something I'd noticed on the chart, and added the afterthought. "Sometime today, we must have crossed the Greenwich meridian. Some crossing!"

Then I walked some distance away with my water bottle, to add a little more piss to the collection I had surreptitiously started after our midday camp. There wasn't much of it but it could, I supposed, yet save my life. After that I lay down. It was past eleven o'clock and I didn't wake again until after four. This was the longest unbroken sleep I'd had for ages.

In the hour or so before dawn I lay still, enjoying the warmth of my sleeping bag and trying not to swallow. Close by, I could hear the two camels rumbling, regurgitating and chewing the cud in those complex digestive processes of their own. Ould Mohammed was huddled by the side of his saddle, completely muffled by his blanket. Light seeped over the horizon in a grey-blue metallic band. Slowly this was surmounted by a blood-orange band, which in turn was topped by a very thick white band. Gradually, above all this, the blackness of the sky turned to blue, which flooded steadily towards the west, dousing the stars one by one. I shook ould Mohammed and then tried to eat some more rations, but the pain was so great that I gave up and spat them out.

We were on the move not long after six o'clock and I blessed what promised to be an overcast day, which would reduce the heat of the sun. It was hot enough and glaring by eight o'clock, but those branding rays were not to break through the high, thin cloud until just before noon. Urgently I flicked my camel's shoulder with my stick to keep him at a good trot. Everything else in me was so totally concentrated upon holding our course that I was anaesthetised from the pain in my throat, in my skull and in the lousy saddle-rubbed sores of my body. Occasionally I looked back, to see ould Mohammed riding farther and

223

farther behind, his spirit apparently almost gone. Then I turned to my front again, for nothing at all mattered but my need to reach that horizon, and the horizon that would lie beyond it, and the succour that eventually I might find to the east. For nearly five hours I continued thus, more a robot than a man, my eyes screwed upon that dip in the sandy ground ahead, then the one which followed it, after that another and another and another.

I had overrun the marks in the sand, unnoticing, before I realised what they were. It was an effort to bring my camel to a standstill and I did it irritably, as though someone had just interrupted my concentration. But when I had turned the bull and walked him back, there was no mistaking what my delayed reflex had registered. I had just crossed a broad set of tracks made by a number of camels. Groggily I dismounted to look at them more closely, though I can't imagine why, for tracks were the province of men reared in the desert, who had studied them from infancy.

It was true that I had become a nomad of sorts. I was a good camel rider by now, good enough to wind my headcloth on, all four metres of it, while riding at the gallop, without tripping up the camel or tying myself into knots. I could eat all the appalling food of the desert without turning a hair. I had even acquired some of the mannerisms of the desert: there is a way of tossing an empty tea glass back to the man who will refill it, with a supremely indolent flick of the wrist, to denote superiority, and I had this off to perfection when I wished to put ould Mohammed in his place. But the tracks of camels or any other beasts were still almost a closed book to me. I could recognise them, but that was all.

Yet these tracks, I could see, must be fairly recent. Their outlines were still sharp, and this could not have been so if they had been made before the sandstorm died down the previous day. The question was whether they had been made late on Friday afternoon, in which case whoever had ridden these beasts would by now be something like eight hours away and possibly travelling faster than we were, or whether the tracks were new this morning, in which case we might have some chance of catching up with them. If we had little hope of catching up, then we must continue on our present course, for the tracks came from the south and went slightly to the west of north. In that direction, I knew, the nearest well was at least four days away. Unless it was likely that we could overtake these riders, we would simply be going out into open desert again, and we would certainly die.

Slowly ould Mohammed shortened the distance between us, his shoulders hunched and his head nodding, showing no sign of recognising that I had stopped and dismounted. But when he saw the tracks, he was electrified. With a rusty shout he brought his camel to earth and almost went full length in his haste to dismount.

"Look, look," he shouted, pointing with outstretched arm. "Camel tracks. They passed one hour ago. Only one hour. We must follow them. Hurry, hurry!" He turned to snatch at his camel's headrope again, preparing to mount.

I stood still, wondering what to do. I had no faith left in my companion's judgement of anything; I had no trust in his competence at all. He had almost run me through the front door of the military camp after Tombouctou, his arrogance and ignorance had got us into difficulties on the way to the well of Abelbod, his crass stupidity in losing the water had put us now in peril of our lives. What were the chances that he had got something right this time? I was not impressed by his flamboyant display of urgency, for he had put on the same show when leading us off on the wrong tack before Abelbod. Perhaps it was no more than an acknowledgement of my own tracking ignorance, compared with which he must certainly be my superior, that made my mind up after a moment's hesitation.

I took a deep breath and nodded. OK—we would follow the tracks.

Ould Mohammed was off at a gallop before I was in the saddle again. As my beast came up on his feet I clouted him to get moving fast, but he, mistaking my intention, went down again, and I almost crashed to the ground. I brought him up once more and set him into a gallop, but felt myself about to topple from the saddle within a few lunging strides and hauled him down to a trot, shouting at the pair of us to steady on; if I fell and broke a limb now I really would be in a pickle. Ould Mohammed was several hundred yards away, thrashing his beast to a frantic pace, himself bouncing dangerously in the saddle like a pebble on a drum. In a few minutes, it seemed to me, he had been transformed from an old man on the edge of his grave to a young buck hell-bent on plunder. Before long he was a speck in the far distance. Then he disappeared beyond a great leisurely roll of the sand sea.

I had been trotting for a long time when something dark appeared against the white and blue of the skyline. My heart started thumping, something was bursting to free itself inside my chest, for this must be ould Mohammed, he must have stopped, he must have found them . . . but in a little while I saw that there was no movement in the dark shape. It was just an outcrop of rock. A little later, another shape came over the horizon and again there was a bursting within, but again it was rock.

An hour had now passed since we set off along the tracks. Things were becoming blurred. I was struggling to fix my attention, myself, on the object of this ride through a great confusion of the senses. I was alone. I had lost ould Mohammed. Where had he gone? Why had he left me? Which of these tracks were his and which belonged to somebody else; or were they all one? Which should I follow if they went in different directions? I asked myself these questions very slowly and deliberately, but I heard no answers.

It was now two hours since we had turned off our

course. It took me several minutes to work that out after looking at my watch.

I wondered why people were mocking me. They kept appearing in small crowds on the extremities of this world; once they popped up far to my right and I started to ride towards them. But as I drew near they changed into the shadow of a cloud racing across the blinding sand, so I turned back again. Other people became rocks as I came near to them. This wasn't fair of them. Why did they pretend so much?

The world was camel tracks and me. We would go on together till the end of time. There was nothing else.

Another dark speck on the skyline, but it didn't fool me. It was another move in the game. That was all.

But it was ould Mohammed. Unmistakably now; I could even pick out the blue of his robe. He had dismounted, and there was a group of people near him. No, there wasn't; it was another outcrop of rock. Then the outcrop broke in two; there was light between the two halves.

I started to gallop and began to babble, "Please let them be people, please let them be people." A quarter of a mile away now, and I could see men carrying something towards ould Mohammed's camel. The bursting sensation again in my chest, something fighting to get out. I could hear a small boy crying, "Thank you, God, Thank you, God," over and over again, and it was me, trying not to cry, my face twisting like a child's, wanting to be brave, not managing very well, giving myself horribly away.

Besides ould Mohammed, four men were there. As I rode up to them, my face under control again, they walked towards me, their hands raised in greeting. Cumbersomely my camel came down, and very awkwardly, like a puppet, I lowered my body from the saddle. When I put the weight on my feet, I reeled forward and nearly went full length. Then I recovered and saluted them. Suddenly, one of the men whirled on his heel and raced back a few yards to

227

pick something up. He returned and thrust into my hands our cooking pot, half full of water.

I shall never forget the look on his face as he held the vessel to mine. There was something puzzled about it, something wide-eyed and anxious and watchful. It was the look a father might have when he watches his own child being born; or the look anyone might have as he watches someone beloved quietly and readily slipping into death.

"*Shrabt, shrabt,*" he said, very gently. "Drink!" and held the cooking pot while I tilted it to my mouth.

There was all manner of filth floating on top of that water; morsels of rice from the dirty pot, strands of hair from the guerba, fragments of dung from the bottom of some well. But the water itself was clear, and I could sense the coolness of it even as its level tipped in the cooking pot before touching my lips. It was the most wonderful thing that had happened to me in my life; just seeing it tip, lapping the sides of the pot, knowing that it was all mine. I sucked at it greedily, and almost passed out with the pain, so that one of the other men quickly put his arm round my shoulders. I tried again, more carefully, and it oozed down my throat in a fiery trickle. I stood there a long time, drinking in this invalid fashion, until I felt myself swooning again and lay down on the ground.

We had been unbelievably lucky. These men were the rearguard of an encampment whose people had set out from the south two or three days before on a fairly desperate errand of their own, for their animals had eaten all the pasture in that area and they were hoping to find more to the north. The women, the children, most of the men and the goats had passed this way before the sandstorm, and their tracks were obliterated by the wind. The four had been delayed by the need to round up camels which had strayed over a wide area. They had reached the well of Asler at the start of Friday's storm and had sheltered there until it passed, setting off again the same afternoon. They had ridden over the ground where we first saw their tracks some four hours or so before we got there. If they had not been herding a dozen camels, and therefore proceeding more slowly than usual, we would never have caught them.

We made a fire of dung and brewed unsweetened tea, and they talked with ould Mohammed while I lay prostrate, in a daze. My companion's capacity for revival seemed far greater than mine. He was sitting up, gesturing grandly, recounting our adventures and holding his audience's attention as though the only hazards he had faced in his life were a distant and much enlarged memory. After a while the men left us, having transferred half a skinful of their own precious water to one of our guerbas. We would have to be careful with it, but it should see us through to safety.

The first thing ould Mohammed said to me when they had gone took the form of a question. "How many days is it?" he asked, "since we left my tent?"

I had no idea, and I was too weak to work it out, but I understood its significance very well. He was recovered enough to start thinking of the present I would give him if we reached Tessalit within fifteen days. This didn't, somehow, seem the right order of priorities in the circumstances.

"I think it's eleven days," he said, very calmly.

I got up and walked away from him, suddenly wanting to be alone. Then I burst into tears, with great heaving sobs that I could not stop, with "Thank you, God," again and again from the half-braised lips of the little boy that was me. How very, very fortunate I was and how very beautiful living was. What were all my people doing this Saturday afternoon in February? I stood with them there for quite a long time, until calm returned and I was just gazing at the shadows of cloud across sand that had bewildered me so much that morning.

The men had suggested that our best course was to make for the well of In Emsal, only a mile or two outside the oasis of Aguelhok on the highway. Still having no exact idea of our position, I had got one of them to point the direction to me, while I took a bearing along his outstretched arm. We therefore started riding at 55 degrees but, after an hour or so, ould Mohammed announced that we must go due north. I was prepared to concede his superiority as a tracker but nothing more, and I very roughly told him to shut up and keep moving. At once we flamed up into a raging argument. He mimicked my use of the compass again and told me it was responsible for losing our way. I got a couple of grudges off my chest about his negligence in general. We were both badly overstrung by what had happened to us and needed to work out our pent-up emotions on the other. Our shoutings died down and we plodded on in disagreeable silence.

I knew what I was looking for. The chart showed that running alongside the highway from north to south, there was a ridge of rocks. As soon as that appeared on the horizon, sanctuary would not be far away. The men had said we ought to reach In Emsal sometime the next morning, but I was wary of accepting the estimates of nomads without allowing a considerable margin for accuracy. Mentally, I adjusted myself to the prospect of not refilling our guerbas until late the next day.

The sun was beginning to set when we rode out of the sand sea and onto the gravel plain. At the far side of it there were many trees, and as soon as we reached them we camped for the night. It was an eerie place after the barren emptiness of the sand. It represented life, for many of the trees were in leaf, and we ought to have found people and animals among them. It was deserted; nothing at all stirred in it, as though all life had fled from the place under threat of some plague. But at least it meant that our camels would eat well for the first time in several days.

Ould Mohammed dumped the guerba containing water on the ground. I picked it up and hung it from a tree. He said that we would have a great meal of boiled rice and meat, but I told him to forget it; we couldn't afford the water for cooking and we must eat cold again this night. The fool had learned as little as any Bourbon, but I was determined not to take the slightest chance of facing another day without drink. At this ould Mohammed lost his temper again, accusing me of wasting water for shaving, of drinking more water than he did anyway. We had another bitter row, and it didn't exhaust itself until I tossed him a package of the emergency rations, which, I had already noticed, he seemed to relish as much as meat. I found difficulty in getting my own first mouthful down, so I ate a couple of raw potatoes instead.

As I settled down for the night, I knew that I wanted more than anything else now to go home, to get away from all this, especially to get away from this disagreeable, stupid, incompetent and dangerously sick man. It would be very easy to do this. I could pick up a truck going north along the highway, and I would be in Algiers a few days later, back in London within the week. But that would be too chicken for words, wouldn't it? I *must* get to Tamanrasset, even if I could manage nothing more. Maybe I would go on from there. Maybe I wouldn't. I was beyond thinking of it at the moment. As I lay back with my head on my arms, I realised that something was missing from the sky. For the first time in many weeks, the moon was totally obscured by cloud. It was just as well that we hadn't been trying a night ride to safety this evening.

We set off early on Sunday, ould Mohammed cocky again, myself cautious. I judged that we would probably reach the well or Aguelhok itself within four or five hours, but he was confident that we would be there in two. In little more than an hour we came upon tracks, so many of them that I could not imagine in which direction they were leading, for they crisscrossed each other, pointing towards almost every degree of the compass. There was no pattern to them, and the only obvious thing was that they were all very old. It had been some time since camels passed this way, and I was disinclined to follow any of their pad marks.

At almost the same moment, I saw the low range of

hills I had been seeking. We started arguing again, ould Mohammed wishing to turn north along some of the tracks. But I insisted that we reach the highway now, where there would be little problem in finding our way to Aguelhok. We arrived at the top of the rocky ridge, and there below us was a broad swathe of vehicle tracks. It didn't look like a highway to me, and it seemed probable that the main route ran parallel to it, on the other side of more trees which grew beyond. But certainly, we could not be far from our goal.

Carefully I explained to ould Mohammed what our position seemed to be, and he agreed that we would do well to follow the vehicle tracks to the north. We had been riding along them for no more than twenty minutes when he pointed ahead and shouted, "Look, I can see it."

I could see nothing at all but the tracks, the ridge to our left and the trees to our right. Then he pointed to the ridge, said he had seen a man up there, and started off in that direction. I followed him and, when he paused on the ridge, caught up. There was no one in sight. Suddenly, ould Mohammed hit his beast into a gallop and raced off down the hill, heading due west. The man was going back into the open desert. I raced after him and only halted him by barging my camel across the path of his. We had another raging argument there and then, with more mimicry about the compass from him and more recrimination from me.

It struck me that ould Mohammed had perhaps gone crazy. He was, after all, sick. He had eaten little for two or three days and he was badly dehydrated. He had also been riding all morning with his bald head exposed to a fierce sun, the howli hanging round his neck like a scarf. I handed him the last of our water and he drank it thirstily. While I was screwing the top back on the water bottle he raced off again, still heading for the desert. Again I caught up with him and this time I tried to reason with him gently, as though he were a child.

For a moment his mad resolution seemed to weaken and he said, in a quavering voice, "We must return to the road."

"Yes," I said, "we must. It makes most sense that way."

Then he flung out an arm again. "Look," he shouted, "there's the town—that thing sticking up there."

There was nothing at all to be seen but the trees through which we had ridden that morning. He was pointing roughly in the direction of Tombouctou. I told him there was nothing to be seen, and once more he raged at me.

I felt myself fumbling for some point of stability on which I could brace myself against the torrent of absolute exhaustion that threatened to engulf me. I didn't think I could stand much more of this. I knew I was very near the end of my tether. There was no anger or resentment left, only a drop of any spirit, and I needed that to get me through this new crisis before I was overwhelmed.

It was without any feeling at all that I told ould Mohammed, "You go that way if you want, but I'm going to the road."

He was silent for a moment. Then he told me to stay in the shadow of a tree for half an hour, no more. If he hadn't found the well of In Emsal by the time he returned, he would come back with me to the highway. Then he galloped off, towards the baffling network of camel tracks that we had left when heading for the ridge.

I sat leaning against the trunk of a thorn tree and watched his figure dwindle in the distance. He started by riding to the west, but then he swerved to the north. After that I lost him among the vegetation. My mind whirled with anxiety. What on earth was my responsibility to ould Mohammed? Somehow I ought to have prevented him from riding back suicidally into the desert, but I couldn't see how I could have stopped him physically.

I began to work out a plan, in case he didn't return. I would stay put until late afternoon, for another two and a half hours, by which time the day would be cooling off. I would then ride east until I struck the highway—surely sometime in the evening. There I would rest until first light and move north. I had an idea that in our various arguments we had bypassed Aguelhok, that it was somewhere just to the south. Going north, however, would be a better bet, because some twenty miles above the oasis there was a well called Abanhok; in that direction I would have certainly one and perhaps two chances of safety. If I went south, and I were wrong about the position of the oasis, I would have nothing more to hope for than a passing vehicle.

The time passed very slowly. My white bull was restless, refusing to couch for more than a few minutes, so that I had to get up at intervals and bring him back to my tree. I dared not let him browse freely, for I could not afford the energy that would be needed to retrieve him later from some distance. I was consciously holding down a lid on my fear, which was beginning to bubble up inside again. I was gazing glassy-eyed at the haze of rock and dead trees to the north, where ould Mohammed had gone.

Suddenly, I heard an old familiar sound which had been missing from my life for the past three months. Moving towards me from the south came the roaring whistle of a jet aircraft. I looked up as it passed overhead on its way north, but saw nothing that betrayed its position. It was more a comfort than a distress to visualise the supercivilised ease of the people sitting up there: the dainty trays of food that were probably being served at that moment, the cossetting attentions of the stewardesses, the miniature bottles of hand cream and after-shave lotion displayed in the airborne lavatory. But how very ironic, I thought, that a Boeing or a Caravelle should choose this moment to come my way for the first time, when I was weighing up my chances yet again of utterly basic survival.

It was three o'clock and ould Mohammed had been away for nearly two hours when I saw his figure galloping back. I'm afraid my first thought was to wonder whether he would be penitent. As he rode nearer, I saw that he had no baggage, but I was by then too fuddled to grasp the significance of an unburdened camel. He must have been less than a hundred yards away, and I still motionless against my tree trunk, when I realised that there was a guerba, a full guerba, bobbing behind him athwart the saddle. The bloody man had found the well.

He leapt down like a cavalier, gabbling triumphant phrases that I couldn't take in. I got myself up and staggered over to where he was untying the water skin. I put my arms round him and hugged him as a reflex more than a conscious act.

"Sorry, sorry," I said. "You were right and I was wrong."

He looked embarrassed and made a great fuss of urging me to drink. In the next few minutes, I gulped two whole water bottles full, about four pints, and the pain of drinking didn't matter any more. After that we made a fire and brewed some tea, while he told me about In Emsal. It was not far, he said, and some Tuareg were camped there. He had dumped the baggage, watered himself and his camel, filled the guerba and come racing back.

We rode very slowly the way he had come, into trees that became fuller and thicker with leaves than any I had seen for a long time. A couple of men rose to greet us as we arrived in the clearing where the wellhead was. Here was life again. Some goats were foraging among the trees, standing on their hind legs with their forelegs high up the trunks while they snatched and nibbled at the lowest leaves. Birds were skimming through the air and strutting over the ground—a kind of guinea fowl and something like a large blackbird, with a dark green body and a ruddy underside. Water, probably enough water to last me to the end of my days, was being sloshed extravagantly from buckets into troughs for the camels. I emptied another canteenful down my throat. Then I collapsed in a heap.

11

THAT SUNDAY EVENING, I lay for a long time in the shelter of a large and bushy tree. I flowed in and out of sleep, not thinking very clearly about anything when I was awake, not even conscious of any vast relief that I was safe. Insofar as I was concentrated upon anything, it was upon the minutest things around me: the froth on a glass of sweetened tea, handed to me by a Tuareg, the brown crust of baked blood on the remnant of our six-day-old meat, the circular patterns made in the sand by grass which the wind had flattened and twirled round on the rooted axes. My only movements were to reach for my water bottle and pour the contents down. Each time, within half an hour, I was conscious of my raging thirst again, but it was not an emotional need I had to satisfy; it was the dehydrated tissues of my body, gradually shrunken since Anechag, that had to be slaked. In the twenty-four hours after my arrival at the well, I was to drink twenty-three pints of liquid. Not much of it emerged as urine.

Ould Mohammed's recuperation was much swifter

than mine. After resting for an hour or so, he suggested riding into Aguelhok to buy tea, sugar, dates and other badly needed provisions. He would, he said, be back before nightfall, and it would then be unnecessary for us to enter the oasis in the morning. We could bypass it on our way north and join the highway just short of Tessalit in a few days' time. It seemed a good idea, though the experience of the previous three days had driven from my mind all awareness of threat from the Mali authorities. I would have welcomed them as brothers on Friday afternoon—when ould Mohammed and I had missed the well of Asler and I had known we were lost—even if I had seen them advancing towards us in full battle order.

The sun disappeared and the night settled down. After a while I wondered vaguely whether my companion had run into trouble; I might have worried, had I not known that his notions of time were much more elastic than mine. I was half asleep when I started at the distant sound of an engine that was growing louder. Sitting up, I could see two beams of light fingering the sky, swinging this way and that, dipping and rising. A little later, headlights appeared far away among the trees, glaring full on for a moment, then swerving at an angle, then coming towards us again.

Slowly I rose to my feet, as the vehicle probed the area for our presence. The Tuareg who had given me tea walked over from where he had been eating a meal with his family beneath the next tree. He said something in Tamachek which I didn't understand, but which clearly expressed concern. I didn't reply. I knew what was coming by instinct and I could now feel my guts tightening with anticipation.

The vehicle stopped about fifty yards away, and I could hear voices talking loudly above the rumble of the engine. Then it turned towards where we stood and came to a halt much closer, its headlights still full on. They glared so powerfully into my face that I could see nothing of the men in the vehicle, whose outline suggested a proto-type of the Jeep. And then, from the perimeter of this blinding light, four soldiers emerged slowly out of darkness. Three of them wore the kepi, as popularised by Fidel Castro, above their battle dress; the fourth affected a grubby white headcloth in the style of the old Arab Legion. Each carried an automatic rifle and all four were pointing at me. Well apart, two on either side of the vehicle, the men approached very slowly, half crouching on bent knees, as though they were stalking a dangerous animal, or someone who might suddenly attack. They stopped about five yards away. I stood perfectly still, waiting for the next move.

Another man appeared, an officer in a plum-coloured beret, walking easily. As he stopped, outside the arc of potential fire, I greeted him and asked him what the trouble was. There was no trouble, he said, very shortly. Were all these things mine? he asked, indicating the baggage strewn round the tree. They were, I said.

He gave an order to the soldiers, and three of them stepped forward and started to gather my things together. I bent down to pick up my money belt, and the soldier with the headcloth, who had remained covering me, rushed forward and jabbed the muzzle of his gun into my side. I gasped with the pain of it and all but overbalanced. The officer asked me what was in the belt and, when I had told him, he picked it up and held onto it. Then he turned to the Tuareg, who had been standing bewildered, and roared at him to help the soldiers, giving the man a great shove in the back to start him moving. The officer was a Negro from the south, a fellow with three deep tribal scars cut on each cheek. I sensed a great deal of racial venom in his attitude to the nomad.

The four guerbas, bulging with water and hanging from the tree, were unslung and emptied onto the ground. I wanted to hit someone for that. They were pitched into the open Jeep, alongside my other possessions. Headcloth motioned me to get in, with a jerk of his rifle.

It was only then that I saw ould Mohammed sitting on the floor. I could not tell in the darkness whether he was frightened or composed. He was certainly subdued, and he said not a word as I climbed in.

The soldiers sat balancing on the sides of the Jeep as we drove off, and Headcloth kept his rifle firmly pointed at my chest. I reached for a cigarette in the large breast pocket of my boubou. Before my hand was halfway there, he had poked the gun into my ribs, with a warning shout to the officer. I think perhaps that if a superior had not been present it might have gone ill with me, for Headcloth obviously had an itchy finger and relished the opportunity to knock his prisoner about. I imagined that he was obtaining more than normal pleasure at the capture of a European.

For myself, I was tense more at the prospect of something awful happening accidentally than at anything else. After what I had recently been through, I felt that I was in no great peril at all. I had just escaped from the desert with my life, against rather heavy odds, and I was in no danger of death unless some trigger-happy idiot made a severe error of judgement.

Suddenly, we became a hunting party. A pair of gazelles sprang out of some bushes, across the beam of the headlights and, with a concerted whoop from the soldiery, the Jeep was after them. The officer, as excited as anyone, shouted an order to the soldier balancing beside me. He raised his gun just past the back of my neck. The Jeep stopped, one of the gazelles standing hypnotised by the light, twenty-five yards away. The gun cracked five times, deafeningly. The gazelle turned and ran for maybe a hundred yards, the Jeep careering after it. The animal sat down and started to lick its side. We stopped again and the marksman scrambled down, to crouch in front of the gazelle at little more than point-blank range. He fired twice more before he killed it. Unconfined joy from the military, who leapt down to drag the carcass to the vehicle and lash it to the back—all except Headcloth, who stayed put with commendable vigilance, his eyes scarcely leaving me, his gun still levelled at my chest. He seemed uninterested in ould Mohammed's presence.

We came out of the trees towards a settlement of mud buildings and headed for a gateway lit by a solitary arc lamp. A tall and rather elegant-looking Negro, neat in khaki drills and sweater, stood there waiting for us, an Alsatian dog at his side. This was the Commandant of Aguelhok. I was marched in close order behind him towards a door of corrugated iron. I wondered for a moment whether this was a cell, but it turned out to be the Commandant's office. I got a push in the back as I crossed the threshold, doubtless from Headcloth, but the Commandant was very correct. He indicated a seat opposite him, across his desk, and he switched on an angle lamp.

The officer who had captured me made his report and the Commandant asked me what I was doing in the desert. I told him, then suggested he should look at my passport and, most particularly, at the photostat of the letter from Paris to M. Bagayoko, which had already done me such good service in Tombouctou. It was extracted from my money belt and the Commandant read it carefully. The soldiers, all this time, had been gathered close around me, as though ready to pounce. But now the Commandant made a dismissive gesture, and their bodies relaxed with—was I imagining it?—a suggestion of disappointment. All but the officer in charge walked out to the yard, where, it seemed, ould Mohammed was standing unguarded.

The Commandant apologised to me for the trouble I had been caused. If I wished, his men would now convey me back to my camp by the well. Alternatively, I was at liberty to remain in Aguelhok for the night and continue to Tessalit in the morning. If there was anything else he could do for me, he was at my disposal. There was, I said, something he could do. He could write a letter to his colleague commanding the garrison at Tessalit, explaining the position, so that I might avoid a repetition of this misunderstanding. He did this at once, handed me the letter and ordered his men to take my baggage down to a house where my companion and I might lodge for the night.

Our things were dumped outside the store where ould Mohammed had first come to obtain provisions. Then the ancient Jeep drove back to the barracks. Only Headcloth stayed behind. A number of men had gathered and started to question ould Mohammed about the night's events, and Headcloth was quite clearly loitering in order to overhear the conversation. I strolled up to him, insulting him amiably in English (there was nothing like it for relieving bruised feelings), buttoning up a loose pocket flap on his battle dress as I did so, in order that he might look approximately like a soldier, finally telling this little bucket of pig swill that my pleasure in his company for the evening was now exhausted. I smiled at him fondly and he stalked off, uncomprehending.

It was he, ould Mohammed told me afterwards, who had hauled my companion into the barracks after seeing him spend much money in the store. When questioned by the military about the source of his wealth, the ass had again spun the story about my being an Arab who was awaiting him at the well of In Emsal. It was small wonder that the troops had been sent to bring in a suspicious-sounding prisoner.

For it was already clear, in the attitude of the soldiers to the Tuareg at In Emsal and to the locals in Aguelhok, that there was great hostility between the Government authorities, who represented Black Africa below the Sahara, and the people of the north, who belonged essentially to the desert. In Tombouctou, indeed, I had heard rumours of civil war up here—presumably the reason that the commissioner in Tombouctou had placed the oases of Kidal and Tin Zouatan out of bounds to me. The nomad populations of this area had suffered much as a result of the

241

drought and, having failed to receive assistance from an impoverished Government in Bamako, were said to have turned upon Negro masters who had once, not so very long ago, been their own slaves.

There was no doubt about the military attitude up here. Next morning I visited the canteen in the barracks, in the hope of obtaining some coffee. It was a bleak shed, with scarcely anything on its shelves but packets of matches, a stack of flashlight batteries, a half-empty bottle of Ricard and a bottle of Johnny Walker, almost full. The walls were covered with crude mural paintings of soldiers drilling and soldiers firing guns; mostly they were of troops firing from the cover of sand dunes. They were here, above all, to keep primitive nomads in order.

We did not leave Aguelhok until the afternoon. The Tuareg from In Emsal had been bullied into bringing my camel to the oasis at first light, and he, decent and be-wildered man, handed it over to me without complaint. But ould Mohammed kept disappearing to drink tea with different people. I sat for hours against the wall of the store, somewhere between a dazed lethargy and the old tension of wanting to be on my way before I lost the momentum of progress. A truck was being loaded ready to start the journey across the Tanezrouft into Algeria. Three young French students were waiting to go with it. They expected to be in Marseilles in four days, home in Paris within six. I much wanted to travel with them, but I knew that I wouldn't. I had to go back into the desert on a camel, or my journey would have been a waste of everything I had so far done.

I now knew precisely what the most fearful thing consisted of; I had measured it, I had touched it, I had almost been destroyed by it. I had to go out to meet it anew, at once, or I would never dare look upon it again. If I turned my back upon it now, I would be pursued by it to the end of my life, always running away from the subject of my fear. And this would not be fear of

242

death by thirst and dehydration, or fear of being lost in a wilderness of sand. It would be fear of encounter. Nothing more. Fear of encounter with a person, with a task, with anything at all intimidating that might cross my path. If I could go into the desert again to face another encounter with what I knew to be there, as exactly and clearly as if I had fashioned it myself, I could walk forwards for the rest of my life into all the deserts of my mind. And this, with love, would be the most precious gift in the world.

My determination faltered once or twice during the journey up to Tessalit. For three and a half days we plodded slowly up the highway, and almost all the time I was tugged between a will to continue and a yearning to be out of all this.

The road, a broad and deeply rutted track furrowed out of the desert and marked by old French kilometre stones whose paint was almost faded away, bore much less traffic than I had imagined. On no day did more than six vehicles pass us in any direction. Mostly they were heavy trucks, swaying dangerously beneath their overloaded cargo of goods, animals and human beings. Three times, private cars came slithering down the highway, their wheels spinning against the loose gravel and sand, a great plume of dust trailing for a hundred yards or more in their wake, their engines racing cruelly, as though the drivers were overanxious to get a move on to safety. They were all Europeans, mostly in couples, and though I waved to them cheerfully as they went past, I doubt if they associated my scrofulous appearance with a fellow Westerner. A brisk nod was all I got from anyone, and then it was eyes front again to face the hazards of the road. I wondered whether any of them would have stopped if, as might have happened a few days earlier, I had staggered onto the highway desperate for water.

There were more aircraft in the sky now than there were vehicles down below. Ever since Nouakchott I had

243

wondered at their absence, but clearly all the traffic from Central Africa to Europe crossed the Sahara along a pretty narrow corridor, and at last I was traversing it. Each day we heard up to a dozen flights passing high overhead, but not once did I see any trace of a plane. There were no vapour trails, presumably because the air even at thirty thousand feet was too dry to produce one.

Once, as we sat eating our midday meal, ould Mohammed looked up at the whistling noise above. "How is it," he asked, "that an aircraft can find its way when it doesn't have a guide?"

He was unconvinced when I told him that it relied, as we had done for most of the time, upon the much-derided compass.

More than ever he was disposed to bicker at the slightest difference of opinion—about which tree we should camp beside, about what we should eat, even about the estimated distance of the rocky hills which were appearing more frequently to the northeast. He was still incorrigibly negligent. When we came to move on after a midday camp, I found that a guerba which had been left hanging almost full in a tree was more than half empty because he had failed to secure the cord around the neck properly.

On the second day out of Aguelhok my white bull went lame, his left forepad cut by a stone. Ould Mohammed said that the beast could still carry me to Tessalit, where I could get rid of it, but the animal limped so badly under my weight that I decided to walk instead. He continued to ride the brown, berating me loftily for my slowness on foot.

I was in no great shape myself. At the first camp we made after the oasis, I was violently sick in the night, with abdominal pains. It was, I thought, the result of shoving too much food into a stomach that had become shrunken in the previous week, for I had gorged myself on all the good things we acquired at Aguelhok, dates and nuts as well as a haunch of the gazelle which ould

244

Mohammed had cadged from the soldiers. It was several days before my intestines recovered their old equilibrium, which was based upon a dosage of drugs that would have dismayed any general practitioner. The heat seemed to have reached new heights, and walking in it was a deadening affair. Where the skin was exposed to the direct rays of the sun, it felt as though a burning glass were being held over it, and I was drinking more copiously than ever before to damp down the smouldering furnace of my throat.

At least, for the present, there was no danger of going dry again. With a well of sweet water upon which we were able to draw between Aguelhok and Tessalit, our progress was soothed by the healthiest sound in the world, the *swish-slosh* of filled guerbas swinging on either side of the saddles.

Thus we came to the last outpost of Mali. The highway curved into a winding gully lined with succulent-looking palms. Just beyond was a spread of mud buildings, crouched in the shelter of tumbledown boulders, monumental in size and domineering in scale. The Commandant of Tessalit received me cautiously, but after he had read the letter from Aguelhok I was treated as though I were kinsman (or, at least, henchman) of the powerful M. Bagayoko himself. Ould Mohammed and I were provided with a room in the building used to shelter road travellers crossing the border, during their overnight stays for customs and security clearance, and the custodian of this place was told to attend to our slightest needs. Meanwhile, the Commandant said, he would have his men scour the oasis for two fresh camels that I might buy to replace those I had brought from Tombouctou.

Next day, two white bulls had been mustered for my approval, but I did not need the Commandant's advice that they were miserable beasts for anyone contemplating such a journey as mine. Their bones jutted sharply at the shoulders and the rump, one of them had broken teeth, neither had much hump, and both—heavily marked with the brands of several previous owners—looked worn by the effects of the drought. The Commandant apologised that there was nothing better to be found in the area and suggested that, tired as my own two camels were, it would be safest if I continued to Tamanrasset with them, together with these new and inadequate specimens. With four camels I should be able to spread loads thinly, giving each beast in turn a day of carrying nothing at all. There seemed no alternative to this plan, so I accepted it.

The arrangement provoked a final contretemps with ould Mohammed. Since Aguelhok he had been pressing me daily for the present I had half promised if we reached Tessalit within a certain time. Although we had overrun it by several days, it seemed to me that, after what we had been through together, it would have been churlish to refuse. I had decided to give him one of the camels in addition to his outstanding wages and had made the mistake of telling him so. Now I had to inform him that the camel would be continuing with me. Ould Mohammed had by then wheedled out of the custodian a saddle of his own; he was proposing to ride the camel home down the highway and along the road to Tombouctou which I had originally been instructed to follow.

He did not fly into a rage when I broke the unwelcome news to him. Much worse, he became a cringing beggar, a broken old man, who laid his hand upon my arm and told me pitifully that I had dealt him a grievous blow. I hardly thought so, for he had just collected 70,000 francs from me, which represented wages plus a 10,000-franc bonus in place of the camel. He had, moreover, tried to cheat me at Aguelhok over the amount he had spent in buying our stores. And at Tessalit, I had discovered that a great deal of food had been removed from the communal tassoufra and transferred to his own private bag.

But the thing that turned me against him most was the discovery of his own meanness. The custodian had given

246

ould Mohammed a good saddle, freely and generously. He had, what's more, been required to lackey for my companion on an epic scale, for on reaching the shelter ould Mohammed had done little but sit on his bed in a clean robe, smoking Gauloises, holding court to all and sundry and issuing orders to anyone who might accept them. The Commandant had told me that we were not obliged to pay the custodian, for his was a Government service provided for the benefit of all travellers, but that the man would doubtless welcome whatever gift we offered. Ould Mohammed, who by my reckoning had at least 75,000 Mali francs on his person (about £75), which made him a prince among men in these parts, gave the custodian precisely 100 francs—or tenpence.

He had served me well just before reaching In Emsal, but otherwise he had been an almost disastrous choice of travelling companion, the only bad turn that Sid' Ahmed had done me. For all my gratitude at his finding the well the previous Sunday, I disliked him very much and was profoundly relieved to see the last of him. When he asked me to write him a letter of recommendation to any other Nasrani who might seek his employment, I carefully issued a warning, to whomsoever the letter might concern, that they travelled with ould Mohammed entirely at their own risk. I would have liked to believe I was writing without malice; but I doubted it.

12

IBRAHIM AG SOWANAKI had been found for me by the Commandant with the same sense of urgency that had produced two camels the day after my arrival in Tessalit. Whatever reservations I might have about the physical capacities of the beasts, there seemed room for none at all when I set eyes on this man. At twenty-seven, he was much younger than most of those I had travelled with, and his build was different, too. They had been short and wiry, for the most part, but Ibrahim was tall and slender without being thin. He was a handsome man with aquiline features that in another culture could have made him at least a useful income. He had the steadiest pair of eyes I had seen and a mouth that might curl in scorn but never, I guessed, shift at opportunity. I was immediately taken by his walk, a fine and proud carriage, in which the shoulders lay a shade back, the legs strode with confidence and the arms swung very freely, more from side to side across his trunk than backwards and forwards as usual.

He was a Tuareg, and communication would be more difficult with him than with anyone else I had known. His own language was Tamachek, of which I knew nothing. At the outset, we had no more than a couple of hundred words in common, a dash of Arabic seasoned with a pinch of French. Yet I had no doubt that we would get on well together. He looked an exceedingly straight man to me. Twice on this journey, my first impressions had been unsound: I had been badly taken in by Mohamed ould Moctar ould Hmeida and, smarting from that experience, I had been unreasonably suspicious in my first dealings with Sid' Ahmed ould Eli ould Simmad. My first snap judgement of Ibrahim Ag Sowanaki, however, turned out to be faultlessly accurate.

Apart from new camels and fresh provisions, it was also necessary to obtain more equipment in Tessalit. With luck, we might reach Tamanrasset in three weeks, and in the last few days before getting there, we would pass through two small oases. Up to that point, however, there were but three wells available, and one of these was rumoured to be dry. Because of this scanty supply and because of the increasing heat, we needed to carry much more water than ever before. This time I would travel with six guerbas, instead of four, and I also obtained a special packsaddle on which one camel could bear water and baggage, but no rider.

My companion introduced a novel item of his own. Every man with me could be remembered by some piece or other of his personal belongings. With Sid' Ahmed it had been a shotgun and an axe; with ould Mohammed it had been a long pole for foraging among trees; with Mohamed it had been nothing more than a chewing stick and a dandy's taste for European shirts, which he selected with a fine sense of colour, to be worn beneath his boubou. With Ibrahim the Tuareg it was a great broadsword which he strapped to his belt as we prepared to leave Tessalit.

We set off on February 16, late on an afternoon which was smoky with the makings of a sandstorm. As our tiny caravan padded away between the buildings, a raggletaggle of soldiery bobbed alongside, advising and joking and wishing us well. On the outskirts of the village, ould Mohammed emerged from a house, shouldering a half carcass of lamb which he had doubtless fished from someone's charity with an artful cast of his hard-luck tale. He paused to watch us go by, and we barely acknowledged each other's presence.

We headed for the miniature mountains, a mixture of black rocky ridges and piles of shale, which I could now see crammed close together away to the northeast. For a day or two there would be no problem with navigation, because a dusty track led through these rocks as far as the Algerian border camp of Timeiaouine, and Ibrahim had traversed it once or twice. Beyond that he had never been, but I foresaw far less difficulty in finding our way than ould Mohammed and I had experienced in riding from Tombouctou. The charts showed a great deal of rocky and other high ground between here and Tamanrasset, ending in the genuine mountains of the Hoggar. The bulk of it inclined northeast on almost exactly the bearing we needed to follow ourselves. If we did but navigate crudely from point to point of its outlying spurs to our right, with the emptiness of the Tanezrouft sands to our left, we should slowly feel our way to our destination without becoming hopelessly lost, like blind men fingering their way carefully along the outside of a building. The one overriding need for absolute precision would be, as always, in the location of these precious wells.

We made our camp a couple of hours after leaving the oasis in a half gale of wind that slung dust into the rice as we were eating. I was again very ill that night, though whether it was from another bout of overeating or from some variation of my perpetual disorder I could not tell. Ibrahim hobbled the camels while I made the fire and started to brew the tea. When he had returned from this errand, he looked gloomy. The camels, he said, were in very poor condition. Three of them were so feeble that he did not believe they would reach Tamanrasset. If we were to have a reasonable chance of getting through, there was only one solution. We would have to walk.

Riding would, in any case, have been out of the question next morning, for we were threading our way through a very narrow passage between rocks. On every side enormous black boulders crowded in upon us, their texture uncommonly like the rough gabbro of Skye, which would tear you to pieces if you fell on it but which never failed to provide a climber with reliable hand- and footholds. We negotiated chasms and gulleys without number, some of them so strewn with heavy rubble that we had to unhitch the four camels from their long train and lead them one by one up or down these obstacles. It was punishing work in the great heat that flared out of those rocks, which emitted a metallic smell much like that of a clean oven that has been burning for some time.

After the midday camp we came out onto a gravel plain and walked across it for hours, while the heat waves undulated just above the surface ahead, transforming distant mountains into mushroom shapes or unidentifiable objects that were detached and floating freely above the earth. I was badly spent by nightfall, and my feet had become as sore as ever they were at the beginning of my journey, on the march from Chinguetti to Tidjikja. The canvas of my shoes was beginning to rot and tear, and the sand here, of much coarser grain than I had known before, easily worked inside and rubbed harshly against soles which had become softened by several weeks out of sandals.

The white bull from Tombouctou, on the other hand, was by then limping much less severely. Ibrahim had relieved the pain of its cut pad by rubbing it with rock salt as an antiseptic and then packing the wound with fragments of its own wool, which he had chewed up into a dressing. Throughout the day he had been watchfully checking each camel in turn, to see that ropes did not chafe, that loads were evenly balanced, that no new cuts had appeared. Nor did he confine his attentions to the animals. Twice during the midday camp he had got up to examine the guerbas, to see whether any had sprung a leak. Not even Sid' Ahmed had shown such care over detail.

Our second full day out of Tessalit saw us start with fingers numbed by cold, yet within two hours I was trailing a good hundred yards behind the train, my energy draining fast again in the overpowering heat. Wryly I compared my condition now with that of the man who three months before had been impatiently driving Mohamed and Sidi Mahmoud out of their apparent lethargy. I was now very thankful indeed to rest at any excuse. The worst moment in every day came after the midday camp when, already dog-tired, one faced the effort of loading up with nothing but four hours of slog to look forward to. The only good moment came after unloading for the night camp, when twelve hours of rest stretched seductively ahead. That afternoon, I began to trip and fall down again, my walk deteriorating to such a weak-kneed shamble that when Ibrahim suggested I ride for a little while, I gratefully mounted the stronger of the two Tessalit beasts. I rode for an hour, but in that time I had to dismount three times to evacuate scalding bowels. In this condition I wanted nothing more than to reach Tamanrasset and concede my defeat. After dark, when I had recovered some strength, I weighed up my chances of getting through to Murzuk in Libya before the weather made further progress impossible. I no longer thought of reaching the Nile.

That night I was awakened from a dream, an experience that would have been strange to me at home but which was not unusual in the desert. On this occasion I was watching a policeman strolling across heathland somewhere, I sensed, in the southern counties of England. He bent down to seize a clump of grass and, tugging at it, rolled back a great stretch of turf as if it were a carpet. There, lying on a bed of peat, was a collection of snakes, writhing and hissing most horribly. At which the constable leapt in the air with a shout and went rushing away across the landscape.

This was not, essentially, much different from a dream which (as things turned out) was even odder, and which I had experienced on the most critical night of my life, when ould Mohammed and I had missed the well of Asler. The location of that fantasy was some room in the House of Commons. Sitting in a chair was the British Foreign Secretary, Sir Alec Douglas-Home, somewhat unlike his real self, with a thick head of iron-grey hair. Three other men were present with him, two of them completely anonymous figures, the other instantly identified by me as Lord Lambton. The Foreign Secretary asked these three to examine his hair, which seemed to him a little matted and sticky. One of the men bent down and pulled gently at a tuft. Whereupon the top of Sir Alec's head came away as neatly as if it had been trepanned to reveal, in the upper half, meat which was cooked and grainy like a side of pork and, underneath, a cavity. The poor Foreign Secretary went white as a sheet, murmured "Good Lord," and was led out of the room by the others.*

We marched into Timeiaouine next morning, climbing over a reef of rocks to find the military camp and its attendant civilian dwellings spread across the wadi below. The camp looked as businesslike a fortress as anything once occupied by the Foreign Legion. There were watchtowers above its gateway manned by sentries, and there was a military bustle of soldiers inside the square, while, outside the walls, twenty or thirty army camels, all of them magnificent beasts, were couched in lines upon the sand.

At our coming, a squad of troops emerged and crowded round us, curiosity mingled with suspicion, but I had no cause for alarm here. I was armed with a letter of introduction from the Algerian Ambassador in London to

* A couple of months later, back in England, I opened my newspaper to read about the cause célèbre involving Lord Lambton. For some time I wondered why the name seemed familiar to me; then I recalled the dream and verified from my notebook that Lord Lambton appeared in it. I have ever since, unsuccessfully, been trying to think why he, of all men, should have figured in the dream. As far as I can make out, I had not been consciously aware of his existence until the day I opened my paper.

all civil and military authorities in the land. With this, I knew, I should receive nothing but assistance in Algeria. At Timeiaouine I was given a royal meal by the commander of the fort, who seemed even more sceptical than I was about my chances of reaching the Libyan border. He told me that within a week or two it would be far too hot to travel.

"You'll see," he said, "if you try it. March is a killer in the desert."

We walked on. We walked through a series of bitterly cold starts to each day which were swiftly overtaken by heat that did not cease to scorch the flesh until the sun was sliding out of the sky to the west. Each day I was tottering badly towards the end, far behind Ibrahim and the camels, so that he had them half unloaded by the time I caught up with him at the place where we would camp for the night. I rarely took the ropes myself, for I was increasingly unable to match the pace of my companion and the beasts. Every hour or so, Ibrahim stopped so that I might come up to make a compass check and indicate the next point on the horizon for which we should aim; then he forged on again, the leading headrope hauled fast over his left shoulder or, as he himself began to tire each afternoon, tied in a noose around his waist so that his arms were free to swing.

At one of these stops we turned, hearing a thump behind us. The brown from Tombouctou, Sid' Ahmed's old camel, which was third in the line of four, had couched himself as though he assumed we were halting to make camp. Ibrahim and I exchanged a glance and a shrug, got the bull to his feet and walked on.

On the evening of the sixth day out of Tessalit, we descended a ridge of slaggy rock into the first area of grazing we had seen apart from Timeiaouine. Camels were browsing here, and Ibrahim, who had taken to leaving his broadsword lashed to a saddle, stopped to buckle it to his belt. For a moment I wondered whether he expected hostility from anyone we might meet, but was told that it was normal for a Tuareg to be properly dressed when he met strangers, the sword being regarded as a symbol of manhood more than a potential weapon. We had made our camp under a high dune when three men appeared, bringing to our fire small bundles of kindling which they offered like posies, as a gesture of friendship and a practical gift. Ibrahim said they had a few sheep somewhere among the trees and were willing to sell one if we wished.

He slaughtered the lamb they fetched with the bowie knife I had brought from England. As he cleaned it in the sand afterwards, he examined its blade with approval. "It's a fine knife, this," he said.

That was the only time he came anywhere near asking for anything beyond the 50,000 francs we had agreed upon as his wage for travelling with me.

We awoke next morning with grit lashing our faces and a screaming wind driving sand in sheets all around. It was patently hopeless to move in such conditions, for we could see no farther than the nearest bush. We munched a few dates and then covered ourselves in blankets though, even with goggles on, the sand crept into my eyes and had my nose streaming as if with a bad cold. I fell into a kind of coma, conscious of nothing but the battering, abrasive elements, noting the ponderous passage of time by my watch. Occasionally I put it to my ear to catch the low, whining hum of its electric cell, a sound that had given me comfort through many dark nights, a promise of continuity from and to the world that was mine. About noon, I felt a hand on my shoulder. Ibrahim, bending over me, shouted that the storm was beginning to slacken; if I wished to move, we might try now.

Laboriously we extracted baggage that had almost vanished under the drifted sand. We roused the camels, all couched nearby with their rumps turned towards the wind, and began to haul them in pairs through the still flying grit. We traversed the dune that had offered little in the way of shelter from the storm and moved onto flat gravel for an hour or so to the well of Iraldiouine, along a track deeply worn by the nomads from whom we had bought the sheep. There we carefully filled the six guerbas to their fullest extent, Ibrahim working the wellhead and pouring water into the skins while I led one of the camels backwards and forwards to haul the bucket up and down the shaft. We needed every drop we could carry away with us, for there was but one more well before the small oasis of Silet, and that was the one which by all accounts might now be dry. Then we pressed on for perhaps a couple of miles, until a tree appeared in the thickening haze ahead. The storm seemed to have acquired a second wind, blowing as fiercely as in the morning, and at the tree we couched the beasts and started to unload again. We rolled into our blankets once more, and passed more hours sheltering blindly from the blasting of the sand.

Next day dawned cold and clear, and a new world lay endlessly ahead. We had thus far been marching close to the rocky massif that ran northeast towards the Hoggar. The flat gravel stretches we had crossed were no more than bays standing in to the massif between headlands of rock. But now the massif itself curved away in a great arc to the right, off our direct course, and we were confronted with a passage across what looked like an eternal plain. Its dimensions were only emphasised by the presence, low on distant horizons, of isolated peaks and tabletops of rock. These made for confident navigation, for they were marked on the chart, but their greatest effect was to provide such scale to the entire panorama as to reduce two men and four camels to their proper proportions in this towering and barren universe. We were insects creeping forward to a rim of the world that might never be reached, across pure and unbounded space in which we had no hope at all of encountering anything else that lived and could offer comfort by its presence. It was appalling; but, at the same time, it was exciting, with a spellbinding quality that penetrated even the dulling of the senses that it imposed.

For over three months I had laboured across the Sahara, and there had been few moments when I had experienced the magnetism of the desert to which so many men before me had succumbed. But now, in its utmost desolation, I began at last to understand its attraction. It was the awful scale of the thing, the suggestion of virginity, the fusion of pure elements from the heavens above and the earth beneath which were untrammelled and untouched by anything contrived by man.

It was also, in this place, the texture of the desert. This plain was fundamentally dark brown, but on it lay stones with colours that swirled across the spectrum. Some were translucent white, others a dazzling green, and alongside either you might see a pebble dyed a deep ruby or a more gaudy red. Most beautiful of all, though, were those stones, so smooth that it was delightful to stroke them, whose darker patterns had a ceramic quality fired by the terrible heat of the Sahara's summer.

A passage across this desert would have been a pleasure to anyone travelling in a vehicle, so flat and unimpeded was its surface. For any creature moving on foot it was criminally hard. On our first morning across this reg, I noticed spots of blood on the ground, and I was not sure whose it was. Ibrahim's sandals, thin to start with, now had holes in the bottom. But, as well as the white bull from Tombouctou, whose pad Ibrahim had doctored from the start, the brown had also sustained a cut. He was, moreover, perpetually foaming at the mouth. Thrice in one day, when we passed solitary clumps of grass, we almost rammed them down the throats of the two animals from Tombouctou, for they showed no signs of fending for themselves. If the brown were not the first camel to die, then probably it would be the feebler of the two whites from Tessalit; Ibrahim thought this one might not even reach the next well. Since Timeiaouine, it had barely bothered to eat even when we came across pasture, preferring to sit and gnash its broken teeth as soon as it was hobbled, and now we ignored it; we could not waste sustenance on a camel whose death seemed imminent.

Crisis was near, but it was without tension. We had faced the fact that we would lose camels from the moment we set out. We now very carefully and brutally planned for their loss. Thus, at midday camp, Ibrahim twice rose wearily from his meal to rouse the two Tombouctou camels from the ground and make them feed with the stronger of the Tessalit bulls, the only animal that seemed in reasonable fettle. My old riding camel from Tombouctou, the white with the cut pad, now carried nothing at all on its back, while the broken-toothed Tessalit bull bore the packsaddle and all the water. As soon as he died, this load would be transferred to the unburdened animal. We were applying, in the desert, the law of the jungle, and odds already heavy against the weakest were weighed even further in favour of the strong. It was a shameful code, but only in this fashion would two men survive.

I never doubted that I would survive, although I was fully aware that physically my plight was almost as great as it had been on that awful day when Sid' Ahmed had been obliged to bully me into going on. My feet were now swelling rapidly so that it was difficult to get them into my shoes, even though these had rotted so much that normally they would have been too loose to wear. They were still letting in so much gravel through the torn canvas that sometimes I had to stop every few minutes to shake it out. After the first hour's march every morning, I felt as if my pelvis were being ground to powder against some ball-and-socket joint in my trunk. I was retaining food only by consuming twice the prescribed dose of drugs each day. Perpetually my mouth burned and my throat ached with dryness. I barely noticed, except at rest, the lice that were feasting in abundance upon my scraggy flesh.

One made what mental shifts one could to relieve the staggering tedium of these hours. The multicoloured stones helped as much as anything, and attention was naturally fixed upon them when the head drooped so much with exhaustion. Nor had I seen so many mirages before. In the distance, on every side, there appeared to be sheets of water. To the west a sand dune floated above the plain like a low cloud, and a range of rocky hills had also levitated from the earth. As much as dry lips would allow, I whistled and hummed when my steps flagged to a saunter, in order to quicken my pace. Always these were military tunes and always they were accompanied by an image. I did not think of Grandad now when I tried "The British Grenadier"; instead I saw an actor playing young Churchill on a ceremonial march at Sandhurst. When I switched to "Colonel Bogey," my private mirage was of Alec Guinness, worn out but still upstanding, at the bridge on the River Kwai.

I thought of refreshment, and dwelt much on the memory of a waterfall which hung from the hillside behind a cottage in the Lake District, where A and I had spent the last summer holidays with my children. It was not—what was that beautiful phrase of Francis Kilvert's?—it was a smooth pouring of plenty from a brimming pool over a sill of rock. What *was* that phrase of Kilvert's? For hours I searched the recesses of memory until I had it. The waterfall's sound was not "the clink and trickle of the brook"; its name was Dash.

Many times my mind floundered dully and obsessively for long periods around some utterly trivial thing which seemed immensely important to me where I was. I spent the whole of an afternoon contemplating the cheese and onions that I would cook for myself as soon as I regained my own kitchen, dwelling fondly upon the minutest details of the dish and its preparation. For thirty-six hours I intermittently ransacked my head for the name of an undistinguished Australian who had played at fullback for an unexceptional Rugby League club some twenty-five years before. I reviewed all the colonial footballing heroes of my childhood, one by one, and the relief, the sense of accomplishment, when at last I nailed my quarry, would have been farcical in any other context. His name was Bob Bartlett; and, to cap my feat, I remembered that he was a centre and not a fullback.

On February 25, we reached the well of In Azaoua. It lay at the head of a ravine which we had followed to find it, and I had not before seen a water hole as primitive as this one. Lacking even a flange of stones, crudely built around the rim, which even the most rudimentary wells had so far possessed, it was nothing more than a hole in the ground, almost hidden by a rubble of rocks. It was not, in fact, dry, but there was very little water in it. It was so shallow that Ibrahim could climb into the cavity, yet when he stood upright his head was above ground level. I passed down the tin mug, and slowly he scooped up enough muddy liquid to fill one guerba. The other five were each rather less than half full. We should have little water left by the time we reached Silet.

As we tied the guerba to the packsaddle, there was a movement round the nearest bend of the ravine, and a small caravan came into sight. There were eight camels, heavily loaded, and a small flock of goats, all in the custody of a man, a youth and a tiny boy. They were, they said, travelling from Kidal to Tamanrasset to sell the goats and the cargo of dried meat. We exchanged greetings before Ibrahim and I moved off, leaving the newcomers to extract what water they could from the pitiful well.

Late that afternoon the gravel plain ended at a great barrier of sand. Painfully we toiled up its slope, then across a plateau so soft that the feet submerged ankle-deep at every step. Both men and beasts were almost done with exhaustion by the time we came to the far side of the plateau, where we were faced with a hazardous descent. Below stretched a vast basin of sand with a group of trees in the middle, bounded on the far side by range after range of dunes. We were standing two hundred feet above it, on the brink of a drop that was very steep indeed. The obvious and prudent course was to unload the beasts, lead them down one by one, then return to manhandle the baggage after them. Neither Ibrahim nor I had the strength left for that. We looked at each other, not needing to speak our minds.

"We try?" he asked. I nodded.

We unhitched the train and Ibrahim set off down the steepling brow with the first loaded camel. After a little while I followed with the second. We were taking a terrible risk that the exhausted beasts might stumble, or merely fall over, in which case they would surely break their legs. We had to lean back hard against their heads to restrict momentum while they, slipping and lurching on splayed legs which sank knee-deep in the sand, came roaring and grunting behind. It took us half an hour to get them down, but we managed it without accident.

The light was beginning to fade from the sky, and we were camped by the trees, when we saw the caravan descending the plateau in our tracks. The man and the youth led each camel in turn, one on either side of its head, down the slope. The tiny boy scrambled down alone with the goats. He could not have been more than five or six years old, and in the society from which I came he would have been guarded and cuddled by anxious parents. I had a son little older, a sturdy boy who played boisterously with his mates but who, nonetheless, could be transformed instantly into a sobbing infant whose agony could be extinguished only by a parent's embrace and the whispered reassurance that all was not lost. Yet this nomad child was required to live as a man in conditions from which I, half the time, shrank with faint heart. I had seen his like many times before. His infant tears would be chastised or ignored as unmanly, and whatever emotional agonies he suffered, he would have to bear them alone. He would mature by imitation rather than by encouragement. By the time he was ten he would be admitted to the circle of men as they idled around the teapot, the girls and the women held at a disdained and familiar distance. This was the other side of the coin in which his life was minted. I had marvelled many times, and been irritated often, when listening to one of these child-men offering weighty opinions upon any topic under the desert sun, his grey-bearded peers hearing him attentively before agreeing or disagreeing with as much consideration as if he were in middle age.

The three brought their animals towards our trees, made their camp at a little distance, then came over to share our meal. When they had returned to their blankets, Ibrahim suggested that we start marching again before dawn. It was a sensible course, in view of the growing heat of each day, though that was not quite the point he was making. The camels, he said, were failing fast, and if we were going to reach Tamanrasset we would have to increase our daily mileage. The stage was not far off, he thought, where at any camp we made, one or more of the camels might not be induced to rise from the ground again. We must therefore extend the distances between our camps.

At a little after three o'clock we prepared to start under a moon that was something from fantasy. Never in my life had I seen it looming as large as when it topped the horizon. It seemed to fill a quarter of the heavens, a full circle which itself was encircled by a colossal and golden penumbra. It was a moon from a children's picture book, with the colour of a Gloucester cheese. There was a sleepy farewell salute from the bundle of blankets nearby as we set off. It was unlikely that we should see the three again, with a four-hour start, in conditions ideal for a night march. There was not a breath of wind, though it was excessively cold. Even with my howli muffled thickly between chin and eyes under a bare head, my face was numb for hours, as well as hands and feet. Had I been snowballing in an English winter, I could scarcely have been colder. In this condition we attacked the dunes and it was heavy work, headhauling the beasts one at a time up the steeper slopes, the brown bull and the broken-toothed white frequently falling to their knees. Dawn found us on the gravel reg again, and all day we plodded across its flat and featureless surface, blistered now as fiercely by the sun as we had been frozen by night under the moon.

Slumped that evening against the unloaded baggage, I was beyond responding to the sunset. On days without number I had been revived by the magical half hour of the sun's decline: most beautiful of all were those evenings when the horizon glowed with green, yellow and blood-red rays, in which the very thin crescent of a new moon rose a trifle above the ground before slipping back again in pursuit of the sun, without the strength yet to climb into the sky. On this evening the colours stained some wisps of high, stratospheric cloud that a remote wind was unravelling towards the west. But I was too weary to delight in it.

I awoke at 3:30, shivering in spite of a great blaze of grass that Ibrahim had started beside us; its light leapt and flickered upon the four camels, which we had couched on the spot before going to sleep. There was a stiffness in my body that came not from the cold nor yet from long exertions, but seemed to issue now from the deepest fibres of my being in a translated protest of the soul at the very thought of movement. I felt as though I were inhabiting a spent and useless contraption of tissue and bone which no longer had any relevance to me and what I really was. Was this, I wondered, why the mystics came to the desert: to be so alienated from their own flesh, at a distance that was beyond repugnance, that they might dwell, without alternative, upon and within the boundaries of the spirit?

We marched until after seven o'clock across the barren reg, in close order, with Ibrahim on the leading headrope and myself bringing up the rear. My old white from Tombouctou was the first camel in line, the two beasts from Tessalit in the middle, Sid' Ahmed's brown bull behind them. When camels are healthy and led in a train like this, their heads tend to strain forward and low to reduce the pull of the ropes on their nose rings. They look a bit like a line of angry geese as they pad along. When they are exhausted, their heads are held high on curving necks, trying to resist the awful dragging of their bodies even when their nostrils are almost being pulled out, the pain of the one seeming much greater than that of the other. Our camels were now marching like this. I was belabouring them from behind with my riding stick in an effort to keep them going, offering them a third pain that might be worse than the other two, to reduce the strain on the ropes and persuade them to go forward.

There was nothing but pain in this desert, for human

beings and animals alike. Life was pain. Only in death was there relief.

We stopped for half an hour to make tea and eat dates. Then we marched on as before. The brown bull, which had carried nothing for two days, now began to move at an angle to the other three, his head still tethered to the saddle ahead, his rump swinging out to the right. He went forward in little rushes each time I clouted his haunch. Suddenly I heard a sound like that of a breathless runner, panting hard. It came not from his head but from under his tail, where his anus had started to throb violently, working in and out like a piston out of control. At the same time I was aware of an appalling smell, which I had come across once or twice before. Somewhere inside, this poor creature was already as putrefied as the overblown corpses I had passed outside Tombouctou. Then he went down with a thump, the headrope breaking with a twang. Ibrahim stopped the train at my shout and came back to help me get the bull to his feet again. We refastened the broken rope and continued, but almost at once the beast went down again. We raised him once more, and something very curious happened. Before we could attach the severed ends of rope, the brown bull cantered forward, past the two camels from Tessalit, to the beast which had shared the long journey from Tombouctou with him. He rubbed his shoulder against that of the white. Then he turned at a right angle, facing it, and sat down again.

Ibrahim shrugged. "He's finished," he said.

I had been unmoved when one of my camels foundered before. This time I felt sadness hanging like a weight on my throat. The brown bull had been such a gallant animal, with much more spirit than any other beast I had used. Most camels roared with indignation when being loaded, but he had been a snarler and a snapper, too, twisting his head right round to menace the rider about to mount. On the move, most beasts bore their riders along at a steady lope, but there had always been something frisky about his trot. He had travelled an intolerable distance to serve my pur-

264

pose. Now I was abandoning him in the middle of the most barren wilderness we had crossed together, just as the day's heat was beginning to burn, where there was not a vestige of shade from either rock, dune or vegetation as far as the eye could see. Ibrahim said that he would be dead by nightfall. As we moved off, two men and three camels now, the brown bull turned his head slowly to watch our going. Then he turned away again, his back to the sun, his head pointing to the west.

We marched on, and by that day's end I wondered how much farther I could continue myself. Waves of nausea flowed through my stomach and there was a heavy ache around my kidneys. My left leg had started to drag, so that I was consciously trying to bring it forward with each step. At our midday camp I had felt as though the sun were burning a hole through my skull, thickly wrapped in a headcloth though it was. When we moved away I hung the map case on one of the saddles. I had never done this before, but now it seemed far too much to carry. By the time the sun was setting, we had been walking for more than twelve hours—almost fifteen if we counted the stops. Ibrahim wanted to continue for another two, but I couldn't take any more and said so peevishly.

His own strength was draining, too. His face was now strained, and his lips, I noticed, had changed colour to grey. Yet not once had he faltered in anything; never had he responded to cross words of mine with anything but his usual calm and careful attention to whatever he was doing. He was almost as different from my previous companions as I was myself. Not only did he eat his food with a spoon, but he took his share in a brass dish of his own, which he also used as a drinking vessel; I never saw him sup water straight from the neck of a guerba, as others were accustomed to. Where others had lain close beside me at night, for mutual warmth, Ibrahim had always rolled into his blanket at some distance. He was the one man who had consistently refused to take anything from the tassoufra containing our shared supplies, even when I asked him to, always waiting for me to apportion the food. He was the only person I had heard say "Thank you" for anything. I could not tell to what extent these habits were Tuareg ways in general, to what degree they belonged singularly to Ibrahim Ag Sowanaki, who had a wife and three children, four camels of his own and a small garden in which he grew vegetables for the military garrison at Tessalit.

We started the next day's march in the night again and, when dawn came, there were three or four great mountains ahead, all but hull down on the horizon. I was reminded how once, in the Navy, my ship had approached Gibraltar from the Atlantic and how I had watched the great rock slowly rise from the depths of the sea, first a misty pinnacle, then a solid bastion, finally a towering cliff. The sensation this day was much the same, though the approach of the mountains was much slower. It was late in the afternoon before we were hard against them. Two of them barred our way, set close together, perhaps fifteen hundred feet high. As we made for the gap between them, we passed great outcrops which had been eroded marvellously into sensuous and bulbous shapes that might easily have been original studies for Henry Moore. The two mountain shoulders, we could now see, consisted of colossal black boulders piled on top of each other, some so finely balanced that they looked as if a fingertip would send them crashing down. We could also see that the gap, which at a distance had promised enough width to drive anything through, was in fact very narrow indeed, barely a passage at all. It was no more than a hundred yards long, but was itself a rubble of black boulders which offered a decent scramble for an unhindered man.

The camels made it plain that they were unwilling to try it. I hauled hard on the headrope of the Tombouctou white, while Ibrahim thrashed it from behind with his stick. Weary as the beast was, it kicked viciously with its rear quarters, narrowly missing Ibrahim's head. It was otherwise immovable. I told Ibrahim to do nothing while I tried another tack. Still pulling firmly on the rope, I began to murmur to the camel as though it were a child. Slowly it started to come forward, roaring and grunting with fear. Then it had to rush down a rock to avoid slipping, almost knocking me off my stance as it came. But, committed, it came forward in more rushes and careful pauses while it felt nervously for a foothold with a foreleg. Within half an hour I had it through the gap. The broken-toothed beast from Tessalit was persuaded to follow the same way. Only the strongest of the camels refused to budge in response either to beating or gentling. Ibrahim said he would lead it back round the mountain and meet me somewhere on the other side.

A couple of hours later, with the sun almost gone, I saw him emerge far behind me, from the shelter of the hillside. He was not alone. There were more camels with him and a figure riding the leader. It was the youth we had first met at In Azaoua, with most of the beasts in the caravan. There was no sign of the man or the small boy, They, he said, were following him somewhere behind, with one camel and the goats. We pressed on in twilight, into rising stony ground. We had been moving for an hour in darkness before we found a clump of trees and stopped. It was then that Ibrahim told me we had no water left. Nor had the youth; his supplies were on the camel accompanying the father and the child. But they never appeared.

Ibrahim and I set off at dawn. The youth said he would wait for the others to catch up. Presumably they had camped when night fell, not wishing to lose our tracks in the darkness. Our camels were twitching and shaking as we loaded them up, the broken-toothed beast swaying perceptibly on his feet. God knows how he had got this far, for neither of us had expected it. By the middle of the morning we were beginning to stagger as badly as the beasts and there was no tension on any of the headropes, for neither of us had the strength to pull them from the front. We were just managing to walk, and that was all. Ibrahim complained of pains in his head, and mine was throbbing dully, as it had for several days. I was no longer walking straight, but progressed in long ellipses like a drunken man who is determined not to show it. When Ibrahim said we must ride, I did not even nod. I waited for the beasts to couch, hauled myself slowly up, and hung onto the saddle as my camel got to his feet. We rode for perhaps an hour, the relief tremendous, towards a full-blooded range of mountains which was beyond our immediate goal. It was the edge of the Hoggar, and Silet was somewhere on this side of it.

We walked again, casually, incapable of anything more as the creeping paralysis of dehydration spread through our limbs. A hot wind flared murderously at us from the west. I had known its scorching threat for many months now, and the sound that betrayed it for the monster that it was: it was a dull sound, a muted booming, as though half a dozen old-fashioned bombers were flying high above, or a convoy of heavy lorries were rumbling several miles away. It would be a killer, this wind, during March in the desert. It was the first day of March now, and the wind had me within its range.

Almost unconscious even of my mind, I was aware of trees somewhere ahead, somewhere beyond Ibrahim and the camels, who seemed to be a great distance ahead. Then there was a tent. Ibrahim was squatting by it, drinking from his brass bowl. Then a small boy was running towards me, trying not to spill what was in the bowl. The water in it was the colour of diluted blood.* This was the most beautiful thing in the world, more beautiful by far than the stained glass of Chartres, than a fugue by Bach, than the moment after ecstasy with the woman you loved, or the moment when your son scrambled to squeeze the breath out of you and say, "I think you're smashing, Dad." There was nothing in the world as beautiful as this bowlful of water.

It was a little before two, and for the next three hours we lay inert beneath bushes, drinking much water and eating dates. We had been there some time when a liquid blur in the heat haze was transformed into substantial shape and

---

* Water from a new guerba is sometimes tinted by a residue of oil or other substance used in dressing the leather.

eventually became a group of camels proceeding along our tracks. The youth was still mounted on the leading beast, but of the father, the child and the goats there was still no sign. We couched the beasts while the young fellow drank his fill outside the tent. After speaking with him for a while, Ibrahim told me the others were coming, and I relaxed into semicoma again.

As the heat wore out of the day, we thanked the people of the tent for their kindness and moved on, the youth and his camels with us. Within the hour we were in the oasis, a sprawling, rudimentary settlement of tents with only a small collection of buildings in the middle. There the camels slaked their thirst and we refilled our guerbas, at a watercourse that did service as the well of Silet. I had seen nothing like this before. It had evidently been channelled from some spring which issued from the earth among a clump of palms. In England it would have been called a ditch, a sluggish thing half-choked with weed, containing the odd tin can, but the water itself was clean and sweet enough. Kneeling by it that evening, as the camels sucked at the surface and shook their jowls endlessly around me, it seemed the greatest bounty I had known for a long time. When the beasts were done, we ambled on a little way to make our camp on the far side of the settlement.

Only then did I really begin to worry about the missing pair. Neither Ibrahim nor the youth had showed signs of alarm, and I had easily accepted their assurance that the others were following us. Too easily, perhaps. I was still unsure where the limits of endurance lay for people born and bred in the desert, though I was clear enough now about my own. Reason told me that the man and the child had water, as well as goats that could give them milk and meat. Our tracks were vivid enough to follow and there had been no wind strong enough to wipe them out. Yet the fact was that they had not now been seen for a day and a half. They could quite easily have had some accident, the father falling from his camel and breaking his leg or worse. That tiny boy, younger than my son Michael, might still be out there alone in that awful emptiness which had come close enough to imperilling me again. Guilt suddenly engulfed me in a wave. I should have insisted on staying put this morning until the others appeared, or I should have insisted that we turn back to look for them. It was absolutely no excuse that I was too weary to think straight, that I relied on the judgement of Ibrahim and the youth. I had an instinct—I had believed I had an instinct—and it had failed most miserably.

I turned to my companion in the darkness. If the two didn't show up in the morning, I said, we must do something to organise a search party from the oasis. That, said Ibrahim, wouldn't be necessary: the youth could attend to them; we must go on. Something thudded sickeningly close to my heart. This man, whom I had come to admire and to love as if he were my brother, had betrayed himself with a few words; just as I had betrayed myself with wilful indecision. I said nothing and tried to sleep, with Ibrahim on one side of me and the youth on the other. When I awoke, it was long past dawn and the youth was missing. He had gone, said Ibrahim, to look for the others.

I told him to wait until I returned. Then I walked back to the oasis. I remembered seeing a Land-Rover parked outside the buildings in the centre. I now hurried to this place, past men who eyed me curiously as they paused in their bricklaying of a new wall. In the main structure I found two people in western dress, dapper officials down from Algiers to advise the local people on planting crops in the oasis. They examined my papers and watched me keenly as I explained what had happened and what I feared. Would it be possible, I asked, for some men to take the Land-Rover across the ground we had covered, beyond those two mountains in the distance? I told them as best I could where the youth had parted company with the missing pair after the noon camp two days before. A foreman, one of the locals, was summoned and went off to fetch the vehicle. I paused, wondering whether I should go with him.

One of the agriculturists said, "Thank you. We'll find them." As I shifted, still half undecided whether to leave, he added, "They're very tough, these people, even the little boys. Tougher than you. . . ." He grinned, disarmingly. "Tougher than me, too."

It was midmorning when Ibrahim and I set off again, slogging towards the range of mountains whose scale and height were almost exactly that of the English Lake District. By midafternoon we were amongst them, creeping up a long hill of slaggy rock whose summit was littered with a great number of cairns and grave slabs. How very symbolic, I thought, of what this journey had become. Behind me lay the corpses of two camels that had died on my behalf. At any moment now, they might be joined by another, or even two; there were spots of blood on the rocks again, and the broken-toothed bull was rearing his head back continuously in that desperate, straining effort that heralded the end. Somewhere out there, in the place from whence we came, that small boy might even now be dying in a heap of dust, the Land-Rover too late to help him, or even failing to find his body at all. I was haunted by the chance of tragedy and my own part in its making.

I was suddenly, furiously, abysmally certain that I could go no further than Tamanrasset. I had, at last, discovered beauty in the desert. It was around me now, the familiar beauty of mountains. But all I could feel was agony, suffering, pain, mindlessness, endlessness, futility. Under the dreadful, drilling heat of this appalling sun I had become an automaton that marched. I was scarcely recognisable as a human being, with the responses that alone distinguished us from the animals. I wondered whether I had forfeited a little of my soul to the desert—maybe the greater part of it.

We stopped among the cairns. Ibrahim, as he had never failed to do from the first day of our passage together, was testing ropes, examining feet, sweeping away ticks from the underbellies of beasts which no longer had the strength to do it themselves, so that the insects hung vilely in thick clusters, surfeited with blood. Ibrahim himself needed rest as badly as any camel. His lips were now cracked open, with

271

blood dried around the edges, and the tip of his nose had turned grey. His face was as taut as any of the ropes he was fixing. As we began to move slowly downhill, towards the long gash of the Oued Abalessa, he told me to hit the broken-toothed white, at the back of the line, in order to keep him going. I did so, and there was the awful crack of hard wood upon bone that was no longer covered in anything but hide.

We camped that night in a grove of trees before one of the most breathtaking views I could remember in many years of roaming the world. Far ahead was the full flourish of the Hoggar, an enormous mountain range of jagged peaks that radiated the light of the setting sun, glowing white against the deep blue sky. It was like looking at a bundle of Matterhorns, each vying with the next for prominence, stature and elegance. They were formidable in their presence and they were operatic in their grandeur. Deep inside that bastion of rock was the place where Charles de Foucauld had made his hermitage. Something stirred within me, a genuflection to his memory, to be sure, but also a desire to touch and clasp those rocks and know them well. I would not reach the Nile now. The Hoggar would be my prize.

We walked down to Abalessa next morning. I had known no oasis more fruitful than this. There were small fields on the outskirts, head high in crops that were thick and ripening and vividly green. The place was superbly irrigated, with a stream that wound around and between the houses. There we watered the camels again and topped up the guerbas. We left almost as soon as we had finished and moved into a line of thorn trees to make our midday camp. When we had unloaded the baggage, two of the camels began to snatch at the abundant leaves. The broken-toothed bull, which we did not bother to hobble, meandered very slowly to the shade of the thickest branches and settled down without a sound. We never got him up again. We did not even try very hard this time. He could go no further, and we knew it. Ibrahim thought that, sitting in the shade, the bull might last a couple of days longer before he keeled over and died. No more. Someone might come across him, just as I had come across a camel awaiting death by the well of Chig so very long ago. But they would leave him be, too, as I had done the other.

We rearranged the baggage, discarding some things that were heavy and no longer of importance to us. In a couple of days we should reach Tamanrasset. Already I could feel myself becoming limp in the knowledge of danger past. We were safe now, whatever happened. There was another well between this place and journey's end, if we needed it.

"Supposing," I asked Ibrahim as we prepared to leave, "supposing these two camels drop dead tonight. What shall we do?"

He looked at me as levelly as he had always done. "You carry some food," he replied, "and I carry some water. We walk to Tamanrasset." He would have said the same thing in the same tone, I knew, if we had lost all our camels a hundred miles ago.

We walked to Tamanrasset. We left the broken-toothed bull beneath the thorn tree and began the long trudge up a wadi, over the wretched coarse-grained sand that flayed the soles of the feet. Our two remaining beasts now moved better than before, without the almost dead weight of invalids pulling at them from behind. We entered rocky hills again, following a track that rose and fell around headlands and into gulleys, the main range of the Hoggar hidden for long hours as we worked our way through its foothills, then appearing once more as we crested some summit and passed over to its other side. It would have been exhilarating had mind and body not been so desperately fixed upon movement, any kind of movement, even the awful dragging movement of limbs that no longer functioned as they ought. Relief now consisted not in rest but in the knowledge that each step forward took us almost within sight of our goal. In that and in our water, which we could drink as freely as we wished.

Yet I, at least, was still conditioned by the long months

273

of scarcity, in which each mouthful was a rare and blessed gift that might disastrously be withdrawn at any time. In the afternoon of our second day from Abalessa, we stopped to check the loads. Being by then too weary to stretch for my water bottle, which hung high upon my saddle, I asked Ibrahim to draw me some water in his bowl, which dangled lower down among the guerbas. I drank half of it and then, in a reflex, I handed him the rest. He did not, as it happened, wish to drink, having taken some a little time before. But, mistaking my gesture for one of excess, he tossed the rest onto the ground with an arrogant, princely turn of his wrist—the motion of a man who has everything he wants, casting out a surplus. I let out a cry of shock, and for a split second I could have hit him. I looked down at the dark puddle on the ground. No man on earth, it seemed to me, had any right to waste something so precious.

On Monday, March 5, we moved away from a camp we had made for the night behind some rocks by the side of the highway that ran through Tamanrasset on its way south across the Sahara from Algeria to Niger. It was much more used than the westerly route up which ould Mohammed and I had laboured three weeks before; several trucks had gone up and down it during the night, and in the space of an hour this morning we had to step aside half a dozen times to allow great petrol tankers and other heavy vehicles to thunder past and smother us with dust. Presently we cut away from the road and headed for the long slab of mountain which stood well behind Tamanrasset. We came to the perimeter of the airport, the most sophisticated thing I had seen since Dakar, complete with a control tower and a tarmacadamed runway. We ignored the warning notices and plodded straight across. A line of electricity pylons began at the other side, and we followed them over several ridges of sand. We marched past the municipal garbage dump, and I had not seen anything so loathsome for years; it defiled this place much more than the wasteland of refuse outside Nouakchott, for everything here was beautiful, whereas there all had been barren. The town itself was all

274

but concealed, even at this distance, in a small forest of trees, every one of them heavy with leaves.

We walked through the trees and suddenly, as if some magician had waved his wand, I found myself leading two camels and a companion in torn and dusty desert clothes down a surfaced street. It was lined with trees, whitewashed halfway up their trunks. Inside the lines of trees were pavements. There were tables set out at intervals along these pavements and people were sitting at them, drinking coffee. They stared at me openmouthed, as though I were a strange animal they had never seen before. I walked on, not daring to speak to any of them, not at all sure where I was going or what I was seeking. Towards the end of the street, I noticed a long low building with a courtyard and a crude sign which called it an hotel. In a reflex from a world apart from the one I had just crossed, I stopped and couched the camels. It was not the ending I had wished.

13

I SPENT MOST OF the next ten days lying on a bed in the Tin-Hinan Hotel, trying to gather enough strength to face the journey home to England. It was a refuge well appointed by whoever had built it, though its comforts were somewhat reduced by the time I got there. Tamanrasset was suffering a water shortage, and the lavatories of the hotel reeked so abominably as to make me regret the passing of primitive ablutions in the desert. It was two days before I was able to wash, and then it was only possible in the municipal steam baths, where a black man and I hove buckets of warm water over each other with childish abandon. The only other occupants of that moist and sombre cavern were lean and straggle-haired youths from Europe and America, the itinerant residue of what was once identified as the hippie culture. They were amiable enough, but neither of us felt at ease in their company.

Tamanrasset, I slowly discovered, was a curious junction of several cultures. On entering the town along its main street, quite unaware that camels did not normally pass that way, I had instantly been reminded, by the pavement tables and the coffee drinkers, of Zermatt. The atmosphere was one of indolent ease enjoyed by strangers who had come to revel, in greater or lesser degree, in the proximity of nature at its most overwhelming and its most unspoilt. There were French, Germans, Italians, Swiss, Americans and English here in profusion. All of them were on the great vagabond route across the Ṣahara, from the Mediterranean coast to various destinations in Black Africa. The most daring of them had careered down the highway by Land-Rover and its various equivalents, or sometimes in vehicles so overworked to start with that they would have been risky conveyances for an extended journey in their countries of origin. The most impecunious, a kind of hitchhiker, had arrived on those ill-used lorries which lurched gallantly for several days from top to bottom of the two trans-Saharan highways and offered, for a relative pittance, a dust-laden and windy position among sheep, goats and shifting local populations. The most affluent and the most nervous had been parcelled into safari groups that would take off into the desert from some point on the highway, in half a dozen well-equipped vehicles with experienced crews, for a fortnight's investigation of the nomad life and the wide-open spaces in between.

Alongside these people at the coffee tables sat a purely Algerian species that was neither one thing nor the other. It was hard to tell whether they belonged to Tamanrasset or whether they had descended from the industrial towns of the northern seaboard. They were all male, they shared the boisterous truculence prevalent among Arabic-speaking young men, and they dressed with a casual nattiness, all tight pants and flowered shirts, that one normally associated with Italy or Greece. Some of them affected the Castro kepi and looked most revolutionary, as indeed they probably were. They had a share in the local wine racket carried on by the air crews who lodged, on overnight stops, at the Tin-Hinan. They were young men just past a cultural

277

crossroads, but they had not yet learned to carry the liquor that their parents would most certainly have abhorred. Pools of vomit frequently appeared on the pavement outside the hostelry on the nights the air crews flew in.

And then there were the men who belonged distinctly to the Tamanrasset of old, or even to an existence which would have made that place a marvel of sophistication and comfort. I saw, one day, five men walking down the main street. They were very dusty, in brown nomadic dress, and it may have been their first visit to the town from the encampments of the desert. They were hand in hand, all five of them, their heads turning in all directions to take things in. They didn't move onto the pavement until a huge Berliet petrol tanker nearly ran them down. It was their innocence that was most striking. A genuine sense of wonder was conveyed by the movement of the heads and eyes but, most of all, by the way they held hands—not firmly, but as a gentle reassurance that they were all in this together.

Most of the men about town, who gave it colour with their swathing blue robes, were well accustomed to its cosmopolitan life. But they held themselves aloof from it. They sold trinkets to the tourists at pretty prices from shops that were well stocked with prosperity. But they did not share the gaseous life of the Gargote et Buvette des Africains, the Restaurant de la Paix or the coffee tables on the pavements.

Nor did I. For the first few days I could do little but raise myself from my bed to eat meals. I wobbled unsteadily when I walked to the post office, crowded with tourists, and after half an hour there I was reeling with faintness. I wrote out a cable to tell everybody at home of my presence here and my failure to go further, my mind ticking very slowly, like a retarded metronome, as I filled in the form. Within a few days I received replies, encouraging me to forget the failure. One of them was from A, fond enough and promising to meet my plane in London; but a note had subtly changed in her tone; things, I realised, would not be quite the same again.

I knew already that I was afraid of going home. I was reluctant to go back as a defeated man, and I was nervous of the world to which I must return, even though the memory and the promise of this had strengthened me more than anything else in the previous four months. It would be strange, going back, after my exposure to the desert, and I wondered how quickly I would accommodate myself to it. Tamanrasset, with its bastardised culture, was a foretaste of things to come and, in this form at any rate, I did not like it. I had no wish at all, for the moment, to speak with people who shared my own natural ways, or something close to them. Our immediate reference points had become separated and I was too tired for the effort I must make to readjust mine. They would, moreover, probably ask questions about the desert, and I did not want to talk of it just yet.

So I shut myself in my room and, instead of drinking coffee with them upon the shaded pavements, I opened the tassoufra and ate a few nuts and dates alone. Later, I sat alone in the courtyard and asked for a glass of apricot juice. As I raised it to my lips, the scent was so powerful that I stopped in the act of opening my mouth. It was rich, delicate, fruitful and very heady. My nose had known nothing so tantalising and delightful for months; indeed, the desert was almost devoid of smell.

Listlessly, I worked out the navigational details of my journey. I took the dividers for the last time and measured the distances between the places where I had camped each night. They totalled 1,857 miles and, allowing for the fact that my companions and I had not often moved in straight lines, it meant that I had probably travelled some 2,000 miles. Since Tessalit, Ibrahim and I had come 373 miles between camps and, apart from two brief periods of riding, we had walked every inch of the way. At least, I thought, I had not given up too easily.

Ibrahim, suspicious of the Tin-Hinan, had preferred to seek lodgings with a distant kinsman of his in town. He came to my room each day to see how I was faring and to report his progress in selling the two camels. He obtained a very decent price for them in the end, considering their condition, and seemed puzzled when I told him to keep the money. It was his by right, for no other man I had known would have got those beasts to Tamanrasset. From the beginning he had attended to the animals with the care of a mother for her children, and it was no fault of his that two had died. I owed him a great deal more than anything I could give him. I kept my own saddle, the tassoufra, the satchel in which were stored the tea things, a couple of the guerbas and the bucket. The rest of our equipment and what remained of our stores I handed over to him.

When I put my Sheffield bowie knife into his hands, his eyes widened with pleasure. He reached for his belt and loosened his short Tuareg knife. I must, he said, take that in exchange; my son might like it. He incised his own name upon the blade in the characters of Tamachek, and we were very pleased together.

Neither of us had been sure how Ibrahim would make his way home. But I discovered that within the week a military patrol would be crossing the desert westwards in vehicles, travelling to the Algerian border post of Bordj Moktar, north of Tessalit on the other Saharan highway. The military agreed to take Ibrahim with them; once they reached the western highway, he would have no difficulty in finding a truck to carry him the last miles down to Tessalit. He would be home within a few days, before I was myself. Just before he left, he asked me to send him copies of photographs I had taken of him. I said I would. And, he added, if I ever came back to the desert and wanted to continue my journey, I must seek him out and we would travel much farther next time. We would, I agreed; we would do that. Then we hugged each other farewell, impulsively. It was the first time we had touched, and there was much warmth in our embrace.

Next day, I walked down to the place where camels were bought and sold. I wanted to see the two that had been mine, and their new owners. There was no sign of them. As I went back up the main street, I saw a familiar figure sitting at a table. It was one of the agriculturists from Algiers whose assistance I had sought in Silet for the missing father and child. I crossed to him, with an old fear pumping my heart. He had almost forgotten about that matter, he said, but, yes, the two were safe. The Land-Rover hadn't found them, but they had walked into Silet the day after I left, having spent the previous two nights with some nomads they had met. They should be in Tamanrasset in a few more days. He chatted on, affably, but I was not really listening. My mind was absent with relief. At least I could go home without a conscience haunted by the spectre of betrayal.

There was one more thing I wished to do before I took flight to Algiers and then to England. Some sixty miles north of Tamanrasset, high up in the mountains, was Assekrem. This was where Charles de Foucauld had made his hermitage for years until his death in 1916. I had long hoped to visit it one day, from curiosity about the man and out of admiration for the ethic he had formulated there. He had been a cavalryman in his youth, a conventional rake who was eventually cashiered out of his regiment for keeping a mistress by the shores of Lake Geneva. In disgrace, he had turned to exploring Morocco; during a period when it was necessary for any Nasrani to disguise himself, he had travelled as a Jewish rabbi.

De Foucauld had been an atheist until this time, but the piety of Moslems restored to him the Catholicism of his childhood. He returned to France and gradually felt his way to the monastic life, but this did not satisfy him. It was not until he became a hermit in the solitudes of Algeria that he was at ease with himself and his God. First at Beni Abbès, later at Tamanrasset and at Assekrem, he won the respect and affection of Moslem nomads and French soldiers alike, but he never converted anyone to

Christianity. It was not his intention to try. He was there, he wrote, to love poor people as though they were his own flesh and blood. Nothing else. Assekrem was where he drew the spiritual strength to attempt this love.

There was a tourist bureau in Tamanrasset, and from there I hired a Land-Rover and its chauffeur. We drove out into the desert east of the town and then turned north along a track through the mountains, which wound airily around cliffs and beside gorges, climbing all the time. I had rarely been as excited by any landscape as I was by this one. There was something of the Dolomites in these straight towers of rock, but they were much thicker from base to peak than anything I had seen in Italy, and they were fluted vertically, like a series of organ pipes, challenging any mountaineer to wriggle and jamb his way to the top, up the cracks in between. Volcanic in origin, they were essentially fountains of lava which had petrified as it poured down from craters which rose higher and higher in successive eruptions. After two and a half hours, we reached a saddle in the mountains, slung between two stumpy hills of slag. One of them was Assekrem, and we were at about ten thousand feet.

A refuge where visitors could stay had been built in the saddle. High above it, a tiny roofline was visible against the sky, and this was the hermitage itself. Leaving my driver to his own devices, I began to climb the steep track up the mountain of loose stones, which said *clank-tonk* at each step, like a great crateful of empty bottles. I went slowly, for the day was very hot and my legs felt as though they had dragging weights beneath the knees. I paused many times to gather my breath anew. The hermitage, when I got there, was tucked beneath the mountaintop, sheltered just below its edge. Two stone huts had been constructed, joined by a short terrace on whose wall a couple of vivid Tuareg blankets were draped to air in the sun. This place had been inhabited since 1955, when the Little Brothers of Jesus, the religious order which grew out of de Foucauld's philosophy years after his death, had come to Assekrem and restored the ruins of his anchor-hold.

Jean-Marie had lived there for well over a decade, part hermit, part custodian, part practitioner of de Foucauld's code. He was a stringy old man whose hair was swept straight back to emphasise the beaky nose and the thin beard on the point of his chin. He wore the long baggy trousers of the Tuareg and, above these, a grey pullover and a windjammer. When I arrived, he was doctoring the sore ear of a small boy whose father had brought him up from an encampment some miles down the valley. Two Tuareg women squatted nearby, watchfully waiting their turn to sell some knickknacks they had stitched together, though why this old Frenchman might wish to buy, except to provide the women with income, I could not imagine. He sat with them, eyes twinkling as he went through the motions of barter, knowing the rules and their boundaries very well, prepared to be exploited, though not by very much.

His greatest local reputation, I guessed, was as a medicine man. The shelves just inside his doorway were almost as well stocked as a decent chemist's shop, with rows of cardboard boxes variously labelled *Vitamines*, *Rhumatisme*, *Pansements* and the clues to a quite remarkable range of druggery. They lay alongside other shelves loaded with hammers, chisels, pliers, saws and the tools of half a dozen crafts. Somewhere up on the hilltop was the wind gauge and the rainwater tube, with which Jean-Marie kept track of the elements. The hermit of Assekrem was an Algerian Government meteorologist, too. He had a white donkey, Tamerlaine by name, which brought his supplies and his jerry cans of water up from the refuge, where they were dumped from a Land-Rover sent by his brethren in Tamanrasset from time to time.

We ate together, Jean-Marie, the four Tuareg and myself, squatting on a blanket in the hut along the terrace from the house. The women joked and joshed with Jean-

Marie, and he kept them at a little distance with gentle reserve. He was a very calm old man, much contained within himself.

After the meal, I climbed the last few feet of track to de Foucauld's chapel on the top. It was a small square shed, dry-stone-walled inside and out, like the others. The threshold was three steps up, from both the ground outside and the chapel floor, to keep wind and dust at bay. A corridor was hung with white monastic cloaks, and beyond it was a small library. The bulk of the collection was the writings of de Foucauld, and there were faded sepia photographs of him on the walls, but there was also a large mixture of books about the Sahara. The only other objects were three more instruments of meteorology.

Behind heavy Tuareg curtains, along the corridor, was the opening to the chapel proper. An altar of rough stone, nothing but a supported slab, stood free from the eastern wall. If you struck it sharply, it rang like the stones on the hillside. Hanging from that wall was a Christ figure, agonised in metal upon a crude stone cross, above a segment of Tuareg leather work. Two thick candles stood in brackets on either side and, to the right, the red lamp of the Blessed Sacrament reserved. There was a Bible on a bracket by the door, and an office book on another bracket attached to the north wall. There was nothing else but an ikon above the Bible. The floor was covered in rush matting, with four goatskins on top. The roof of the chapel consisted of branches held down by corrugated iron and stone. There were two small windows, the only sources of light, one in the roof above the altar, the other in the outer wall nearby.

I sat down with my back propped against the west wall, facing the altar. For a long time I did nothing but absorb the details of the room, hearing the wind rushing round the walls outside. I said nothing more positive than "Thank you, thank you," time and again, in a whisper. I was trying to perceive something special to this holy place, but no great shaft of illumination enlightened its gloom. I was conscious of lassitude, weariness, a difficulty in focusing my mind. I tried to recall sharply the moments of crisis on my journey, so that I might say "Thank you" with more purpose, but the images would not come. Perhaps I was rejecting them out of a residual fear.

Strangely, for a man who had been reared as I had, it never occurred to me that I might utter any of the Church's formal prayers. It was only possible for me to speak as I had become over many years—to say "Thank you" or "Please show me" or "Help me . . ." without any name for the object of my gratitude and supplication. Even "Our Father" had to be examined so carefully for cant, for hypocrisy, for the minute nuances that I could not honestly accept, that it would have lost its point in the protracted stumble of being-said. Was this, I wondered, sheer arrogance, to insist on exactness in such a thing, an adolescent refusal to compromise with what was not clearly defined? Or was it merely lack of faith?

I lay there for an hour or more undisturbed, before I moved at all. I rose feeling tired, with a tide of depression lapping gently round the ankles of my soul. Perhaps several days here would have changed things, though I doubted it. I went outside and stood for a little while on the tabletop of Assekrem. The view was stupendous, with mountains rising like stalagmites all round. The wind came across the summit in sweeping gusts, noisy and inflamed. There was a sudden uprush beyond the end of the chapel: like smoke, a flurry of dust rose into the air past the mountain's edge. This *was* a holy place, and would have been even if no man had ever trodden it. In the sunlight, the adjacent peaks were khaki. To the east they ran in thick confusion as far as Libya, where I had wished to go. Beyond that lay more sand seas, stretching for a distance that I dared not contemplate. Somewhere beyond all sensing it lay the River Nile, not even a dream any more. I was reconciled to its loss now.

I went down to say good-bye to Jean-Marie and to

offer a lift to the Tuareg. I felt empty as I paused for a moment on the terrace and took a last look round. I knew I could not go on. I did not wish to go back. But I must do this, I must return to my own people. Only with them could I replenish what had been poured out of me in the ride across Mauritania, in the collapse before Tombouctou, in the sandstorms near the well of Asler, and in the long march with Ibrahim by the edge of the Tanezrouft.

I patted Tamerlaine's head and thought sadly of my camels. Then I started down the track to begin my journey home. I had made a kind of peace with myself. The rest of it would have to come slowly, in whatever lay ahead. This place was another reference point, to be used in times to come. It was one of many, and without them I would have been quite lost. The best of them spoke to me, who was without faith, as they had spoken to Christian, to Jew, to Moslem alike, through many ages.

I will lift up mine eyes unto the hills. . . . Lo tira mippahad lay'lah . . . Bismelleh er Rahman er 'aDheem. . . .

Appendix

EQUIPMENT LIST

It may be of some interest to other desert travellers to know what equipment I took to the Sahara from England. Apart from my own clothing and some reading for pleasure (referred to in the text), the list was as follows:

Bubble sextant, Mark IX
Nautical Almanacs, 1972 and 1973 editions
Sight Reduction Tables for Air Navigation, Vols. I and II
U.S. Navy star identification chart (planisphere)
Prismatic compass (ex-WD model)
Silva compass
Bulova Accutron 3 wristwatch
Variety of dividers, protractors, graph-paper pads, etc.

Charts

35 sheets of Carte Internationale du monde (1:1 000 000), carte de l'Afrique (1:1 000 000), published by Institut Géographique National, Paris; and Editions 2 AMS and 4 AMS (1:2 000 000), issued by Army Map Service, Washington, D.C.

Medical kit

500 tablets codeine	100 tablets Tofranil
100 tablets Lomotil	100 tablets Valium
100 tablets Nivaquine	4 tubes Acromycin
100 tablets Piriton	4 tubes Acriflex
100 tablets tetracycline	500 tablets salt

Variety of bandages, dressings, slings, etc.

Miscellaneous

Agfa Super Silette 35mm camera
4 rolls Kodacolor film
Weston Master 2 light meter
Aquapac water filter, with reserve cartridge and pump
6 packs Turblokken compressed food rations
Sailmaker's palm, needles and thread
Sheath knife
Housewife

WORD LIST

boubou	Mauritanian national robe
cram-cram	prickly grass
couscous	dish of cooked grain
dawa	medicine
el Fateha	opening verse of the Koran
el Shehahda	Koran verse on the oneness of God and the primacy of his prophet Mohammed
guerba	goatskin water bag
ghudda	food
howli	headcloth
humpy tent	tent made of grasses bundled across sapling frameworks
kherubgeh	game played with balls versus sticks
loakh	large curved boards used to write on
marabout	holy man
oued	wadi
ould	son of
rahhla	camel saddle
reg	flat gravel plain
serwal	baggy trousers
tassoufra	leather bag for food carried behind camel saddle
wadi	dry riverbed or valley
zrig	drink made of camel's milk, sugar and water